José Bergamín
A Critical Introduction 1920–1936

Writer, critic, and cultural activist José Bergamín (1895–1983) was unjustly relegated to the sidelines of contemporary Spanish intellectual life for reasons that have more to do with his political dissidence and long periods of exile than with the interest and importance of his written work. This book represents the first attempt to come to terms with that work.

Professor Dennis's study focuses on the period 1920–1936, the so-called silver age of Spanish literature, during which Bergamín rose to prominence alongside a group of superlatively gifted writers and friends, among them Federico García Lorca, Rafael Alberti, Jorge Guillén, and Pedro Salinas. It sets out to explain the nature of the relationship Bergamín had as a critic and prose writer with the major poets of the 1920s and 1930s, and at the same time systematically examines the singularity of his own work as an aphorist, essayist, and dramatist. Professor Dennis also devotes attention to explaining the sense of Bergamín's initiative in founding the important journal *Cruz y Raya* (1933–1936) and the role this publication played, both culturally and politically, during the troubled years of the Second Republic.

This book not only fills a notable gap in our understanding of pre–Civil War literary and intellectual life in Spain, but also lays the foundation for all future research into the work of this fascinating and enigmatic writer.

NIGEL DENNIS is professor of Spanish at the University of Ottawa and author of *'El aposento en el aire': Introducción a la poesía de José Bergamín*, *'Diablo Mundo': Los intelectuales y la República*, and *'Perfume and Poison': A Study of the Relationship between José Bergamín and Juan Ramón Jiménez*. He is also the editor of a collection of Bergamín's essays entitled *Prólogos epilogales*.

José Bergamín in Uruguay, ca. 1950
(presented to the author by Bergamín's family)

José Bergamín

A CRITICAL INTRODUCTION 1920–1936

NIGEL DENNIS

UNIVERSITY OF TORONTO PRESS

Toronto Buffalo London

© University of Toronto Press 1986
Toronto Buffalo London
Printed in Canada
ISBN 0-8020-2561-7

University of Toronto Romance Series 55

Canadian Cataloguing in Publication Data

Dennis, Nigel, 1949–
José Bergamín
University of Toronto romance series, ISSN 0082-5336; 55)
Bibliography: p.
Includes index.
ISBN 0-8020-2561-7
1. Bergamín, José, 1895–   – Criticism and
interpretation. I. Title. II. Series.
PQ6603.E69Z59 1986   868'.6209   C85-099748-8

Back cover: José Bergamín, ca. 1940 (presented to the author
by Bergamín's daughter)

This book has been published with the help of grants from the Canadian
Federation for the Humanities, using funds provided by the Social Sciences
and Humanities Research Council of Canada, from the Publication Fund of
University of Toronto Press, and from the University of Ottawa.

Ahora comprendo por qué
tu pensamiento es tan claro:
tan claro que no se ve.

J.B.

Contents

Introduction and Acknowledgments

This is the first full-length, broadly systematic study of the work of José Bergamín. The fact that it has taken so long for someone to write a study of this kind is in many ways surprising, since Bergamín has generally been recognized, especially in recent decades, as a key figure in the Spanish literary and intellectual world this century. While critics have tirelessly swarmed around his more eminent contemporaries, and while books have been written about other less challenging writers of his time, Bergamín has been set aside and has remained largely an unknown quantity both in Spain and abroad. The question, 'Who is José Bergamín?' with which Paul Ludwig Landsberg began his presentation of two essays by this writer to a foreign public in 1940 is still being voiced today, perhaps with greater urgency than ever before.[1] There are several immediately discernible reasons why an adequate answer to this question has not been given before now. The long periods of exile Bergamín has endured, the inaccessibility of many of his books and articles, the general disorder of his published work, his own antipathy towards literary critics, his status as persona non grata in Franco's Spain: all these factors have made it difficult for a clear overall assessment to be made.

These difficulties have been compounded by the very nature of Bergamín's literary personality, which one critic has aptly described as a 'desafío permanente para taxónomos' (permanent challenge to taxonomists).[2] Many people have remarked on how his originality and independence, combined with the extraordinary range of his written work, have made it impossible to fit him comfortably into any established category.[3] I myself have taken the liberty of recycling an image Bergamín himself once used – though in an entirely different context – and of comparing him with 'un cangrejo cocido' (boiled crab), simply because 'no hay por dónde cogerlo' (there is nowhere to get hold of him).[4] The effect has been that while Bergamín has had many admirers, some of whom have been able to illuminate different fragments of his work, his personality as a whole has continued to elude even his most stubbornly loyal readers. Critics have fallen into the habit, therefore, of drawing attention to his importance, of referring to his work in glowing terms, of stressing the desirability of a detailed study of his writing, and without exception, of never taking the matter any further.[5]

Since this is the first study that attempts to resolve some of these difficulties, it has enjoyed certain privileges, but at the same time it has had to grapple with a number of basic handicaps. On the positive side, I have happily not been dogged by the spectre of any other critic who had previously undertaken this task of outlining and making sense of Bergamín's work. This has given me considerable freedom and has guaranteed at least a measure of originality in what I have said. On the negative side, I have been obliged to take nothing for granted and in almost every chapter I have proceeded on the understanding that the reader is unfamiliar with even the most basic data concerning the topics under review. This explains why this book is modestly, but I think accurately entitled *A Critical Introduction*. It sets out to chart essential territory and to offer the kind of critical guidance that I hope will make it possible for interested readers to navigate through the major areas of Bergamín's early work.

This book is introductory and partial in another sense, however, precisely because of the multiple and complex dimensions of Bergamín's literary personality. Bergamín was active for more than sixty years as a professional writer, cultivating different genres, residing in different countries, continually discovering new potential within himself and exploiting it in his work. Inevitably, this has made the global introduction that at one stage I planned to write a practical impossibility. The limits that I have chosen to impose on this study – the chronological ones of 1920 and 1936 – correspond more to a convenient critical convention than to any conviction on my part that they establish definitive boundaries. By calling a halt in 1936, with the demise of *Cruz y Raya* and the outbreak of the Civil War, I have simply tried to make the subject more manageable. I do hope, however, that one of the useful functions that this book will perform will be to invite other critics to look at what Bergamín did during the Civil War and after, identifying the elements of continuity in his work and the new emphases that began to emerge in exile and later after his return to Spain.

Even within these chronological limits I have not attempted to exhaust the subjects tackled, and I am conscious of what I have not found room for. Bergamín's work of the twenties and thirties spills over in many different directions and cannot be contained in a single study. Each chapter, for example, could easily have been expanded into a book, but I have deliberately – and understandably – avoided this temptation, being convinced that a basic foundation needed to be laid before more detailed and refined work could usefully be done. In this sense, I have been haunted by one of Bergamín's most memorable aphoristic dialogues: '¿Tienes dentro de ti todo lo que has aprendido? – Lo tengo a mi lado, en el cesto de los papeles' ('Do you have inside you everything you have learned? – I have it at my side, in the wastepaper basket'). In addition, there are some major aspects of Bergamín's literary background and intellectual formation that are omitted from this book. At the time of writing this introduction, for example, I had completed a book-length study of Bergamín's relationship during these years with Juan Ramón Jiménez (Cassel: Edition Reichenberger 1985), and have undertaken similar examinations of his relationships with Ortega and Unamuno. These subjects are obviously crucial for an understanding of particular attitudes and ideas that Bergamín held in the twenties and thirties. I have excluded them from this book in order not to make it too unwieldy and to avoid blurring the focus on Bergamín's own creative work. I can only suggest that interested readers keep an eye out for these studies, which I believe complement and illuminate further what I have said here.

The internal structure of this book has been determined in large part by the difficulty alluded to concerning the unclassifiability of Bergamín's work and activities during this period. The result is not entirely satisfactory, since chapters are devoted on the one hand to specific genres – such as the aphorism – and on the other to more general issues, such as style or the significance of the *Cruz y Raya* enterprise. In my own defence, I can only say that this arrangement has seemed to me to be the one that best suits the demands of this particular case, and at least has the virtue of describing, in a more or less chronological sequence, the major elements of Bergamín's work in the years prior to the Civil War. The chapters can be read independently since they are practically self-contained and their coherence is not undermined, I would say, by the cross-references they occasionally make use of. Ideally, though, they should be read as a whole so that the larger composite picture can be built up.

*   *   *

This book has its remote origins in a doctoral dissertation presented at the

University of Cambridge in 1976. I mention this circumstance not because this book is a revised version of that thesis – it is probably fortunate that there is little resemblance between the two – but because of the debts I incurred at Cambridge in the early stages of my research into Bergamín's work. I am happy to acknowledge here the help I received in the early and mid-seventies from Helen Grant, the late J.T. Boorman, and the late Edward Wilson. In different ways, these people provided the kind of conditions in which my interest in Bergamín could take root. During those same years, and later, I also benefited from the advice and assistance of a great many Spaniards for whom Bergamín was not, as the manuals of literary history suggested, a relic from a dead past, but a living creative force. Some of these deserve special mention. In the case of Luis Felipe Vivanco and Arturo Soria y Espinosa, both dead now, their admiration for Bergamín, their intimate knowledge of the period I was interested in, and their generosity in providing me with documentary material as well as their own personal insights were invaluable to me. I also had the good fortune to meet Ramón Gaya, the prodigy of *Verso y Prosa*, the animator and illustrator of *Hora de España*, and unquestionably the best critic of Bergamín's work. Our conversations over the past seven or eight years, while not limited to Bergamín, have constituted a unique re-education. Other people like Julio Gómez de la Serna, José Antonio Muñoz Rojas, José Luis Cano, and Ernesto Giménez Caballero gave me the benefit of their opinions on Bergamín's writing. While in Cambridge in 1974 and 1975, Pedro Grases took a generous interest in my work and was subsequently responsible for tracking down for me dozens of articles that Bergamín had published in South American periodicals. Jordi Maragall gave me much encouragement while he was living in Madrid in the seventies, and although I never met Corpus Barga personally, my correspondence with him shortly before his death confirmed the need to reinstate Bergamín in the Spanish intellectual world. This conviction was strengthened by my meetings in Rome with Rafael Alberti and by the letters that Jorge Guillén was kind enough to write to me.

For readers who find these litanies of gratitude tiresome or embarrassing I could perhaps recommend that they turn at once to chapter 1. I would in the meantime like to mention also some younger and as yet less eminent Spaniards who throughout the seventies, and in some cases in this decade too, have shared my enthusiasms and given me practical help. Arturo Soria y Puig, for example, has inherited his father's integrity and generosity. Alberto Porlan was my first really informed guide in the labyrinth of Spanish intellectual history in the pre-war period. Carlos and David Pérez Merinero ran many errands for me in Madrid libraries, and with their own pioneering work on César Arconada set an honourable example to follow. Francisco Laporta has provided constant encouragement and hospitality.

Since moving to Canada in 1976 I have been able to maintain the momentum of my research into Bergamín's work, thanks to a number of people. In particular, I owe a great deal to the expertise of Lorraine Albert of the Morisset Library of the University of Ottawa who has managed to solve even my most baffling bibliographical problems with professional ease. Ian Gibson has in recent years become my most reliable and entertaining informant in Spain concerning Bergamín's activities and has frequently taken time away from his own work to supply me with valuable material. I am also indebted to those Hispanists working in Canada who have given me official and unofficial support, especially Ignacio Soldevila Durante, K. Sibbald, Victor Ouimette, and Peter Bly. My trips to Spain in recent years have been made possible by the generosity of the University of Ottawa and above all by the help provided by the Social Sciences and Humanities Research Council of Canada. It was while in receipt of research grants from this institution in 1978 and 1979 that most of the work for this book was done. I am glad to acknowledge here the fact that without the facilities made available by those grants, this book would never have materialized. I also gratefully acknowledge the help received from the School of Graduate Studies and Research of the University of Ottawa.

The one major debt that I have not so far mentioned and which I doubt if I shall ever be able to repay adequately is to José Bergamín himself. It is not a debt that is reflected directly in this book, though it is true that despite his allergy to literary critics, he tolerated my academic curiosity with gracious good humour and over the years placed a great deal of inaccessible or unpublished material at my disposal. If I have preferred not to quote him as an oral source, it has simply been in order to let his texts speak for themselves and to base this book as exclusively as possible on published documentary sources. In any case, what I have learned from him has gone far beyond the business of ascertaining a date or locating a particular edition. Quite apart from his work as a writer, Bergamín sets an unfussy, natural example of intelligence and sensitivity, of courage, independence, and inventiveness. If this study helps in any way to give him a measure of the recognition he undoubtedly deserves, I shall regard the years I have devoted to writing it as well spent.

*   *   *

At the suggestion of the publishers of this book I have rendered into English a fair number of Spanish quotations that, because of their historical, biographical, or critical relevance, may be of interest to the general reader. Readers with a specialized knowledge of Spanish and of the period I cover – to whom this study is primarily directed – will appreciate my reasons for not attempting to translate any of Bergamín's creative writing.

Sketch of the young Bergamín ca. 1920 done by his friend
Benjamín Palencia, who went on to become one of the major painters
that Spain has produced in this century.

Taken in 1936, shortly after the outbreak of the Civil War, in the HQ of the Alliance of Anti-Fascist Intellectuals in Madrid (over which Bergamín presided). The photo draws attention to the front-rank position Bergamín occupied at the time.
He appears here with two major writers: Rafael Alberti and Manuel Altolaguirre.

This photo from 1936 gives an idea of the prestige Bergamín enjoyed outside Spain in the 1930s (and later). With him are the writer Claude Aveline and his life-long friend André Malraux.

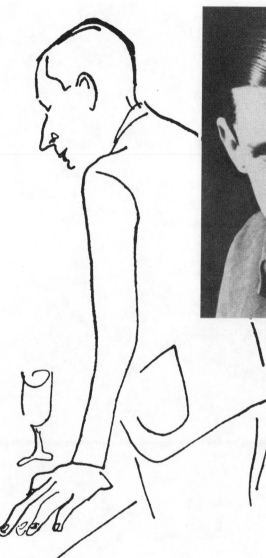

A rare photo, originally
published in Switzerland
in 1940, that evokes
something of the passion
and intensity of
Bergamín's activities
during the Civil War.

A sketch, suggesting Bergamín's dissidence,
done in 1937 by his friend Ramón Gaya.

This photo, reflecting Bergamín's humanity and humour,
is taken from a book on Malraux and shows Bergamín in exile
for the second time in Paris, ca. 1970.

JOSÉ BERGAMÍN

1

'Tras el fantasma':
A Biographical Sketch

Mis huesos ahora ya son
la sombra de lo que fueron:
lo que me sostiene en pie
es un fantasmal espectro.

J.B.

The Bergaminos were originally inhabitants of northern Italy. By tradition they were shepherds in the mountainous region around the city of Bergamo, which they themselves founded and named. The family later moved to Venice where their surname was changed from Bergamino to Bergamín. Although the exact date is not certain, it seems that at some stage in the mid-nineteenth century, Tomasso Bergamín, through his admiration for Garibaldi, became involved in the struggle for Italian unity and was forced to flee the country. He was twenty years old and chose to seek refuge in Spain where, soon after arriving, he married an Andalusian girl from Málaga. A few years later, the couple fell victim to a cholera epidemic and died leaving two young sons. One of these sons became a Jesuit priest, though he subsequently became disillusioned with the order 'dont il ne supportait plus les accomodements avec le ciel et le siècle.'[1] The other son, Francisco, was adopted by a distant relative on his mother's side and taken to the tiny village of Pujerra, in the Sierra de Ronda, where for several years he tended a herd of pigs. He eventually returned to Málaga, alone and in mysterious circumstances, and having languished for a time in the care of local fishermen, he was found by Francisco de la Rada y Delgado, a famous lawyer of the time, who took him under his wing. Thanks to this benefactor's help, he received a basic education and went on to study law. At the age of twenty, he set up his own practice in Málaga where he began by defending – free of charge – the smugglers and *bandoleros* of the region. He also married an Andalusian girl, from Antequera, who numbered among her relatives several well-known bullfighters. The family ended up by moving to Madrid where, by dint of sheer personal effort, Francisco Bergamín forged for himself an outstanding career in law and politics, occupying ministerial posts in several governments under Alfonso XII.[2] As the writer Claude Aveline puts it: 'Venise, Garibaldi, une conspiration; l'Andalousie, les Jésuites, une rébellion; Madrid, le Barreau, l'esprit libéral; plus, su sang du toréro. Quelle réhabilitation pour les théories de Zola et son histoire naturelle d'une famille!'[3]

José Bergamín was born in Madrid on 31 December 1895, the youngest of Francisco's nine sons and daughters.[4] He spent the first twenty years of his life in the rambling, labyrinthine apartment that his family occupied in the Plaza de la Independencia.[5] While growing up there, he came under the influence of a number of factors that would later determine in large part his outlook as a writer. The first of these was, unsurprisingly, the example set by his parents. In a revealing, unpublished autobiographical note, Bergamín has himself drawn attention to the importance of the inheritance – of attitude and belief – that he received from them:

Mi padre, abogado y político famoso, nos daba su ejemplo de infatigable trabajador. Huérfano desde los cinco años, se había construído su vida con sólo su esfuerzo personal y poseía una amplísima cultura. Autodidacta, su ejemplo me enseñó a serlo a mí, y, a la par, aprendí de él a no darme ninguna importancia a mí mismo. Por este camino le seguí, dando algún paso más: que fue el de no tomarme nunca en serio: ni a mí mismo ni a los demás; diría que ni a Dios ni al Diablo, que nos dan ese buen ejemplo no tomándonos demasiado en serio a nosotros. Por mi madre, andaluza como mi padre (de Antequera, mi padre de Málaga) de espíritu y sentimiento cristianos, y de práctica católica, recibí formación poética, muy popular, con un sentimiento cristiano-católico en que se arraigó toda mi vida. Y que, con el tiempo, se fue profundizando y afirmando más.[6]

(My father was a lawyer and a famous politician, and as a tireless worker set us children an example. Orphaned at the age of five, he had forged a path in life for himself thanks only to his own efforts. Furthermore, he was an extremely cultured man. He was self-taught, and I followed his example. From him I learned not to attach any importance to myself. I even took this a step further and never took myself seriously – or anyone else for that matter, not even God or the Devil, who also set a fine example by not taking us too seriously. My mother was Andalusian, too, like my father: she was from Antequera while my father was from Málaga. She was endowed with a Christian outlook and sensibility, and was a practising Catholic. From her I received a very popular, poetic upbringing, imbued with Christian-Catholic feeling. My entire life took root in this feeling and as the time has gone by, this sentiment has grown stronger and deeper.)

In view of Bergamín's subsequent activity as a creative writer, restless Catholic thinker, and political activist, the relevance of these early and lasting parental influences is worth bearing in mind. The second factor that needs to be taken into account is less predictable. Like most children of his background, he spent a good deal of time in the company of family maids and servants. The unspoiled freshness of their imagination, coupled with the richness of the traditional language in which they expressed themselves, made a deep impression on his sensibility and prepared the ground for his own lyrical exploitation of the potential of popular idioms – characteristic of so much of his writing – and for his militant defence, enshrined in his polemical essay 'La decadencia del analfabetismo' ('The decline of illiteracy'), of the unsullied, childlike spirituality of the common people. In an as yet unfinished autobiography, he alludes to his constant exposure as a child to the daily conversations of the maids of the household:

Estas cosas, como su diálogo, con sus diferencias de tono y de acentos, según la región de España de la que llegaban, creo que fueron educando mi oído – dada la profunda atención de mi silencio infantil – en una riqueza de lenguaje español, a la que debo más, tal vez, que a mis devoradoras lecturas posteriores de adolescente, la formación imaginativa de mi propio vocabulario parabolero. Un cierto gusto, diré que barroco, por las palabras, y por sus infinitas posibilidades de expresión imaginativa, por su enorme poder de evocación fantástica, creo que lo debo al contacto vivo de aquel lenguaje popular que escuchaba de niño, oyendo la charla inagotable, como fuente viva de figuraciones y sentidos poéticos, de las mujeres de los pueblos, que venían a servir a Madrid, desde todos los rincones de España: gallegas, vascas, asturianas, levantinas, castellanas, andaluzas ... Así se enriquecía nuestra tradición malagueña propia – digo la de mi casa andaluza – con todas aquellas aportaciones vivas de lenguaje y creación imaginativa de todas las vertientes populares de España.[7]

(I would say that this contact and those conversations I listened to – with their differences of tone and accent according to the region of Spain from which the maids came – gradually sensitised my ear (given the rapt attention of my silences as a child) to a wealth of Spanish to which I perhaps owe a greater debt in the formation of my own parabolic vocabulary than to my later readings as a tireless adolescent. I believe I owe a certain taste I have – that could be termed baroque – for words, for their infinite possibilities of imaginative expression, for their enormous power of evocation, to that living contact with popular speech that I had as a child. I absorbed that inexhaustible flow of words, that living spring of figurative and poetic language that issued from the women who left their villages and went into service in Madrid and who came from all the corners of Spain: Galicia, the Basque provinces, Asturias, Levant, Castille, Andalusia ... In this way our own traditional family ties with Málaga – I refer to the Andalusian household in which I was raised – became enriched by the intermingling of languages and creative imaginations that came from the entire popular stock of Spain.)

Bergamín attended a traditional Catholic school where the only notable talent he showed was for the study of foreign languages and for literature in general. He was helped in his acquisition of French and a smattering of English by family tutors, to whose guidance he also owed his early knowledge of the classics of European literature. His consuming interest in the written word is evident in his own precocious but unflagging attempts at creative writing:

Empecé a escribir, si no me equivocan mis recuerdos, desde los nueve o diez años. Desde los catorce o los quince emborroné papeles y papeles; recuerdo haber escrito, ya hacia los diecisiete o dieciocho años, dos libros de poemas, una novela y un poema dramático.[8]

(If my memory serves me correctly, I began to write when I was about nine or ten years old. From the age of fourteen or fifteen onwards, I scribbled away ceaselessly. By the time I was seventeen or eighteen I remember I had written two books of poetry, a novel, and a dramatic poem.)

Despite a marked aversion to formal academic study, Bergamín did attend university, though with haphazard regularity. He has said on a number of occasions that it was precisely because of his great love for literature that he decided not to study it at Madrid University, fearing the damage that might be done to him by contact with unimaginative teachers of the subject. Instead he chose law, but having graduated, he appeared in court only once to exercise his profession. He found the proceedings so tedious and boring that he vowed never to return. For a while, in 1921, he worked as political secretary to his father, who was at that time Minister of the Interior. Among the people who worked alongside him during this period was the young Manuel Altolaguirre, sent to Madrid from Málaga by his father, who was a friend of Francisco Bergamín. If Altolaguirre's testimony is to be believed, little time was devoted to the official tasks that were supposed to occupy them:

7 A Biographical Sketch

Otras eran ya nuestras aficiones. Andando el tiempo nuestro campo sería el de la literatura y en lugar de atender a los litigios, comentábamos lecturas recientes, conversaciones a las que debo mucho de mi formación literaria.[9]

(We had other interests already then. As time went by, our field would be literature, and instead of attending to the cases before us, we spent our time discussing the books we had just read. I owe a great deal of my literary background to those conversations.)

Bergamín's own literary formation owed much to his tirelessness as a reader. Throughout his teenage years, he devoured almost anything that fell into his hands. Although his early tastes were inevitably eclectic, some of the authors he encountered were to make a permanent impression on his own creative and critical outlook, and it is interesting to hear Bergamín himself document the most important of them:

Mis primeras lecturas juveniles a las que toda mi vida he seguido fiel, fueron: Goethe (en francés, que aprendí a leer al mismo tiempo que el español), Julio Verne, Tolstoi, Ibsen, Heine, Shakespeare, Byron, Hugo ... Y en español: La Celestina, casi todo Menéndez Pelayo, Bécquer (culto familiar andaluz), y Rubén Darío, Valle-Inclán, Felipe Trigo ... Seguidamente, leí a Unamuno, Azorín, los Machado, Juan Ramón Jiménez ... También en mis primeros años juveniles aprendí yo solo a leer el italiano, leyendo la Divina Comedia y el Decamerón (éste último lo había leído ya en español) y a D'Annunzio. Pero la preponderante influencia en mis años jóvenes fue la de la literatura francesa 'finesecular,' desde el romanticismo al 'simbolismo': con predilección por Nerval y Baudelaire; más tarde por Gauthier. Guiado por Los raros de Rubén Darío y por la lectura de Rémy de Gourmont, mi mundo juvenil vivía esa literatura apasionadamente; y aquellas lecturas culminan en Gide y, sobre todo, en Barrès: éste último es el que decisivamente influyó más en mí. Entretanto, eran mis lecturas fundamentales de juventud: Pascal, Ibsen, y los rusos – Tolstoi y Dostoevski: y sobre todos Nietzsche. A más de Goethe y Heine; más tarde, Novalis, al que leía por Maeterlink, que también fue importante lectura juvenil mía. En el fondo de todas estas lecturas de mi juventud, hay tres esenciales que apoyaron mi pensamiento para toda mi vida: los Diálogos de Platón, la Etica de Spinoza, y la Crítica de la razón pura de Kant.[10]

(The first authors I read as a youngster were those to whom I have remained loyal throughout my life: Goethe (in French, which I learned to read at the same time as I did Spanish), Jules Verne, Tolstoi, Ibsen, Heine, Shakespeare, Byron, Hugo ...

And in Spanish: *La Celestina*, almost all Menéndez Pelayo, Bécquer (an Andalusian passion of my family), and Rubén Darío, Valle-Inclán, Felipe Trigo. Immediately after these I read Unamuno, Azorín, the Machado brothers, Juan Ramón
Jiménez ... During those youthful years I also taught myself to read Italian, and
made my way through the *Divine Comedy* and the *Decameron* (I had already read
the latter in Spanish), and the work of D'Annunzio. But the major influence on my
youth was fin-de-siècle French literature, from Romanticism to Symbolism, with a
special preference for Nerval and Baudelaire, and later for Gauthier. I was guided
in those years by *Los raros* of Rubén Darío and by reading Rémy de Gourmont, and
within my juvenile world I lived that literature with great passion. That reading
culminated in Gide, and above all in Barrès who was to have a decisive influence
on me. At the same time, a number of other writers left a deep impression on my
youth: Pascal, Ibsen, and the Russians Tolstoi and Dostoevski. More important
than them all: Nietzsche. I should also include Goethe and Heine, and later
Novalis, whom I read via Maeterlink, another important writer for me at the time.
Beneath all these encounters which shaped my youth there are three essential
texts on which my thinking throughout my whole life has been based: Plato's
Dialogues, Spinoza's *Ethics*, and Kant's *Critique of Pure Reason*.)

It is an extraordinary and highly revealing list. Most immediately striking
is the absence of any systematic exploration of the Spanish classics of the
Golden Age. Since Bergamín's reputation, particularly as a critic, is linked
to his knowledge and appreciation of the writers of the sixteenth and
seventeenth centuries, the predominance of foreign writers in his list is
surprising; but it simply puts the evolution of his literary tastes into
perspective. The basic influences were European, while his fascination
with the Golden Age came later – when he would personally do so much
to rehabilitate neglected writers in the thirties, especially in his journal
Cruz y Raya.

It is also significant that Bergamín should confess that 'mi mundo
juvenil vivía esa literatura apasionadamente,' since this points to a
fundamental reciprocal relationship that has always characterized his
understanding of the function of literature and its relation to life. He was
once asked, for example, to describe or define '¿qué es o qué significa para
mí la literatura?' ('what is literature or what meaning does literature have
for me?') and gave the following reply: 'Tomar conciencia de la vida
gracias a la lectura, desde la niñez, de algunos libros determinados. La
Literatura existe o vive, está viva para nosotros, cuando la *vivimos* como
una cosa nuestra; individual o colectivamente. La vida se literaturiza como
la literatura se vive. Sin esta acción recíproca, la literatura no existe'

('Becoming aware of life by virtue of reading, from childhood onwards, a particular set of books. Literature exists and lives, is alive for us, when we *live* it as something of our own, individually or collectively. Life becomes literature just as literature becomes life. Without this reciprocal action, literature does not exist').[11] For Bergamín, therefore, literature is not distinct from life but rather provides an access to it. It becomes subsumed into life just as life is subsumed into literature. This is true not just as an abstract scheme, but also as an indication of the trajectory that Bergamín's own life and literature have followed.

These early literary interests also draw into focus the important philosophical or ethical dimension of his thought that would manifest itself first obliquely and then later more militantly in his writings of the late twenties and of the thirties as a whole. If to the names already listed are added those of Bakunin, Kropotkin, and Herzen, who also absorbed the young Bergamín, the concomitant concern with social justice, with a utopian idealism tinged with Christian feeling, can be viewed in its appropriate context.[12] It is the coincidence of allegiance to radical political thought and to popular forms of uncorrupted Christianity that would later sustain some of the most controversial aspects of his social and religious commitment of the thirties.

This deep involvement with literature and his incipient vocation as a creative writer gathered additional momentum thanks to the contacts with writers that Bergamín made as a young man. His friendship with them and their recognition of his literary promise encouraged him to take an active part in the Madrid literary world and to begin publishing his work. While still a teenager, he became friends with writers like Gómez de la Serna, Pérez de Ayala, Valle-Inclán and Benavente, and was soon attending the *peñas* and *tertulias* at which some of them pontificated. He was, for example, one of the founding members of the famous Pombo *tertulia*, which he continued to frequent up until the outbreak of the Civil War.[13] He attended the gatherings at the Gato Negro café, presided over by Benavente and Valle-Inclán, and was a conspicuous member of the 'cenáculo de los *Hombres Jueves*' that for a while met regularly at the Palace Hotel under the supervision of Alfonso Reyes.[14] His interest in the theatre was given added impetus by his friendship with Gregorio Martínez Sierra, whose meetings at the Teatro Eslava he also attended.[15] At the same time, around 1920, he met and came to be on friendly terms with Ortega y Gasset, Díez Canedo, Moreno Villa, and the Machado brothers.

The most decisive factor, however, in his literary formation and in the launching of his career as a writer was his close relationship with Juan

Ramón Jiménez. Bergamín was one of the first of the novice writers – who would be known collectively in the twenties as 'la joven literatura' – to make contact with Jiménez. His fervent admiration for the poet was reciprocated, and Jiménez's interest in the new talent appearing on the literary scene was largely kindled by the insights and recommendations he received from his young friend. It is significant, for example, that Alberti describes Bergamín during the early twenties as a kind of 'secretario permanente' to Jiménez.[16]

The publication of Jiménez's journal *Indice* in 1921 and 1922 not only put Bergamín firmly on the literary map as a young intellectual force to be reckoned with, but also signalled the first public excursion of many of the writers who would subsequently be associated with the so-called 'Generation of 1927': Salinas, García Lorca, Guillén, Espina, Gerardo Diego, Dámaso Alonso, Marichalar, Chabás. If the four numbers of the journal served to affirm the promise of these young writers, its publishing offshoot, the Biblioteca de Indice, played an equally significant role in bringing the most outstanding of them to the attention of a wider reading public. Like the journal itself, this collection was vigilantly supervised by Jiménez himself, whose exacting standards of creative and typographical excellence gave it its distinctive character. In the Biblioteca de Indice, the first book by Pedro Salinas – his *Seguro azar* – was published, along with Antonio Espina's second book of poems entitled *Signario*. The inclusion in the series of a collection of sketches by the painter Benjamín Palencia under the title *Niños* draws attention to Jiménez's interest in the young painters of the day, while the critical edition by Alfonso Reyes of Góngora's *Fábula de Polifemo y Galatea* was to play a crucial role in guiding the young poets of the decade towards the *poète maudit* of the seventeenth century.[17] But clearly it is the publication in 1923 of Bergamín's first book, *El cohete y la estrella*, that is of primary interest here. The book owes much to Jiménez who was largely responsible for selecting and ordering the aphorisms that appear in it, as well as the typographical layout. Jiménez also included as a kind of prologue to the book a 'caricatura lírica' of the author – one of the earliest of this series of portraits that he would later publish under the title *Españoles de tres mundos*.[18] The text itself bears eloquent testimony to the esteem in which Jiménez held his young friend at the time. The publication of *El cohete y la estrella*, despite its mixed reception, situated Bergamín in the forefront of the literary vanguard of the twenties. In 1924, thanks to the prestige gained from this first book, he took his place alongside the other major writers of his own age presented collectively to the French public as 'la jeune littérature espagnole.'[19]

Given the size of the literary world at the time in Madrid, it is not surprising that Bergamín's early friendships with people like Gómez de la Serna and Jiménez, his prominent role in the *Indice* enterprise, and his association with Jiménez Fraud and the Residencia de Estudiantes should have put him in touch with practically all the outstanding young writers of the day.[20] He shared their interest in new literary trends and took an active part in their rediscovery of Spain's cultural past.[21] He also overcame his early reluctance to publish his work and became an assiduous contributor to all the most notable journals of the decade: *Alfar, Residencia, Mediodía, Papel de Aleluyas, Litoral, Carmen, Gallo, Verso y Prosa, La Gaceta Literaria,* and many others. Few of the essays and reviews he published in these journals have been collected, though in many ways (as this book will suggest), they stand as one of his most singular contributions to the decade as a whole. Through them, Bergamín won for himself the role of leading commentator on his generation's creative achievements.[22] The contribution that he made in 1927 to the celebrations designed to commemorate the tercentenary of Góngora's death confirmed his place as a major critic of the time.[23]

Throughout the twenties, Bergamín travelled extensively in Europe. In 1927, for example, he visited England in order to pay homage to William Blake, the anniversary of whose death he felt had passed unnoticed by English poets. It was in London, during this visit, that he met T.S. Eliot.[24] In the following year he married Rosario Arniches, the daughter of the famous *sainetista* Carlos Arniches. Their honeymoon was spent on a Baltic cruise in the course of which they visited Sweden, Denmark, Norway, and the Soviet Union.[25]

Unlike most of his fellow writers of the twenties, whose attitude to politics at the time was either naive or indifferent, Bergamín had always been an alert and informed observer of political life in Spain. Being the son of a famous public figure doubtless gave him an advantage. His conviction that the monarchy in Spain was bankrupt explains his early espousal of the Republican cause: to use his own words, 'por un *no* a la monarquía me hice republicano' ('by rejecting the monarchy I became a Republican').[26] He became involved in the conspiratorial manoeuvres headed by politicians like Sánchez Román and Miguel Maura, and in 1930 spoke alongside Unamuno at a meeting in Salamanca in support of the Republic. When the new régime was proclaimed in the following year, Bergamín made a practical contribution to it by accepting posts in the provisional government. He has described his experiences of the summer of 1931 in the following terms:

Viene la República, colaboramos en el gobierno provisional Justino de Azcárate, Antonio Garrigues, Alfonso Valdecasas, y todos fuimos directores generales. Yo era director general de Acción Social y comisario general de Seguros, el menos social y el menos seguro. Felipe Sánchez Román me pidió que entrara en el Ministerio de Trabajo, donde Largo Caballero era ministro, para preparar la reforma agraria, cuyo proyecto era de Sánchez Román, Agustín Viñuales y Flores de Lemus, proyecto que rechazó el Gobierno por oponerse Alcalá Zamora y Miguel Maura. Yo renuncié el cargo de director general de Acción Social al reformarse el Ministerio de Trabajo y pasar estas funciones al de Comunicaciones, cuyo ministro era el helenista Nicolau D'Olwer. No acepté ser candidato a las Cortes como independiente. No era un político, sino un escritor.[27]

(When the Republic was proclaimed, a number of us accepted posts in the provisional government, Justino de Azcárate, Antonio Garrigues, Alfonso Valdecasas. We were all Directors General. I was Director General of Social Action and General Supervisor of Insurance. Felipe Sánchez Román asked me to work in the Ministry of Employment, under Largo Caballero, in order to help prepare the legislation for agrarian reform, the plans for which had been drawn up by Sánchez Román himself, Agustín Viñuales, and Flores de Lemus. Because of the opposition of Alcalá Zamora and Miguel Maura, these plans were rejected by the government. I resigned from my post as Director General of Social Action when the Ministry of Employment was reorganized and my responsibilities came under the Ministry of Communications headed by the Hellenist Nicolau D'Olwer. I refused to stand for parliament as an independent candidate. I was a writer, not a politician.)

It was indeed as a writer and cultural activist that Bergamín made his mark on Republican life, although the political intention and implications of his activities should not be underestimated. It was in 1933 that he emerged as a really prominent and influential individual force in the intellectual world when he helped to found the journal *Cruz y Raya*, of which he soon became the sole director. Although the journal was unable to realize its full potential during the three short years in which it appeared, there can be little doubt concerning the skill and dedication with which Bergamín promoted an enlightened response among Republican Catholics to the dramatic demands of the time. His generosity towards young writers, both in Spain and abroad, largely explains the success with which *Cruz y Raya* complemented, in a less formal but equally scholarly and illuminating way, the initiatives of Ortega in the *Revista de Occidente*. The anthology section of the journal and its publishing offshoot, the Ediciones del Arbol, were particularly important: they stimulated interest in both classical Spanish literature and in certain outstanding European writers and at the same time brought out superlative editions of the major literary works produced in the last years of the Republic.[28]

The alarming nature of political developments in Spain and in Europe in general in the mid-thirties explains why so much of Bergamín's writing at the time was designed to comment critically on the forces that threatened the survival of the Republic. This characteristically vigilant and outspoken attitude is evident, for example, in his articles in *Cruz y Raya* and the Madrid press of 1933 and 1934, discussing such events as the foundation of the Falange and the repression of the Asturian Revolution.[29] As fascism in Europe spread and as the dangers to the Republic posed by Gil Robles and the Confederación Española de Derechas Autónomas increased, Bergamín found himself adopting more radical attitudes. By 1935, he was openly recognizing the links that existed between Marxist humanism and his own particular brand of Christian idealism. He was involved in the foundation in February 1936 of the Alliance of Anti-Fascist Intellectuals and became its president in August.

The authority and prestige that he had acquired between 1933 and 1936 as a Catholic intellectual committed to the ideals of liberal republicanism found their most militant expression during the Civil War. Soon after the outbreak of war, Bergamín was appointed cultural attaché at the Spanish embassy in Paris at the suggestion of the ambassador, Luis Araquistáin.[30] He became the Republic's most vocal spokesman among French intellectuals and was in close contact during the war with influential writers, such as André Malraux, Jacques Maritain, Emmanuel Mounier, Etienne Gilson, and Georges Bernanos.[31] Continuing the campaign he had waged in *Cruz y Raya* against a corrupt and cynical Catholic Church, he denounced publicly and repeatedly not only the conduct of the Spanish clergy but also the official policy of the Vatican itself.[32] His tireless efforts to win moral and financial support for the Republican cause took him on various propaganda tours of North America, Europe, and the Soviet Union, and it is surprising that he still found time to devote so much creative energy to journals like *El Mono Azul, Hora de España,* and *Madrid. Cuadernos de la Casa de la Cultura.*[33] In July 1937, he played a major role in the Second International Congress of Writers in Defence of Culture held in Madrid, Valencia, and Paris.[34]

The fall of the Republic naturally meant exile for Bergamín and it is significant that it was he who coined the phrase 'España Peregrina'

(Pilgrim Spain) to describe the exodus of Spaniards that took place following Franco's final victories. He moved, in 1939, to Mexico and became an outstanding figure in the community of exiled intellectuals who, while they waited for an opportune moment to return to Spain, sought to continue abroad the literary and cultural initiatives they had been obliged to abandon. Bergamín was made president of the Junta de Cultura Española, founded *España Peregrina*, one of the first major Spanish literary journals in exile, and renewed his activities as a publisher in the important Editorial Séneca, which he directed.[35]

His efforts to become integrated into Mexican cultural life were undoubtedly sincere, and his friendships with writers like Octavio Paz, Xavier Villarrutia, and Carlos Pellicer, as well as his regular contributions to journals like *Romance*, *Letras de México*, *El Hijo Pródigo*, and *Taller*, testify to the success with which they were rewarded. It would be naive, however, to think that the dialogue between the exiled Spaniards and their Mexican hosts was problem-free. There were inevitably tensions and personality conflicts, the nature of which remain to be examined in depth, and it would probably be fair to say that Bergamín had his detractors in Mexico as well as his admirers.[36] The death of his wife in 1943, which left him in sole charge of their three children, may have contributed to a growing sense of isolation and to a mounting despair at the impossibility of maintaining in exile the kind of authoritative response to the plight of Spain that he had achieved in the thirties. It is evident, at least, that when it became clear in 1945 that Franco was not to be ousted by the Allied Forces in Europe, his disillusionment became acute and a period of restless wandering began.[37]

Bergamín moved first to Caracas, where in 1946 and 1947 he taught Spanish literature both at the university and at the Instituto Pedagógico, and contributed regularly to the *Revista Nacional de Cultura*. This was practically his first experience of teaching in a formal academic environment and did not prove to be an especially happy one. He showed little reticence in expressing his lack of faith in university teaching, with the result that the only favourable impression he made in Caracas was among the students. Because of his unconventional teaching methods, his situation soon became untenable and he left Venezuela to take up a special chair of Spanish literature that had been created for him in 1947 in Montevideo.[38]

Uruguay at that time was something of a South American haven, bearing little resemblance to the politically devastated country of recent years. Its quiet colonial air, its warmth and genuine hospitality provided

Bergamín and his family with an ideal environment for the years they spent there. In Bergamín's own words: 'Montevideo fue mi más larga estancia americana y la más feliz, de tal modo que podría decir que fue, con México, mi segunda patria, sólo que más amable y particularmente cariñosa' ('It was in Montevideo that I spent the longest time while I was living in South America. It was also the happiest period of that part of my life, so I could say that, along with Mexico, Uruguay was my second homeland, though its associations for me are warmer and I have a particular fondness for that country').[39] The years spent in Montevideo were especially productive: Bergamín wrote several important books there and a number of his plays were staged. He also continued his close association with the periodical world, contributing to journals like *Escritura* and *Entregas de la Licorne* and writing a regular weekly column for the Caracas newspaper *El Nacional*.

Bergamín visited Europe briefly in 1950 to attend, in the company of friends like Alberti and Picasso, the World Peace Congress. Although he was refused entry to Great Britain because of his supposed murky, subversive past, he did spend short periods in Poland, Italy, and France, and it was perhaps this re-encounter with the Old World that prompted him to consider the possibility of returning to Spain. He also came to realize at this time that if he was to make an effective contribution to Spanish life, he would have to do it from within the country.[40] His decision to return was eventually made in 1954, and he moved to Paris in that year in order to facilitate arrangements. Two of his children had by this time already returned to Spain and the third had established himself in Venezuela. While Bergamín's own application was being processed, he lived alone in the Casa de México in the Cité Universitaire. It was not, however, until 1958, after several of his requests for the necessary permission had been turned down, that he was allowed into Spain. Bergamín's commentary on this point is worth recalling:

El general Franco, en unas declaraciones a un periódico de México, se congratul-aba de mi regreso, también del regreso del General Rojo, que Franco llamaba el *generalísimo de ellos*, y de Miguel Maura, citándonos como ejemplo de españoles que saben perder, a lo que contesté en otras declaraciones: 'Hay que saber ganar.' Mi primera visita fue para Azorín, mi maestro, y le seguí viendo durante años. En aquella primera entrevista en su casa me dijo: 'Voy a hablarle del panorama político para que se entere de la situación española. Los españoles se dividen en tres clases: los indivisos, los tolerantes y los réprobos. Yo soy un tolerante, y usted es un réprobo tolerado, cosa que no le va a durar mucho.'[41]

(In a series of declarations that appeared in a Mexican newspaper, General Franco referred with some satisfaction to my homecoming as well as to the return of General Rojo (whom Franco called '*their Generalissimo*') and Miguel Maura, quoting us as examples of Spaniards who knew how to lose. I replied to this in a statement made elsewhere in which I said, 'It's important to know how to win.' The first person I visited on my return was Azorín, my master, and I continued to see him regularly in subsequent years. During that first visit of mine to his house he said to me: 'I'm going to put you in the picture with regard to the political situation in Spain so you know how things stand. Spaniards are divided up into three classes: the indivisible, the tolerant, and the reprobates. I am one of the tolerant ones, and you are a tolerated reprobate, though you won't be for very long.')

As it turned out, Azorín's words were to prove prophetic.

Despite his natural expectations, Bergamín's return to Madrid was beset with problems. He was plagued by financial difficulties and continued to be dependent largely on the irregular income he received from his contributions to South American newspapers. He failed to become reintegrated into literary and intellectual life and found it impossible to renew many of the friendships he had broken in 1936. Although he managed to publish a number of books, he clearly had little hope, given the arid cultural climate of those years, of regaining the kind of prestige he had enjoyed before the Civil War. The repressive nature of Franco's régime and the hostility with which Bergamín was still viewed in official quarters meant that he was frequently harassed by the authorities. His own tendency to make the most of any opportunity, regardless of the risks involved, to speak out for the same values he had stood for in the thirties only aggravated the situation. In January 1961, for example, he was invited by the bullfighter Domingo Ortega to lecture at the Círculo de Bellas Artes on the subject 'El toreo, cuestión palpitante' ('Bullfighting: the burning question'). He scandalized the audience by giving the topic a loaded, political interpretation and had to be escorted from the auditorium under the protection of Antonio Bienvenida and Domingo Dominguín.[42] The following day, the newspaper *ABC* referred to the provocative nature of the lecture and Bergamín was summoned to the Dirección General de Seguridad. There, in the same office he had occupied when his father was Minister of the Interior, he was unceremoniously interrogated by the Chief of Police. It was an initial sign of the growing official antagonism towards him.

It was, however, two years later that matters came to a head. When reports reached Madrid of the extreme repressive measures taken by the authorities to break up a miners' strike in Asturias, a manifesto was published requesting a clarification of how the situation had been handled. It was signed by over a hundred prominent intellectuals, including Bergamín. For no apparent reason, Bergamín was singled out by the then-minister of Information and Tourism, Manuel Fraga Iribarne, as the instigator of the protest and became the victim of a systematic campaign of vilification and intimidation. He lived under constant police surveillance and when it became clear that the authorities were no longer willing or able to guarantee his personal safety, he took refuge in the Uruguayan embassy. Concern at the treatment he was receiving was voiced internationally: telegrams of protest were sent from the Vatican, from President Kennedy, from his friend André Malraux, then a minister in De Gaulle's cabinet. It was largely due to the weight carried by these protests that Bergamín was granted permission to leave the country and provided with a one-way ticket to Montevideo.[43]

Once again in exile at the age of sixty-eight, Bergamín remained in Uruguay for only a short time before returning to Europe. He spent the next six years in Paris where, thanks largely to the help he received from Malraux, he lived modestly but in reasonable comfort as a permanent guest at the Fondation Louis Weiller. While in Paris, Bergamín enjoyed considerable prestige in the intellectual world. In November 1965, for example, a series of television programs was devoted to his life and work. Given his precarious official status in France at the time and his haunting of the Spanish literary scene, the title that these programs were given – 'Entretiens avec un fantôme' – was particularly apt.[44] In 1966 he was awarded the Legion of Honour in its special grade of Commandeur des Arts et des Lettres, a distinction given to only two other Spaniards, Picasso and Buñuel. In 1969, French television showed a two-hour film entitled 'Masques et bergamasques ou reportage sur un squellette,' which, under the direction of Michel Mitrani, showed several extracts from Bergamín's dramatic works, translated for the occasion by his friend Florence Delay.

Throughout these years Bergamín was again financially dependent on the income he received for articles published in the South American press, particularly in *El Nacional* in Caracas. It was through this outlet that he continued to express his undiminished opposition to Franco and his passionate concern for what he considered to be the survival of Spanish culture. Predictably, he remained convinced that his voice needed to be heard within Spain and he made constant enquiries to the Spanish authorities in Paris concerning the possibility of returning to Spain. It was not, however, until after a change of government in Spain in 1970 that he was able to obtain the necessary permission, receiving the excuse that the previous problems surrounding his applications had been due to 'administrative error.'

Bergamín's second homecoming proved in general to be more agreeable, though the role of political dissident that he has played naturally throughout his life brought him once more into conflict with the authorities. On a number of occasions, for example, provocative articles he published in *Sábado Gráfico* – a weekly magazine to which he contributed regularly between 1974 and 1978 – ended in court cases. By and large, however, public response to his writings was increasingly favourable in the seventies. With the relaxation of censorship, he was able to republish several books that up to that time were virtually unknown in Spain. At the same time, he continued to produce new work, especially poetry. The younger generations of readers and critics became gradually aware of the extent of his contributions to literary life in and outside Spain in the twentieth century, realizing that within the enormously varied collection of writings and within the vicissitudes of his unsettled life, there lay a highly original and creative talent, and a mind of great integrity and clearsightedness.

In more recent years Bergamín was granted a small measure of the public recognition that he clearly deserved. In 1978, for example, he was judged by a group of eminent critics to be 'la personalidad literaria más completa y con mayor proyección sobre nuestra cultura dentro y fuera de España de los miembros aún vivos de la generación del 27' (the most complete literary personality of the surviving members of the Generation of 1927 by virtue of the scope of his work and the range of its impact on Spanish culture both within and outside the country).[45] In 1980, the Centro Dramático Nacional paid homage to his work as a dramatist, staging extracts from a number of his plays in the Teatro María Guerrero in Madrid.[46] When Alianza Editorial published two books by Bergamín in the following year, the Madrid Ateneo hosted a public launching at which critics of the calibre of Caballero Bonald and Fernando Savater spoke in praise of the writer.[47] In 1982, Bergamín received both the Premio Pedro Salinas, given by the Universidad Internacional de Menéndez Pelayo in Santander – a prize he shared with Rafael Alberti – and a special award from the Fundación Pablo Iglesias in recognition for 'el conjunto de su obra literaria y la ejemplaridad de su larga vida' (his literary work as a whole and the exemplary nature of his long life).

In spite of these accolades, Bergamín remained an outsider. He attacked the monarchy in Spain with the same boldness with which he attacked the Franco régime.[48] His intractable Republican sympathies resurfaced in 1979 when he stood for election to the Spanish Senate for the radical party Izquierda Republicana. His decision in 1982 to leave Madrid and to take up residence in San Sebastián was widely interpreted as a political gesture and many saw it as the principal reason why he was not awarded the prestigious Cervantes Prize for which he had been strongly tipped that year.[49] In his late eighties, Bergamín's dissidence was once again tempered by isolation. He chose a voluntary exile within Spain, the sense of which he himself suggested in a poem he wrote shortly after arriving at the north coast:

Fui peregrino en mi patria
desde que nací.
Y lo fui en todos los tiempos
que en ella viví.
Y por eso sigo siéndolo,
ahora y aquí:
peregrino de una España
que ya no está en mí.
Y no quisiera morirme,
aquí y ahora,
para no darle a mis huesos
tierra española.[50]

(I was a pilgrim in my land
from the time I was born.
And I've been so all the years
that I have lived here.
And I'm still a pilgrim
right here and now:
a pilgrim in a Spain
that is no longer within me.
And I have no wish to die
right here and now
for fear my bones will be buried
beneath Spanish soil.)

Bergamín died in San Sebastián on 28 August 1983 and was buried in a small cemetery in Fuenterrabía, facing the sea and the frontier with France.

2

'Ingenio de saeta':
The Aphorist

Como el fantasma agudo de una flecha lanzaron contra mí tu nombre:
aforismo. Y te clavaste en mi corazón.

J.B.

The publication in 1923 of *El cohete y la estrella* constituted the offical début
of a writer described by Antonio Espina in an early review as 'ya muy
significado entre la *élite* intelectual por sus ensayos en algún diario y
revistas de minoría' (already a notable figure among the intellectual élite
because of the essays he has published occasionally in newspapers and
minority journals).[1] It was not, however, an unconditionally acclaimed
début. In his letters to Unamuno in the months following the book's
publication, Bergamín expressed his disappointment at the limited
reception it had been given and the apparent misinterpretations to which
it had been subjected.[2] The earnestly defensive tone he adopted while
confessing his unease to Unamuno may well have prompted the latter to
write his own review of the book, which appeared in the Madrid press in
March 1924.[3] Although Unamuno's review was mainly a personal
commentary – replete with etymological digressions – on a handful of
aphorisms that had caught his eye, the simple fact that he had taken the
trouble to write it, drawing attention to the work, was enough to make his
young admirer almost deliriously happy.[4] His sense of gratitude at having
received this public blessing from Unamuno helped to strengthen the
reverential respect he felt for the man he would describe in the dedication
to his second book of aphorisms as a 'místico sembrador de vientos
espirituales' (mystical sower of spiritual winds).

El cohete y la estrella is a curiously eclectic book. Its tone moves between
the morally sententious and the playfully mischievous. The subjects it
covers range from literature, music, and painting to jazz, sports, and
women. Although it is a collection of aphorisms, it opens with a long,
narrative prose poem and closes with an exact transcription of a popular
Andalusian nonsense rhyme. And yet, as Unamuno realized, it was

'un libro de las más recóndita sinceridad' (a book of the utmost sincerity). As was to become practically the standard procedure in the case of a good deal of Bergamín's writing, it was a question of 'reading between the lines,' of penetrating the facade of stylish, unorthodox, playful poses in order to grasp the true seriousness of the book and the sense of those recurring interests and anxieties that gave it its underlying coherence.

Bergamín's choice of the aphorism as a literary form was undoubtedly determined in part by his own temperament as a writer: his natural preference for the fragmentary, self-contained observation, elegantly and often wittily condensed into a few words. The aphorism was the ideal outlet for what Juan Ramón Jiménez called his 'injenio de ardilla' (squirrel wit).[5] In other respects, however, his choice was symptomatic of a trend in prose writing in general at the beginning of the twentieth century – what Pedro Salinas called 'la ambición de la brevedad' (the ambition to be brief).[6] Between roughly 1910 and 1930, people like Jiménez, Unamuno, Eugenio D'Ors, Antonio Machado, Ramón Gómez de la Serna, and among Bergamín's contemporaries, Benjamín Jarnés, Adolfo Salazar, Giménez Caballero, and Gerardo Diego all cultivated – some more consistently than others – prose forms that were fractured, episodic, asystematic.[7] Some of these writers may well have influenced the way in which Bergamín handled the aphorism. A number of his ingenious metaphors, for example, are reminiscent of Gómez de la Serna's *greguerías*:

El cohete es una caña que piensa con brillantez.[8]

En la oscura noche de agosto el lucero tiene taquicardia. (100)

Los gallos sacuden las alas como los ángeles. (158)

Yet the possible background influences to Bergamín's aphorisms are as elusively eclectic as their substance. The kind of perspective within which they can be read needs to include not only the Spanish writers mentioned above, but also Oscar Wilde, Jean Cocteau, and Nietzsche, and from a more remote past, Pascal and Gracián.[9] Some of the most significant traces or echoes of these writers discernible in Bergamín's aphoristic works will be examined later in this discussion.

Something of the book's underlying intention can be gauged from its title and subtitle: 'Afirmaciones y dudas aforísticas lanzadas por elevación.' There is an implied opposition in the main title between the *cohete* and the *estrella*. The *estrella* seems to denote what is permanent, established, certain, though perhaps enigmatic. Its spiritual connotations are suggested in the text with which the book opens, a lyrical paraphrase of the biblical episode concerning the three wise men and their encounter with Herod (19–20). At one point, Herod threatens the wise men in the following way: '¡Os digo que tenéis la vida pendiente de un hilo mientras no me descubráis vuestra estrella maravillosa!' – to which the *rey negro*, described by Bergamín as 'más astuto que los otros y algo burlón,' answers 'lo que tenemos pendiente de un hilo, señor, es la estrella maravillosa.' He extracts from his robes 'unos grandes picos dorados' and explains 'la lleva siempre el que va delante de nosotros.' The wise men are released, but Herod orders the massacre of the children, who die clutching the toys that have been left for them.

The star would appear to represent everything that is implied by the coming of a Messiah, and yet at the same time there seems to be an element of trickery, sophistry, or sleight of hand at play. Hope and expectation are frustrated, erased by a loss of innocence and subsequent disillusionment. The aphorisms with which the book begins suggest that the interaction between the *estrella* and the *cohete* is designed to evoke this tension between belief and doubt. The short-lived *cohete* is launched into the eternity of the night sky, its brief flash of hope – and perhaps of despair too – temporarily emulating the steady light of the stars. The restless individual conscience interrogates the unchanging but unknowable certainties of the heavens. The quest for faith is met by an enigmatic silence:

En la azulada noche alta, el niño que miraba a las altas estrellas ve surgir un cohete repentino, y su corazón se inunda de alegría inocente y pura. (21)

Mientras contemplo el cielo estrellado de la noche, mi mano guarda apretadamente un taquito de cartón quemado. (21)

El cohete interrumpe sin miedo el *silencio eterno de los espacios infinitos*. (22)

The allusion to Pascal in the last aphorism is significant for a number of reasons. First, it serves as a reminder of the assiduousness with which Bergamín as a young man read Pascal.[10] Second, it draws attention to the way in which Bergamín appears in *El cohete y la estrella* as the kind of troubled spirit portrayed in the *Pensées*. When Pascal writes, for example: 'Je regarde de toutes parts, et je ne vois partout qu'obscurité'[11] or 'Nous souhaitons la vérité, et ne trouvons en nous qu'incertitude' (187), he suggests the kind of spiritual anxiety and scepticism that characterizes Bergamín:

El barómetro que marca *variable* es un irónico acusador de Dios. (26)

El escepticismo es provisional aunque dure toda la vida. (58)

La fe no es una comodidad para el espíritu, es un esfuerzo. (58)

The reflection on the continual struggle to conquer faith links Bergamín's outlook to the *agonismo* of Unamuno, too. Bergamín's doubts and uncertainties, like those of Unamuno, are not necessarily destructive. When he wrote later in *La cabeza a pájaros*, 'Si hay una mala fe, ¿por qué no va a haber una buena duda?' (105) and stated that 'La duda y la fe son el ritmo vivo del pensamiento' (101), he simply pointed to the ideal dialectical nature and the constant restlessness of religious belief. Faith, in his view, needs to be questioned continually in order for it to avoid becoming complacency, automatic unthinking practice: 'La certeza es el enemigo de la fe' (101). Again, this is in harmony with some of the opinions Pascal expressed on the subject. Bergamín's *buena duda* has its origin, perhaps, in Pascal's concept of *douter bien*: 'Nier, croire et douter bien, sont à l'homme ce que courir est au cheval' (144). It is this constant and natural oscillation between the two extremes that underlines the affinity between the two writers. What the young Bergamín voices, in effect, is Pascal's *bonne crainte*.

The *cohete*, therefore, rises – like Bergamín's hope and expectation – into the unpromisingly silent heavens, empty except for the passive, onlooking stars. The sense of the image – the lofty quest, the search for truth, permanence and illumination elsewhere than on earth – is most clearly seen in the final aphorism of the book:

Contén el impulso de tu vida hasta poder lanzarla mejor; contra cualquier cosa, si quieres ganarla; si no hacia arriba, inútilmente, para verla perderse en el cielo. (62)

The recurring possibility that the search may be futile explains why Bergamín's scepticism pervades the entire book. He seems to be caught between a genuine yearning for spiritual fulfilment and a corrosive uncertainty in the prospects of achieving it. This tension undoubtedly gives his writing much of its vigour, and is often communicated in the aphorisms as a kind of subversive heterodoxy. As in Unamuno, the intensity of the quest for faith comes across as near sedition:

Poca sensualidad nos aparta de Dios; mucha, nos lleva. (32)

Pecar, tiene arrepentimiento y perdón; no pecar, tiene solamente castigo. (32)

Ese católico virtuoso vive como si no creyera en la resurrección de la carne. (33)

Hay también un virtuosismo de la virtud, que es el peor de todos. (33)

Hay que tener un Dios, una amante y un enemigo – dice un poeta. Exactamente: hay que tener tres enemigos. (26)

Examples such as these suggest that Bergamín wished, in a sense, to 'humanize' religion. He argued in favour of the need to take into account, in matters of faith, the reality of human weakness, the facts of temptation, and inevitable sin. There may once more be echoes of Pascal here. Pascal believed that it was unnatural for man to position himself exclusively at one extreme; the other (or others) needed to be incorporated so that man could move more easily between them: 'Je n'admire point l'excès d'une vertu ... On ne montre pas sa grandeur pour être à une extrêmité, mais bien en touchant les deux à la fois, et remplissant tout l'entre-deux ... La nature de l'homme n'est pas d'aller toujours, elle a ses allées et venues' (163). The most notable expression of this principle in Bergamín's aphorisms is the importance attached to the Devil. In *El cohete y la estrella*, the Devil would appear to represent that other extreme to which Pascal refers – the opposite point of contact that virtue and faith need if they are to avoid becoming exclusive and corrupt:

Encender una vela a Dios y otra al Diablo es el principio de la sabiduría. (24)

NI MÁS NI MENOS. – Si el Diablo tira de ti hacia abajo lo mismo que el Angel hacia arriba, deberás agradecer a los dos por igual la conservación de tu equilibrio. (60)

Such an equilibrium is not necessarily static; it has its 'comings and goings,' to go back to Pascal's idea. This interplay of opposites, deeply rooted in Bergamín's sensibility, creates a kind of constantly ongoing stability, a continually renewed perspective that guides the individual forward.

In these aphorisms, therefore, Bergamín suggests how he moves from faith to doubt and back to faith again, only to repeat the whole process once more. He was later to write in *La cabeza a pájaros*:

No hay fe sin duda, ni duda sin fervor. (100)

El que espera, desespera; y el que desespera es que empieza, de nuevo, a esperar. (100)

Se empieza siempre por creer y se acaba siempre por dudar; pero hay que empezar siempre de nuevo. (101)

It is this dialectical process that defines the dynamic sense of his own faith and explains the coexistence in his work of prayer and blasphemy, of piety and irreverence. He once wrote:

Todo lo que tiene un sentido tiene un contra-sentido. Todo lo que tiene un Dios tiene un contra-Dios: el Diablo. (119)

The Devil simply affords Bergamín the best vantage point from which God can be seen. If God represents everything that he and man in general aspire to – light, life, heaven, immortality – then the Devil embodies, either in abstract or concrete terms, in theology or popular superstition, their *contra-sentido*: darkness, death, hell, and so on. The Devil stands as a reminder of what man can fall victim to if he turns his back permanently on God.[12]

*   *   *

There is much more to *El cohete y la estrella*, however, than this confession of a sincere but unorthodox *escepticismo agónico*. For a man in his late twenties, Bergamín displays a degree of sententiousness that would be surprising in a writer twice his age. The numerous aphorisms in which he preaches, admonishes, censures, and advises reveal an unusual maturity and strength of conviction in the area of moral conduct. Despite their categoric tone, which doubtless reflects the earnestness of the young writer's beliefs, these observations are elegantly expressed and intellectually challenging:

Se puede vacilar antes de decidir, pero no una vez decidido. (29)

Mejor que acertar poco a poco es equivocarse de una vez. (29)

Estar dispuesto a equivocarse es predisponerse a acertar. (33)

Limitarse no es renunciar, es conseguir. (45)

Se puede decir lo contrario de lo que se ha dicho, pero no se puede hacer lo contrario de lo que se ha hecho. (55)

The reflections of this kind that the book contains are not always couched in generalized, impersonal terms. Bergamín's frequent use of the imperative underlines his personal commitment to the ethical and intellectual principles he was advocating, as well as his premature taste for finger-wagging. Some of the most notable examples of this tendency are:

Cuando pienses, mejor o peor, no lo hagas nunca a medias. (56)

No pienses nada, o piensa hasta el fin. (56)

Aunque no vayas a ninguna parte, no te quedes en el camino. (57)

Procura no convertir tu vida en una carrera, y menos que nada en una carrera de obstáculos. (57)

Sé apasionado hasta la inteligencia. (58)

If many of these imperatives are rooted in firm ground and are readily acceptable, Bergamín elsewhere, in his more erratic and questionable judgments, reveals the arbitrariness and dilettantism of a cultured but not entirely stable young man. When Espina described the Bergamín of *El cohete y la estrella* as 'un escritor de talento, pero joven y moderno. Moderno hasta la incoordinación. Joven hasta la arbitrariedad' (a writer of talent, but young and modern. So modern he is uncoordinated; so young he is arbitrary),[13] he perceptively drew attention to the way in which the writer's obvious intelligence was sometimes qualified by an impetuosity that spawned random, precarious, and eminently fallible opinions – 'tiros perdidos en la nube o en el suelo' (shots fired at clouds or falling aimlessly to earth), as Espina called them. It is surprising that these less convincing aphorisms are devoted to literature, since a good deal of the renown that Bergamín would gain in the twenties and thirties was due precisely to the sureness of his instincts as a reader and critic. In other words, although he was soon to demonstrate an uncanny ability to recognize genuine creative talent, he included in his first book a series of judgments on literary figures (the majority of them his near contemporaries) that rested on the shaky foundations of partiality and prejudice.

Some of these literary judgments, it must be admitted, are illuminating and are expressed with considerable wit and originality:

Leyendo la prosa de Gabriel Miró – dulce y compacta como el turrón de su país – se suele tropezar también, a veces, con una amargura de almendra. (*CE* I, 65)

MAESTROS DE OBRAS. – Gabriel Miró construye su literatura como un panal. Ramón Pérez de Ayala la suya, como un nido de golondrinas. (*CE* I, 65)

El lirismo de Rosalía de Castro es el de la gaita; el de Bécquer, el del bordón de la guitarra. (*CE* I, 61)

Other observations, however, contain a mixture of mischief and malice. Ruben Darío is one of the main targets of his strictures:

Con una inconsciencia de arribista, verdaderamente genial, Rubén Darío re-estableció, como si fuese una gracia, toda la ramplonería rítmica que la poesía española había ido eliminando durante siglos. (*CE* I, 62)

Con el chin-chin de sus platillos, Rubén Darío entusiasma el mal gusto negro que casi todo el mundo lleva dentro. (*CE* I, 64)

He shows a surprising lack of sensitivity towards Machado:

Antonio Machado, retórico y neo-clásico en la segunda época de su poesía, parece un guitarrista virtuoso tocando a Beethoven y a Mozart. ¡Qué lástima de guitarra! (*CE* I, 66–7)

The fact that by the time of the Republic, Machado had become one of the poets that Bergamín most admired simply reveals the precariousness of some of his early judgments. His attitude towards Darío has undergone a similar change, and the poet who in 1923 was a paradigm of bad taste and hollow *modernismo* has since become one of Bergamín's acknowledged masters.

The way in which Baroja is peremptorily dismissed is striking only because of its youthful onesidedness:

EL 'RESTO' EN LA LITERATURA. – Todos los libros de Pío Baroja. (*CE* I, 66)

Ortega is taunted and teased in a way that would be inconceivable five or ten years later when Bergamín would be free from the contagious prejudices of Juan Ramón Jiménez and able to judge intellectual merit more objectively:

EL SENTIMIENTO ES TODO. – Cuando ha terminado el banquete, Ortega y Gasset se levanta y con esa voz cascada de piano de hotel que tiene, mientras una mueca le arruga toda la cara en una contracción que quiere ser una sonrisa, dice, dirigiéndose al festejado: *Muchísimos besos a los niños* ... (CE i, 69)

Ortega y Gasset es viejo como el mundo, como todo lo viejo, gastado y estropeado que hay en el mundo. (CE i, 69–70)

Nunca podré llegar a comprender que Ortega y Gasset tuviera unos diez o doce años, aproximadamente, cuando nací yo. (CE i, 70)[14]

Espina was clearly quite right to call Bergamín to task over what he called his 'juicios derivados más bien del apasionamiento sectario y de camarilla que domina en el mundo literario madrileño, que de la reflexión imparcial' (judgments that stem more from the narrow sectarian passions that prevail in the Madrid literary world than from impartial reflection).[15] Predictably, when *El cohete y la estrella* was republished in 1942, the text was purged. As an obvious sign of regret, and as a token of his youthful over-exuberance, Bergamín suppressed every single one of these literary opinions, even those that were entirely positive and uncontroversial and therefore unlikely to be held against him.[16]

*   *   *

Bergamín's second book of aphorisms avoided the weaknesses of the first and built upon its strengths. *La cabeza a pájaros* was published in 1934 in the Ediciones del Arbol of the journal *Cruz y Raya*, which he had begun editing the previous year. Most of the aphorisms, however, date from the period 1925–30, and include many he had published in those years in literary journals like *Alfar*, *Mediodía*, *Carmen*, *Verso y Prosa*, and *Ley*, as well as numerous unpublished ones and others distilled from longer essays written at the time.[17] Given the prominence to which Bergamín had risen in the intellectual world since the publication of his first book, it is unsurprising that *La cabeza a pájaros* was given a widely enthusiastic reception and caused the author none of the frustration and disappointment that he had felt in 1923–4. Substantial reviews were published in the Madrid press by Miguel Pérez Ferrero and Guillermo de Torre, while Pedro Salinas devoted a long and sensitive commentary to the book in the *Indice Literario* of the Consejo Superior de Investigaciones Científicas.[18] The positive response elicited from the younger intellectuals of the day, many of whom had begun looking to Bergamín as a source of guidance in the troubled years of the Republic, can be seen in the eulogies written by people like José Antonio Maravall and Ramón Sijé.[19] The publication of the book merely confirmed a reputation that had already been won and underlined the confidence and authority that the writer had gained since his début a decade earlier.

La cabeza a pájaros is very much a continuation of certain basic concerns that are apparent, albeit in fragmentary form, in *El cohete y la estrella*. It is, however, more systematically organized, being divided into five sections, each bearing a different title and each focusing broadly on a particular subject. The third section, for example, entitled 'Arte de temblar,' is devoted to poetry and brings together a series of reflections that will be examined in a later chapter dealing with Bergamín's work as a critic in the twenties. The fourth section – 'Puente de plata' – centres on music and is characterized by the writer's customary combination of perceptive insight and playful irreverence. On the one hand, Bergamín can be lyrical and suggestive as in the following examples:

La música es la puerta secreta del silencio. Una introducción a la muerte. (139)

La música pasa: el silencio queda. (140)

No te fíes demasiado de la música, que no tiene palabra. (140)

On the other hand, his critical imagination sometimes serves less solemn ends as he mocks and deflates with deftly controlled images or sudden outbursts of mischief:

El pianista se hace un lío con la oscura cola brillante de su gran piano y da manetazos de ciego para salir de las sonoras ondas sombrías que le circundan. (145)

El violín del gran virtuoso es un zapato tan lustrado que rechina de gusto. Porque el violinista pone un entusiasmo de limpiabotas en tocar su violín, en sacarle sonoramente tanto brillo que parezca un espejo: un espejuelo al que van a chocar los melómanos entontecidos como alondras. (146)

¡Cuidado con ese violín, que *tiene gatitas en la barriga!* (145)

Whereas in other parts of the book the comments are generalized and care seems to have been taken to avoid the possible criticism of sectarianism, in 'Puente de plata' Bergamín reflects on specific composers. Had these kinds of judgments been applied to literary figures, as they had been in *El cohete y la estrella*, they would doubtless have been controversial. Presumably music was considered to be a fairly unpolemical subject, however erratically it was assessed. Bergamín's attention roams over composers as distant from each other as Bach and Debussy, Chopin and Ravel. Some of his comments show genuine insight while others are more self-consciously ingenious:

A Chopin, la fuerza no se le va por la boca, se le va por las manos. (149)

The other three sections of the book are entitled 'Molino de razón,' 'La cáscara amarga,' and 'El grito en el cielo' and describe different aspects of Bergamín's spiritual identity. The first section opens with a striking self-portrait:

He tomado en mi vida una cruz que da vueltas como las aspas del molino y muelo razonablemente mi trigo haciendo aspavientos de loco. (92)

This recalls the definition of faith that Pascal gave in his *Pensées*: 'ni sagesse ni signes, mais la croix et la folie' (225). Indeed, the kind of humane scepticism and sensitive anti-rationality that Pascal alludes to in his writing is again evident in many of the aphorisms that deal with religion, developing ideas that were already present in *El cohete y la estrella*.

Bergamín's commitment to his own faith is total and unequivocal:

Dios es cosa, causa de todo, porque todo es causa, cosa de Dios. (96)

O todo es mío o yo soy de Dios. (103)

The Devil, however, continues to be a constant companion, struggling to undermine this allegiance to God. Summarizing an idea that he explored at length in his essay 'La importancia del demonio,' he writes:

Donde no está la voluntad de Dios está siempre la del Diablo. (118)

The implication is of the struggle to resist the Devil's will in order to receive grace and faith and harks back to the dialectical *agonismo* of Bergamín's first book. The Devil is no longer seen as a necessary counterpoint, but rather as the extreme antithesis to God, trying to secure the downfall of the man who seeks salvation:

Mi vida está detrás de la cruz, como el Diablo; por eso luchamos cuerpo a cuerpo, siempre, los dos: por el mismo sitio. (92)

But the idea of the continually enriching oscillation between doubt and faith, evident in *El cohete y la estrella*, is strongly developed in *La cabeza a pájaros*:

Hombre de mucha fe, ¿por qué no has dudado? (101)

La duda no es vacilación: es oscilación y es fidelidad. (101)

En la duda, en las dudas, no te abstengas nunca de creer. (101)

Al que no le cabe duda de nada, ¿cómo le va a caber la fe de todo? (104)

The movement between reason and passion is similarly elevated into a major canon of Bergamín's spiritual beliefs, echoing perhaps Pascal's view of 'le vrai christiannisme' as 'soumission et usage de la raison' (146). Bergamín's reflections on the subject seem imbued with precisely the kind of 'inteligencia de la pasión' that he had responded to in Pascal (70). The latter's concept of faith as 'Dieu sensible au coeur, non à la raison' (147) is reflected in *La cabeza a pájaros* where reason, as a means of access to knowledge, is either rejected or else transformed sentimentally – passionately – into a means of perceiving truths that evidently go beyond logic and rationality:

Razón es pasión, y pasión es conocimiento. (95)

El que no tiene pasión no tiene razón: aunque pueda tener razones. (99)

La razón es la única loca que hay en la casa: una loca muy de su casa. (99)

This constant questioning of the usefulness of reason in matters of faith leads Bergamín, as it did Pascal, to appreciate the 'purity of ignorance':

the sanctity of childlike innocence, uncorrupted by learning. The idea is, of course, present in the teachings of Christ but both Pascal and Bergamín seem especially responsive to it. Where Pascal stated simply, as a corollary to his disavowal of reason, 'la sagesse nous envoie à l'enfance' (146), Bergamín made of the notion one of the most fundamental and engaging (though easily misunderstood) tenets of his religion. For him it was an idea that lent itself ideally to the kind of provocative, paradoxical formulae that he cultivated:

La inocencia lo ignora todo porque lo sabe todo. (114)

Bienaventurados los que no saben leer ni escribir porque ellos serán llamados analfabetos. (110)

La letra entre con fe, con sangre. Y al pie de la letra está el Espíritu crucificado. (122)

The implications of such convictions as these were examined by Bergamín in another major essay of the period: 'La decadencia del analfabetismo.'[20] It is a kind of lengthy postscript to the aphorisms quoted above, and is essentially a lament for the damaging effect on the pure spirituality of the *niño/pueblo* of the misguided reverence for learning and reason.

Bergamín appears, in *La cabeza a pájaros*, to be curiously suspended between the orthodox and the unorthodox, projecting the same kind of dual personality the reader discerns in *El cohete y la estrella*: the genuinely restless thinker held in check by the playfully ironic sceptic. His preoccupation with death and immortality, for example, which linked him to Unamuno among others, explains why he should feel drawn towards the classical paradoxes of Christian belief: life as death, death as life. His aphorisms on the subject are subdued and conventional. What vitality they have stems rather from their *conceptista* exploitation of opposites than from any substantive originality:

Piensa siempre en la muerte para la vida, no en la vida para la muerte. (108)

La vida es mentira; la verdad no es vida, es razón: pasión y muerte. (111)

Bergamín's use of the paradox, however, becomes more suggestive when it is directed elsewhere. His interpretation of blasphemy, for example, as a sure sign of continuing faith shows how unsettling his logic can be at times:

La blasfemia del pueblo es un grito de angustia que Dios oye como una oración. El que blasfema no ha perdido la fe todavía: y si se alza contra Dios es porque cree en El y le ama, desesperadamente, aun sin saberlo. (119)

His attacks on unidimensional faith, cut off from everything else in its 'virtuosismo de la virtud' – to return to the phrase he used in *El cohete y la estrella* – are similarly unorthodox:

Si eres demasiado moral, exclusivamente moral, no podrás ser creyente. (123)

La fe católica se arraiga en la inmoralidad humana como en su propia naturaleza de tierra preparada por la corrupción que le abona; se nutre de ella ocultamente para poder nacer pura, saliendo a respirar al aire libre de los cielos: la común anarquía en que culmina la plenitud de su existencia. (123)

* * *

It may already be evident from the examples quoted above that one of the prime stylistic features of Bergamín's aphorisms is their imaginative revision of commonplaces of all kinds, particularly the fixed formulae of popular speech. In his review of *La cabeza a pájaros*, Salinas drew attention to the way in which Bergamín constantly referred back, in a creative and inventive way, to the proverbs and idioms of the Spanish language:

A lo largo de su obra se alude constantemente a personajes, frases hechas y costumbres populares. Parece haber como un fondo de resonancias de lo popular en lo más remoto de su espíritu. Pero esas frases hechas, sobadas y resobadas por el uso, las somete Bergamín a un proceso de profundización y elevación, las poetiza y las convierte en una expresión cargada para nuestros oídos de familiaridad, y, en cambio, para nuestro espíritu, deslumbrante, de brillo nuevo.[21]

(Throughout his work there are constant allusions to set phrases, popular customs, and figures. In the deepest recesses of his mind there seem to be resonances of popular culture. But Bergamín makes these idioms and commonplaces more profound, elevated, and poetic, and transforms them into expressions that, on the one hand, are familiar to the ear, but which, on the other hand, dazzle the mind with their brand new shine.)

Whereas Salinas emphasized the lyrical aspects of this process, Guillermo de Torre, writing about the same book, referred to its critical nature, its tendency to call conventional ideas into question: 'no sólo ataca a los lugares comunes, a las frases hechas, sino a los modos proverbiales, a los clisés del idioma, tan abundantes en castellano' (not only does he attack commonplaces and set phrases but also proverbial expressions and linguistic clichés, so numerous in Spanish).[22] Since this approach to popular language was to become the hallmark of Bergamín's literary style in general, it is worth examining in some detail.

If Bergamín's fascination with popular language itself stemmed from his daily contact as a child with the maids of his household, his technique of manipulating it, ingeniously and critically, may well have owed something to the immediate precedents set by Unamuno in Spain and Oscar Wilde in England. Although the stylistic affinities between these writers are useful to bear in mind, it is probably unwise to take the comparisons too far. Unamuno, for example, has constantly been cited as the model Bergamín used as both thinker and stylist.[23] It is certainly true that Unamuno's taste for the lapidary and often paradoxical statement was shared by his young admirer and can be seen throughout the latter's writing, not only in his aphorisms. Whether Bergamín consciously or unconsciously responded to Unamuno's call to 'repensar los grandes lugares comunes' (rethink the great commonplaces) is a matter of debate; but the fascination with etymology and the affection for the unsuspected truths that words could be shown to contain if sufficiently coaxed or juggled clearly bound the two writers together. There is evidence, too, to suggest that Bergamín read Oscar Wilde as a young man, and the conception and presentation of his essay 'La decadencia del analfabetismo' may be indebted to Wilde's provocatively entitled essay 'The Decay of Lying.' In this context, Wilde's conviction that 'our proverbs want rewriting'[24] is particularly significant. In his plays and essays, proverbs were cleverly amended: 'Indiscretion is the better part of valour' (4); 'Divorces are made in heaven' (xii). They are also respun to great effect: 'Work is the curse of the drinking classes' (xii). Clichés too are continually subverted and redeployed: 'the survival of the vulgarest' (10); 'hitting below the intellect' (102), and so on. In precisely the same way, as will be seen, many of Bergamín's aphorisms put familiar sayings and turns of phrase to decidedly unfamiliar uses. Like Wilde, Bergamín rearranges conventional wisdom and reorchestrates conventional linguistic and moral norms to serve a more elevated or witty purpose.[25]

There are a number of obvious instances in *El cohete y la estrella* and *La cabeza a pájaros* where the practical wisdom contained in proverbial expressions is bluntly refuted. The proverbs are turned around and consequently made to illuminate a totally different and naturally more subtle and suggestive idea. Consider the following idea:

PIENSA MAL Y NO ACERTARAS. – Se acierta siempre, en arte, cuando se piensa bien. (45)

The cynical popular adage 'piensa mal y acertarás' is usually invoked in order to avoid over-optimistic judgments of other people. Characteristic here is the way in which the correction of the proverb becomes meaningful by being placed in a new context, 'en arte' being the operative phrase. Hence the proverb ceases to have anything to do with personal assessments and is transformed into an aesthetic judgment. The terms of Bergamín's remark are, as Salinas pointed out, entirely familiar, but the new arrangement and revised context they are given engender fresh meaning. A closely related example is

NO SIEMPRE LO PEOR ES CIERTO. – Los carteles de Zuloaga, que no anuncian ninguna corrida. (47)

The writer again subverts the pragmatic pessimism of the popular belief that 'lo peor es cierto' and uses the reconstructed phrase as an instrument with which to pass ironic judgment on Zuloaga's painting.

Bergamín's 'corrections' amount to a re-contextualization of the traditional common sense of proverbs. By simply contending the opposite of a given formula, he radically redirects its meaning. When, for example, he writes

EL SABER OCUPA LUGAR. – El valor de una inteligencia se cotiza generalmente por el cesto de los papeles (62),

he evidently discards the conventional idea of the usefulness of learning ('el saber no ocupa lugar'), but the resonances set up by the component parts of the proverb are retained and simply re-tuned in order to register a different point. In the kind of straightforward inversion that Bergamín offers in 'Más vale un pájaro volando que ciento en la mano' (116) the effect is to substitute a 'poetic' truth for an eminently practical one. In other words, the proverb has been lyrically re-invented. This happens elsewhere, too, where by refuting the soundness of a proverb the writer is able to dignify and elevate its meaning into a spiritual one:

Lo cierto es la muerte; lo incierto, lo dudoso, es la vida: la inmortalidad. Aprende a
dejar lo cierto por lo dudoso. (101)

In this case, unlike almost all the examples quoted previously, the revised
proverbial formula appears at the end instead of being used as a title or
introduction with which to establish at once an unfamiliar context for
familiar associations. Here, the subverted proverb is appended as a kind
of attention-catching postscript to a comment in which specifically
spiritual values are given to notions ('lo cierto' and 'lo dudoso') that in
normal usage have only practical implications. This is a good example of
what Salinas called the 'espiritualización de lo popular' in Bergamín's
aphorisms, a process to which I shall return in connection with his use of
colloquial expressions.

In other cases, Bergamín does not correct or even modify substantially
the structure of a proverb but instead uses it as a point of departure for a
further commentary. It is apparent in these brief glosses that his purpose
is to guide the reader's attention not towards what the proverb conventionally says but towards what it can be shown to mean if approached and
extended in a particular way. In the following example, therefore, the
proverbial expression functions only as a prop:

Más sabe el Diablo por viejo que por Diablo. Lo mismo da. Porque cuando empezó
a ser Diablo empezó a saber: y empezó a envejecer. (114)

Bergamin's point here has nothing to do with the idea of the wisdom that
experience and old age bring. Whereas in the proverb the *Diablo* is purely
figurative, Bergamín resurrects its literal meaning. In this way he is able to
use it in order to convey a deeply held spiritual conviction, namely that
knowledge and learning can be diabolical and corrupting, separating man
– by ageing him – from his natural, childlike, and divine innocence. A
related point is made in similar fashion in the following aphorism:

La letra entre con fe, con sangre. Y al pie de la letra está el Espíritu crucificado.
(122)

Here Bergamín has merely taken the set phrase 'la letra con sangre entra'
as a stepping stone from which to proceed to a more challenging and
complex idea. As a consequence, the proverbial notion of the effort
involved in the acquisition of knowledge is abandoned. The writer uses
the literal sense of *sangre* in order to link up with the image of the

crucifixion, suggesting how spiritual values fall victim to the progress of literacy. The incorporation of the idiom 'al pie de la letra' is an additional sign of the subtlety with which ideas are sometimes expressed in these books. Bergamín divorces the idiom from its figurative meaning and by insisting on the literal sense of both *pie* and *letra* succeeds in establishing a connection between both the *letra* of the proverb 'la letra con sangre entra' and the 'Espíritu crucificado' that hangs, *literally*, at the foot of it. Indeed, the suggestion is of Christ crucified beneath the *letra* proclaiming him to be King of the Jews.

It is easy to see in the following example how the gloss can distort the sense of the proverb by widening and complicating its implications:

Dios aprieta, pero no ahoga. La música ahoga, sin apretar, suavemente, como el Diablo. (143)

Once again the proverb – 'Dios aprieta pero no ahoga' – is merely a pretext. Bergamín is less interested in the comforting advice it contains on the need for resignation in the face of hardship than in using its familiar component parts to formulate a surprising judgment on music. Predictably, the elements in the proverb are taken at their face value and then built upon in order to argue the diabolical effects of music on the unsuspecting listener. Elsewhere the gloss is briefer but still charges the lifeless commonplace with new meaning:

Si te he visto, no me acuerdo; si te he mirado, sí. (110)

En la variación está el gusto de la eternidad – piensa la veleta. (161)

Some unusual effects are achieved by tampering with the proverb in a more subtle way. The resonances that its individual parts set up are still clearly discernible, but they are arranged in a new sequence. For example, Bergamín takes the solemn pragmatism of the saying 'Primero es la obligación que la devoción,' shuffles the words around slightly and produces the unexpected formula:

La primera obligación es la devoción. (98)

There is no better comment on this process than Salinas's:

Bergamín apenas si varía la frase, no introduce en ella elemento conceptual nuevo, escribe sencillamente 'la primera obligación es la devoción,' y el conflicto de la frase queda resuelto de golpe, de plano, sólo por un tratamiento espiritual de aquellos elementos verbales.[26]

(Bergamín hardly alters the phrase at all; he does not introduce any new conceptual element into it. He simply writes 'Devotion is the first obligation' and the tension in the sentence is suddenly and totally resolved, simply by a spiritual treatment of those linguistic items.)

With the minimum of reformation, Bergamín achieves the maximum reorientation, revitalization, and spiritualization of meaning.

The procedure is similar in an aphorism like 'La ciencia propone y la filosofía dispone' (27) where Bergamín takes the given structure and balance of a proverb ('El hombre propone y Dios dispone') and reapplies them to different categories. It is as if he delights in flattering the reader's familiarity with a given formula only to surprise him with a fresh rendering of the relationship it normally describes. This is essentially his technique when handling idiomatic expressions. The idiom is immediately recognizable, but its usual figurative meaning is in some way altered. Bergamín prefers to play upon the literal, delexicalized meanings when formulating his judgments. Consider the following two examples where the idiom appears – as was the case with certain proverbs – as a kind of preamble to the aphorism itself:

CON LA MUSICA A OTRA PARTE. – ¿Adónde podrán ir ya, Señor, los alemanes con su música? ...
El Señor: Es de esperar que no vengan al cielo. (42)

PINTAR COMO QUERER. – Aprender a vivir es aprender a conducirse, y aprender a conducirse en la vida es como aprender a dibujar; primero se copia del modelo y luego se hace lo que se quiere. Por eso hay que aprender a querer, para saber lo que se quiere. (45)

In neither example is the usual sense of the idiom respected. Rather, each serves as a starting point from which Bergamín, by insisting on the literal values of *música* and *pintar*, is able to launch observations related directly or indirectly to these two disciplines. Whereas the expression 'irse con la música a otra parte' is normally used, in the imperative, to get rid of something that is annoying in a general sense, Bergamín exploits its literal, specifically musical connotations. By using the idiom as a title, he amplifies the sense of the dialogue, maintaining a semantic link between the two (by means of *música*) and compressing their critical, condemnatory thrust.

The idiom 'pintar como querer' undergoes an analogous revision. Bergamín divorces it entirely from its traditional associations (of 'wishful thinking,' 'day-dreaming,' and so on) and uses the literal meanings of the verbs *pintar* and *querer* as a vehicle for a generalized moral judgment. This shows the distance that is constantly and surprisingly opened up between the overworked idiom and the richly suggestive reformulation. In a statement such as 'El aburrimiento de la ostra produce perlas' (115), the colourless commonplace ('aburrirse/aburrido como una ostra') is cleverly transformed into a much more provocative idea simply by rethinking the relationship between its component parts.

A technique that is sometimes used balances or contrasts one semantic item – devoid of any obvious figurative meaning – against another, the figurative sense of which is only partially discarded. Consider the following two aphorisms:

De casi todos los sitios en que se entra muy fácilmente por la puerta, se suele salir por la ventana. (28)

A Chopin la fuerza no se le va por la boca, se le va por las manos. (149)

In the first example, a balance is elegantly created between *entrar/puerta* and *salir/ventana* in their literal senses. Yet the meaning of the aphorism depends on the figurative sense of the phrase 'salir por la ventana,' which denotes failure. As often happens, the aphorism resonates with its own ambivalence, produced by this artful fusion of literal and figurative meanings. In the second example, the symmetry and contrast (*boca/manos*) is ingeniously engineered, though once again the connection between the two is precarious: Bergamín has made simultaneous use of both the figurative sense of the idiom 'írsele a uno la fuerza por la boca' and the literal meaning of its component parts.

There are also a number of cases in which *both* parts of the aphorism are used in different senses at one and the same time. The most memorable example is:

Cuando se tiene la *cabeza a pájaros* hay que *andarse con pies de plomo*. (154)

At one level, the aphorism exploits the opposition between the literal senses of *cabeza* and *pies*, simply suggesting physical extremes. Yet both expressions – 'tener la cabeza a pájaros' and 'andarse con pies de plomo' – are figurative ones, the first suggesting a 'featherbrained' disposition and the second, deliberate caution or stealth. Hence the two parts of the aphorism oppose and balance each other at a different level, too. At this second level, the *pies de plomo* function as an abstract antidote to the *cabeza a pájaros*. By operating simultaneously at both levels, Bergamín engenders a subtle duality of meaning, a blend of surface similarity and deep dissimilarity.

While much of this toying with literal and figurative meanings produces ingenious results, some of the ideas that Bergamín constructs out of popular sayings have a distinctly lyrical quality. This is particularly true when some spiritual sense is extracted from an idiom that, according to all conventional criteria, has no religious connotation. The series of aphorisms grouped around the expression 'poner el grito en el cielo' is a prime illustration of how serious ideas can be conveyed by delicate reorientations of popular phrases. Bergamín characteristically side-steps the idea of loud complaining or indignation that the idiom usually expresses. Instead, he sees in the image of the heaven-bound cry – once more an image created by the *literal* meaning of the phrase – a way of capturing not only the idea of faith and prayer, of contact with God, but also the meaning of Christ's exclamation on the cross. Consider the three aphorisms with which the series ends:

La fe es estar siempre en un grito y ponerlo, siempre, en el cielo.

Si no pones el grito en el cielo, ¿cómo quieres que te oiga Dios?

Cristo al morir puso el grito en el cielo. (148–9)

The definition of faith, the invitation to prayer and the depiction of Christ crucified derive not only their ingenuity but also their strength and memorability from this pointed reformulation of a popular saying. Nowhere is Bergamín's masterly re-creation of the *modismo* for his own spiritual ends clearer than in these examples.

Finally, some unexpected and witty effects are achieved when what might be called 'scientific commonplaces' – i.e. fixed mathematical formulae, endlessly repeated like idioms and proverbs – are revised and put to new uses. For example, Bergamín produces a new version of Archimedes's principle when he comments:

Un alemán sumergido en una civilización cualquiera distinta de Alemania pierde de su peso el de un volumen igual al de inteligencia que desaloja. (31)

The substitution of moral categories for mathematical ones in the following example produces a formula that is instantly familiar but decidedly new in meaning:

La conducta recta es la menor distancia entre dos vidas. (59)

*   *   *

From the discussion above, it will be evident that there is much 'agudeza y arte de ingenio' in Bergamín's aphorisms. There is good reason, therefore, to add the name of Baltasar Gracián to those already mentioned as background influences and possible sources of inspiration for *El cohete y la estrella* and *La cabeza a pájaros*. Bergamín's critical revision of proverbial expressions, for example, as well as his subtle word-plays, could owe as much to Gracián and the Baroque tradition in Spain in the seventeenth century as to Unamuno and Oscar Wilde, and it is unsurprising that the two writers have been compared. Torrente Ballester, for example, describes Gracián as 'el escritor con el que [Bergamín] guarda mayor semejanza estilística' (the writer to whom Bergamín is most closely allied stylistically), while Andrés Amorós significantly uses the word 'neogracianesco' to describe Bergamín's aphorisms.[27] Bergamín's stylistic affiliations with the seventeenth century are examined in greater detail in the discussion of his discursive prose, but in order to complete this survey of his aphorisms, it would be helpful to look at some of their formal characteristics that justify this comparison with Gracián.

I have referred above to the way in which Bergamín exploits the double meanings that words sometimes have, particularly words contained in popular expressions and therefore endowed with a figurative as well as a literal sense. This usage indicates the presence in his aphoristic works of a strong element of verbal *conceptismo* of the kind to which Gracián devoted a good deal of attention in his study of *conceptismo* as a whole.[28] Bergamín also manipulates sounds and meanings in a number of other ways, strengthening the degree of purely linguistic ingenuity that his aphorisms have. For example, he plays on the similarity between the sounds of words that have no semantic connection:

Tan poco les dijo que tampoco lo comprendieron. (95)

He links and contrasts words that have the same root origin, thereby emphasizing simultaneously their surface similarity and their effective difference:

El músculo no construye, destruye. (37)

La reforma no es lo que forma, sino lo que deforma. (55)

Lo razonado no tiene nada que ver con lo razonable. (60)

Si eres crédulo no puedes ser creyente. (104)

Una bebida espirituosa no puede causar un daño espiritual. (30)

The emphatic negatives in each of these aphorisms reveal how words that seems to gravitate towards each other by virtue of a phonic relationship are in the end sharply differentiated.

Bergamín's *conceptismo*, however, and his stylistic kinship with Gracián go far beyond this. The two writers also share a notable preoccupation with balance and opposition, what Gracián called a 'simetría intelectual entre los términos del pensamiento' (intellectual symmetry between the terms of the idea).[29] In Bergamín this insistent movement between opposing extremes explains why much of his writing assumes a sharply symmetrical form, in both a conceptual and a linguistic sense. This is true not only of his aphorisms – in which similar or contrasting items are continually played off against each other – but also of several individual books. *El arte de birlibirloque* (1930), for example, is built upon a sustained comparison between the Apolonian Joselito and the Dionysian Belmonte. The arguments of *Mangas y capirotes* (1933) depend similarly on the differences established between Greek and Christian theatre or between Lope de Vega and Tirso de Molina. The kind of reasoning procedures that underpinned books like these are also found in Bergamín's journal *Cruz y Raya*, in the tense but elegant balance and interaction between affirmation and negation, acceptance and rejection.

In the aphorisms, ideas are rarely tackled in isolation. As Luis Felipe Vivanco once pointed out: 'Bergamín, para pensar ... necesita moverse entre los términos de una disyunción' (in order to think Bergamín needs to move between two disjunctive terms).[30] This explains why he constantly uses an opposite or complement of some kind in order to throw into sharper relief the qualities of the items he is seeking to define. Many of his literary and artistic judgments, for example, depend on confrontation:

43 The Aphorist

Bécquer es apasionado; Rubén Darío sentimental. (*CE* I, 61)

La escultura de Rodin baila en un solo pie, por virtuosismo; la de Méstrovic, porque su otra pierna es de palo. (39)

Satie es a Debussy todo lo contrario que Listz a Wagner. (42)

Aphorisms like these are symmetrical not only in the sense that individual artists – and sometimes pairs of artists – are juxtaposed, but also in the careful balancing and contrasting of associated terms. Bergamín often draws together two (or more) items into a common conceptual framework and then suggests, usually ironically, the distance that separates them. For example:

En la literatura francesa se puede elegir a la carta; en la española no hay más que el cubierto. (48)

Sometimes the stark symmetrical simplicity of the comparison is striking. If in this example,

Cristianismo puro: barbarie pura (25),

the balance is between antithetical substantives, the identical adjectives creating that 'common ground' on which the concepts clash, then in the following example, the balance rests on the opposition between both nouns and verbs:

La música pasa: el silencio queda. (140)

Bergamín continually created what Gracián referred to as an 'armónica correlación' between opposing notions, balancing their attributes in condensed, uncluttered, symmetrical fashion in order better to define them:

La fe es única; la duda, múltiple. (101)

La castidad es lo viril; la lujuria, lo afeminado. (36)

Sensualidad es liberación; sexualidad es servidumbre. (33)

El título es cosa del hombre. El nombre es cosa de Dios. (113)

Other types of aphorism are constructed along similar lines. The symmetrical balance of contrasts in the above examples is sometimes slightly altered in favour of a more subtle binary rhythm. In these cases, the second part of the aphorism extends the first instead of merely balancing it, and opens up an additional dimension of the proposed idea:

Existir es pensar; y pensar es comprometerse. (32)

Belleza es expresión; y expresión es, siempre, milagro. (95)

No hay fe sin duda, ni duda sin fervor. (100)

El pensamiento es un estado de gracia. Y la gracia un estado de juego. (95)

Each aphorism has a clear pivotal point on which it turns and seems to invite a syllogistic conclusion that would effectively establish a link between the two extremes: 'existir *es* comprometerse,' 'belleza *es* milagro,' and so on.

At other times the balance between the two parts of the aphorism depends on the initial creation and subsequent resolution of what might be termed an 'interrogative tension.' This is to say that, just like Gracián, Bergamín arouses the interest and expectation of his reader by opening his sentences with some unusual or simply provocative remark.[31] The sentence then closes by explaining or justifying that unconventional beginning. The structure of this kind of aphorism is again symmetrical in the sense that it seems to ascend with the initial creation of this tension, and then descend as the tension is resolved. A few examples will clarify this idea:

El aforismo no es breve: es inconmensurable. (94)

By initially refuting the most conventional quality of the aphorism – namely its brevity – Bergamín unsettles the reader, but the tension thus created is dispersed by the introduction of the concept of immeasurability. As often happens, two terms are viewed within a common conceptual framework – in this case 'size' or 'measurability' – only for the distance that separates them to be emphasized. The same rhythm is evident in the following:

La duda no es vacilación : es oscilación y fidelidad. (101)

Here, the accepted nature of doubt is questioned, creating a tension or hesitancy in the reader. Bergamín plays on the phonic similarity between *vacilación* and *oscilación*, but at the same time underlines the distinction between the two terms.[32]

The frequent use of the chiasmus produces a different effect. Instead of opening up onto some new aspect of the idea, or resolving a point by extending and explaining it, the second part of the aphorism in these cases turns back upon itself, literally reversed, so that the geometrically opposite contention can be maintained. The symmetry and elegant equilibrium of the phrase here depends upon words mirroring themselves. Sometimes it is a question of a straightforward inversion:

Dios es cosa, causa de todo, porque todo es causa, cosa de Dios. (96)

No hay inteligencia sin instinto o instinto sin inteligencia. (97)

At other times the inversion is more ingenious, involving a change in grammatical function of one or all of the aphorism's component parts. There are changes involving nouns and adjectives, as in these examples:

Ni el arte es religioso, ni la religión artística. (29)

Sensualidad: miraje místico. Misticismo: miraje sensual. (33)

La poesía es cosa natural y la naturaleza cosa poética. (97)

Bergamín demonstrates his fondness for this device by taking it to the extreme of composing false versions of the chiasmus, warning the reader against the dangers of reversing a given formula:

Un entomólogo es un coleccionista; pero un coleccionista no es un entomólogo. (31)

Un juguete guarda siempre un enigma. Pero un enigma no guarda nunca ningún juguete. (136)

The use of the chiasmus simply emphasizes the elegant symmetry that characterizes so many of the aphorisms. The inversion of words and ideas produces rhythms and arrangements that are stimulating aesthetically, while at the same time creating unusual perspectives on all kinds of ideas.

Other unusual perspectives are created by the use of the paradox. The importance Gracián himself attached to the paradox as an instrument of *conceptista* thinking can be gauged from the space he devotes to it in his *Agudeza y arte de ingenio*.[33] Bergamín favoured this device in all his writings of the period, but in his aphorisms especially, some of his most original and suggestive insights are expressed in paradoxical terms. For example:

El arte verdadero procura no llamar la atención, para que se fijen en él. (44)

The reasoning behind this comment furnishes an excellent example of how the *conceptista* mind functions. Conventionally one would expect that in order to be noticed, it would be natural and necessary to attract attention. However, it is precisely because this kind of logic is predictable that the *conceptista* chooses to subvert it. Bergamín argues that art that is ostentatious, deliberately drawing attention to itself, is of suspect value: 'mucho ruido para nada.' True art, on the other hand, quietly pursues its own goals. When this reasoning is condensed into aphoristic form – and it is the *condensation* above all that gives the comment its impact – it appears as an abrupt contradiction.

A similar example would be:

Para mentir con facilidad basta ser sincero. (110)

Again, where conventional reasoning naturally associates sincerity with telling the truth, the *conceptista* strategy is to contend the opposite. The conceit contained in the aphorism, as in many others, is precisely the establishment of a logical connection (the logic being unusual but still plausible) between two ideas that are to all intents and purposes incompatible. Clearly, if approached from a suitably unorthodox point of view, it makes sense to say that a liar who doubts his lies will argue with less conviction and success than the liar who firmly believes in his. Similar glosses could be written on the following examples, too, where the surface contradiction can be resolved by reconstructing the unusual paths taken by the writer's mind:

Cuando una mujer tiraniza es cuando muestra mejor que es esclava.(34)

Para poder dudar de algo hay que estar seguro de todo. (104)

Si la música dijera la verdad, mentiría. (141)

El escepticismo es provisional aunque dure toda la vida. (80)

El que lo acepta todo rechaza lo mejor. (111)

There is an obvious danger in trying to relate too closely the formal characteristics of Bergamín's aphorisms with the style of another writer or with a clearly defined (though varied) stylistic tendency such as *conceptismo*. This danger concerns the fact that certain rhetorical devices tend naturally to surface in the aphorism: the paradox, the word-play, symmetry, and so on are used by aphorists simply because they achieve the maximum effect within the constraints imposed by the form. It is as easy to document apparent similarities of expression between Bergamín, Unamuno, Gómez de la Serna, and Gracián as it is between Bergamín, Goethe, Reverdy, and Novalis. It is unwise, therefore, to invest too heavily in such comparisons. If Bergamín's kinship with Gracián seems to be especially convincing it is because, as I shall go on to argue, the affiliation with the Baroque prose style of Spain's seventeenth century is particularly pronounced.

*   *   *

Juan Ramón Jiménez once wrote that 'un aforista es bizarro – espuma ... de jabón, de sastre; otro – agua viva de manantial – eterno' (one type of aphorist is bizarre – a soap bubble; another – fresh water from a spring – eternal).[34] Although this is more a general observation on types of aphorists than a specific critical judgment, Jiménez leaves little doubt as to where his own preferences lie. Like Nietzsche, he believed that the aphorism could be a 'form of eternity.'[35] Given the weaknesses of Bergamín's early aphorisms – their iconoclasm and partiality, their sometimes ephemeral nature – it is in a sense surprising that Jiménez should have shown such enthusiasm for *El cohete y la estrella*. He clearly realized that beneath its *bizarre* posturing lightheartedness there lay a genuine depth of perception and a more permanent capacity to enlighten and question. In a letter he wrote to Bergamín in 1923, following the book's publication, the encouragement he gave his young protegé reveals a recognition of the double-edged character of his aphorisms:

¡Y vuelva usted firme y entusiasta, a terminar otro libro tan alerto y multiestallante – aunque a veces sea el tronido y el buscapié debajo de la mesa de alguien – como *El Cohete!*[36]

(I hope you return full of resolve and enthusiasm, ready to finish another book as alert and volatile as *El Cohete*, even though the aphorisms are sometimes claps of thunder or kicks under the table!)

This combination of critical vigilance and earnest if sometimes playful subversion was to become a major feature of Bergamín's style and outlook. Benjamín Jarnés once proclaimed categorically that 'un libro de aforismos no es nada, si no es un bello cofrecillo de sorpresas' (a book of aphorisms is nothing if it isn't an exquisite little box of surprises).[37] In his aphoristic works, Bergamín's continual 'surprises' – whether outrageous or scandalous, disturbing or haunting – are the measure of the freshness of his perception, the strength of his capacity to rethink, revise, and reorder the common fund of experience. By manipulating ideas and language with such flair and originality, he was able constantly to catch his readers unawares, disconcerting the poets, the philosophers, the musicians, and the believers among them. Bergamín emerges from *El cohete y la estrella* and *La cabeza a pájaros* as an expert in masterminding the conceptual ambush, ever ready to fire a passing shot – *una saeta aforística* – at the conventional expectations of his public.

3

'Gusano de luz':
The Critic

Si quieres expresar la luz, hazte cámara oscura.

J.B.

It must have been rather unsettling for Bergamín to find himself, in the early 1920s, surrounded by a group of friends who were superlatively gifted poets.[1] Even before the publication of *El cohete y la estrella*, he had tried his hand at poetry but, perhaps on the advice of Juan Ramón Jiménez, had decided not to publish it.[2] Bergamín's problem was to know that he had an obvious talent as a writer and yet to be unsure about what to do with it. The success of his aphorisms among certain readers offered only partial reassurance. His cultivation, in the twenties, of a variety of other genres may be interpreted in retrospect as a sign of his search for the appropriate outlet for his creativity and originality. Even if this search was never formulated as a problem, the way in which the uncertainties it implied were resolved points to the place that Bergamín eventually found for himself in that constellation of prodigious talent in Madrid at the time.

Bergamín's solution involved, in effect, the formal renunciation of poetry, the decision – perhaps unconscious – not to try to compete with the poets of his own age on the ground to which they had laid claim. This did not stop him from writing poetry, but it did dissuade him from publishing it. Nor did his decision mean that in his published work his lyrical instincts and his attachment to poetry were suppressed. What it did mean, rather, was that his poetry underwent a series of transformations. In the first place, his style as a prose writer sometimes became what one critic has perceptively called 'una indecisa forma de versificación' (a hesitant form of versification).[3] In the second place, his major energies as a writer were channelled into the role of critic and commentator of poetry in general and, more specifically, of the poetry of his own generation. This, essentially, was the singular contribution that Bergamín made to pre-war literary life in Spain.

This role that Bergamín found for himself is referred to in an important article of 1929 by Gerardo Diego. He described Bergamín as an 'espectador participante de la poesía, frente a la que viene a representar el papel del coro en la tragedia griega, la de su espejo o conciencia pasiva, y, por momentos, activa' (a participating spectator of poetry, opposite which he plays the part of the chorus in Greek tragedy, the role of its mirror or its passive – and sometimes active – consciousness).[4] He went on to link Bergamín with José María de Cossío, another indefatigable critic of the time, and commented: 'Tanto Cossío como Bergamín han escrito versos – y Bergamín obras de creación dramática y filosófica – pero ellos, modestamente, prefieren actuar de animadores o iluminadores – gusanos de luz – de la poesía ajena' (Both Cossío and Bergamín have written verse – and Bergamín has also written dramatic and philosophical works – but modestly they prefer to act as animators or illuminators – glow-worms – of the poetry of others) (193). These critical and creative *illuminations* are to be found in the essays and reviews that Bergamín wrote throughout the twenties and thirties and upon which his distinction as a writer came to rest. If this distinction has subsequently been obscured, it is largely because these texts lie scattered in a large number of publications not readily accessible to the interested public. There still exists no single volume of his writings devoted to aesthetics and to the poetry of his contemporaries. It is only by going back to those texts that it becomes possible to recover the sense of Bergamín's activities in those years in his capacity as 'gusano de luz,' as the critical instrument through which 'la poesía ajena' was illuminated.[5]

For the purpose of this discussion, Bergamín's writings of the period can be divided up into two main categories. The first covers what might be called the theory of poetry and involves general questions of aesthetics. The writings that fall into this category are important, since they shed light on the approaches to poetry that dominated the twenties in particular and which have consistently attracted critical attention. The second covers what could be termed 'practical criticism,' and involves the assessment of individual poets and specific works. The texts that belong to this second category perform a dual function: on the one hand, they establish a connection between general theoretical principles and the enactment of those principles in the work of certain writers; and on the other hand, taken as a whole, they provide a critical profile – a kind of embryonic *catalogue raisonné* – of Spanish poetry as it was developing in the period.

In order to be able to judge the sense of Bergamín's contribution to the long debate on aesthetics in Spain in the twenties it is helpful to chart, albeit schematically, the basic issues that were at stake and the new directions in which poetry was moving at the time. The historical point of departure is Mallarmé, described by Guillermo de Torre in 1920 as 'precursor auténtico y progenitor de las floraciones póstumas que hoy se ramifican en los poetas vanguardistas' (the real precursor and progenitor of the posthumous flowerings that are now spreading among the avant-garde poets).[6] Mallarmé's legacy underpinned much of what was thought in this period: the reaction against the effusive confessionalism of the Romantics, the resolve to restrict the poem exclusively to those elements necessary for its aesthetic functioning. His influence was discernible on the first wave of Spanish *vanguardistas* – the *creacionistas* and *ultraístas* – whose 'higiénica labor iconoclasta' (hygienic demolition work), to use Diego's apt phrase,[7] made the break with the past irrevocable and set in motion a radically revised concept of the poet's mission. This initial militant vanguard was hamstrung by its own obsessive and sometimes immature interest in novelty for novelty's sake, but still managed to establish some fundamental principles. In the first place, it preached the need to abandon the subjective and sentimental, symptoms, in the words of Cansinos-Assens, of 'la senectud del ciclo novecentista' (the decrepitude of the cycle of the 1900s).[8] In the second place, it proclaimed the importance of affirming the autonomy of art. The idea was to create an anti-anecdotal, self-sufficient, non-transcendental poetic art rooted in the pure, eternal, liberated fruits of the imagination: the image and the metaphor. The theory to support this idea was formulated with great clarity and confidence:

El creacionismo lírico es la poesía misma, límpida, desnuda y abstracta. Una poesía libertada del objetivo secular que supone narrar, reproducir, describir o alegorizar los motivos de la vida. Una poesía purificada que asociando imágenes diversas en el fluir de la cerebración abstracta, compone una totalidad lírica, en absoluto independiente de la sensación genitora.[9]

(Lyrical *creacionismo* is poetry itself, limpid, unadorned, and abstract. A poetry liberated from the secular goal of narrating, reproducing, describing, or allegorizing actual life. A purified poetry which, through the association of different images in the flow of abstract reasoning, makes up a lyrical totality, entirely independent of the sensation in which it originates.)

The theory, however, proved much more confident than the practice, and the kind of autonomous, purely poetic reality that was envisaged rarely materialized on paper.[10]

This revision of the goals that poets were encouraged to set themselves leads directly to the twin impulses – *deshumanización* and *purismo* – that have traditionally, though with unnecessary emphasis, come to characterize the aesthetic sensibilities of the decade as a whole. Although both these terms have given rise to misunderstanding, they do represent, both as enactment and analysis, the main direction in which poetry was moving. They exemplify notions that are essentially complementary. On the one hand, for example, they suggest that characteristic 'ausencia del *hombre*' (absence of the *man*),[11] the reticence many poets felt about writing in too subjective a fashion. On the other hand, they describe how poets focused on the external and impersonal, determined to render in aesthetic terms what was 'outside,' transforming and purifying the data culled from experience into an alternative, self-governing, exclusively artistic reality.

Fundamentally, the process being championed was one of aesthetic metamorphosis. As one critic put it, it was a question of '*reformar* la realidad: sustituir la forma real por otra forma que ... depende sólo de la idea, de la iniciativa creadora del artista' (*reforming* reality: of substituting the real form with one that is dependent solely on the idea, on the creative initiative of the artist).[12] The kind of art that corresponded to this principle naturally demanded for its evaluation a new critical apparatus that would enable the reader to appreciate the new intentions behind it. The importance of Ortega's *La deshumanización del arte* (1925) is not simply that it was the first critical approach to 'el arte nuevo,' but rather that it represents a systematic and generously unprejudiced attempt to understand and to come to terms with the tenets implicit in the art and poetry of those years. As will be shown, it was Bergamín, writing *from within* the generation, who expressed some of the ideas that Ortega, slightly older, had formulated from the outside, in his capacity as alert and concerned *espectador*.

Allied to the principles of pure creation and objective beauty, of poetry as 'la finalidad de sí misma' (its own finality),[13] was the notion that this new poetic art was inherently intellectual. What it offered to both reader and writer was, in Aleixandre's words, 'un placer inteligente' (an intelligent pleasure).[14] Rejecting the unconstrained outpouring of emotion, the poet cultivated a more controlled, cerebral means of expression, refining and purifying his material in an attempt to forge a kind of absolute poetic reality. The business of writing involved 'todo el rigor del análisis' (all the rigour of analysis)[15]: the precise elimination of conventional dross, the deft and polished integration and arrangement of those elements needed to give the poem a formal perfection. The result was often, and usually self-consciously, an intricate and finely structured poetic artefact, the kind of 'morada impecable' (impeccable abode) that Diego admired in Guillén's poetry.[16]

This kind of writing threw out a challenge to readers, testing their capacity to decipher and savour the degree of ingenuity and originality that had gone into its construction. It is this sometimes deliberate and self-satisfied difficulty – often rooted in the consciously subtle and wittily audacious – that caught Ortega's attention in 1924–5 and was later to catch Machado's.[17] It gave rise, with good reason, to the idea that in this period both the practitioners and readers of poetry represented a marginal élite. Art became a kind of intellectual test of strength, and Fernando Vela captured the sense of this exclusivist, problem-seeking attitude when he wrote: 'Esta es nuestra anormalidad: que sentimos fruición cuando la obra de arte nos presenta problemas y no soluciones' (This is our abnormality: that we enjoy a work of art that presents us with problems rather than solutions).[18] Such problems could only be solved by the refined and sophisticated. Guillermo de Torre's comment that the new art was a 'jeroglífico y rompecabezas' (hieroglyph and puzzle) only for 'las mentes débiles' (weak minds)[19] serves as a reminder that for most of the twenties this self-congratulatory hermetism in poetry sustained a cultural 'splendid isolation.'

* * *

Bergamín spoke out frequently and intelligently during these protracted discussions on what art and poetry could or should be. One critic, referring to the work of the major poets of the twenties, has gone so far as to say that Bergamín 'se propone con frecuencia formular la teoría estética del grupo' (often sets out to formulate the aesthetic theory of the group).[20] It is certainly a well-founded remark and it is surprising that this insight has never been developed by any critic writing about the period; but it would be an exaggeration to think of Bergamín's theory as the only valid one put forward at the time. Critical awareness of the direction in which poetry was moving was shaped by an amalgam of opinions, and when Gerardo Diego called Dámaso Alonso 'mi constante y encarnizado enemigo poético' (my constant and outraged poetic enemy), explaining that 'nos pasamos la vida riñendo amistosamente' (we spend all our time quarrelling amicably),[21] he drew attention to the lack of a clear consensus among poets and critics concerning the aesthetic goals that were being set. Clearly, no single theory, not even Bergamín's, could account for the variety of approaches or the multiplicity of styles being successfully pursued in those years. Yet Bergamín's views on the subject do demand special consideration precisely because in his capacity as 'espectador participante de la poesía' and constant companion of his friends, he was strategically well placed to judge the sense of their initiatives and achievements.

*   *   *

The two major texts by Bergamín on aesthetics are 'El pensamiento hermético de las artes' and 'Notas para unos prolegómenos a toda poética del porvenir que se presente como arte.'[22] Significantly, they were both written in 1927 and so reflect the intense interest of that year in poetry in general. Equally significant is the fact that whereas critics have consistently referred to other texts written at the same time by other members of Bergamín's generation – Lorca's 'La imagen poética de Don Luis de Góngora,' Dámaso Alonso's 'Escila y Caribdis de la literatura española,' or Diego's 'La vuelta a la estrofa,' for example – almost no attention has been paid to these two substantial pieces by Bergamín.[23] This is surprising, not only because Bergamín himself was actively involved in all aspects of the Góngora celebrations of 1927, but also because he was evidently considered at the time to be one of his generation's leading spokesmen on aesthetic matters. Since his two texts of that year contain his most precisely argued thoughts on this subject and in many ways explain the axiomatic judgments he regularly published in literary journals at the time, they deserve special examination.

'El pensamiento hermético de las artes' is the text of a lecture Bergamín gave at the Museum of Contemporary Art in Madrid. Just as Ortega had done in *La deshumanización del arte*, he took 'art' to mean poetry, music, and painting, though no serious distortion of his ideas is involved if they are applied solely to poetry. What he attempted to do was to define the nature and mechanics of the 'act of creation' in general and to suggest the kind of permanent critical criteria appropriate for its understanding. He begins by focusing on 'el pensamiento poéticamente puro o recién nacido inmortal al que los griegos llamaron Hermes' (175) and argues that the sense of this fundamental creative phenomenon has been obscured by the critical vogue of interpreting 'las artes poéticas' using vitalist criteria. In order to demonstrate their prejudicial effects on the task of critical elucidation, he refers to both 'el criterio histórico' and 'el criterio psicológico.' Bergamín dismisses the first because by charting the relationship between a historical period and a work of art or its author, it draws attention only to the mortality of the work in question, its relevance in a dead past: 'El criterio historicista opera siempre sobre cadáveres; su visión es la de un campo de batalla sembrado de muertos a los que no quiere dejar en paz' (178). In this way, the reader of a conventional manual of literary history becomes, in Bergamín's eyes, the equivalent in the field of literary studies of a tourist surveying the aftermath of the battle of Waterloo. The weakness of the psychological, subjective approach is that the work of art is only activated and becomes meaningful by the imposition upon it of the reader's or critic's own sensibility: 'la obra poética – dice el criterio psicologista – es un pretexto imaginativo contemporáneo de mi propia sensibilidad' (184). The work of art exists, therefore, only in potential, and the realization of that potential depends exclusively on the reader. The range of living resonance that the work may acquire is determined in a totally arbitrary way: by what the reader, with his erratic personal concerns, has cared to or is able to give it.

Rejecting the partiality and inconsistency of these two criteria, Bergamín posits an alternative: an absolute, rational tool of evaluation which, in his view, is the only one capable of doing justice to the absolute, rational procedure that he believes to be the essence of every work of art. This alternative is already implicitly suggested in his references to the shortcomings of the historical and psychological perspectives in criticism: 'a un criterio de valoración racional, el único posible, se sustituye un pretendido criterio de valoración histórico, vitalista o imposible' (179); 'racionalmente, no hay perspectivas que valgan' (182). In other words, he affirms that the central ingredient in both the creation and understanding of art – the latter necessarily corresponds to the former – is rationality, reason, intelligent rigour. Upon the basis of this single criterion, Bergamín builds an argument that touches upon many of the concerns characteristic of the decade and restates them in a new and suggestive way.

Bergamín maintains that the act of artistic creation is the process whereby the spontaneous and unclear impulses of inspiration are subjected to the 'precisión racional del pensamiento' (205). The result is a 'realidad poética imaginativa' (206), independent of its creator and therefore free of the limitations imposed by the latter's transitory nature: 'la objetividad imaginativa es la razón de su existencia poética: su constitutiva racionalidad' (206). Art that is anchored in life, merely reflecting a state of feeling or consciousness, is necessarily as mortal as the mind from which it springs, or as Bergamín ingeniously puts it: 'las artes poéticas se hacen, de este modo, transitivas, verbales: se convierten en personas vivas y declinan, verbalmente, en el tiempo que las condena a muerte' (189). Against this notion of the provisionality of an art that is personal and subjective, Bergamín sets the ideal, permanent value of *truth*: 'las artes poéticas ... no tienen vida, porque tienen verdad; no pueden despertar intereses vivos, sino, exclusivamente, verdaderos' (190 –1). In order to stress the incompatibility of these two elements, he extends his idea and opposes *illusion* to *truth*, viewing the former as the sustenance of life while the latter transcends life. He argues that the mistake of 'las artes poéticas' has sometimes been to 'hacerse ilusiones de realidad en vez de hacerse realidad de veras' (192), an opinion he later clarifies by saying, in typically elegant and epigrammatic fashion: 'las ilusiones son el alimento de la vida: para la muerte; las verdades lo son del pensamiento: para lo inmortal' (210).

Because of its basis in a rigorously impersonal rationality, the 'objetividad imaginativa' of art constitutes a reality in its own right, outside time. This is implicitly confirmed in a revealing allusion to Mallarmé, described by Bergamín as 'un poeta, acaso el más puro poeta, es decir, el que hizo en Francia una poesía más racional (real, impersonal, sustantiva), una poesía más verdadera ...' (192–3). Bergamín acknowledges Mallarmé's achievement: the suppression of the subjective, the rational creation of an autonomous, substantive poetic reality. These ideas are, in turn, incorporated into his own view of art as a self-governing, impersonal, artistic reality: 'las artes poéticas tienen realidad verdadera o pura cuando son, exclusivamente, cosas o causas de razón, cuando existen impersonalmente, como únicamente pueden existir, como construcciones imaginativas' (197). The substantive nature of this rational poetic reality – 'cosa de razón' – is further alluded to in an important paragraph where Bergamín writes: 'las artes poéticas son artes de hacer y no de engendrar ... las obras poéticas hechas, lo que los escolásticos llamaban certeramente *artefactos* (una pintura o música o poesía), son cosas porque no son engendros' (197).[24]

Bergamín recognizes and explains the difficulty that characterizes this type of art: 'la dificultad de las artes poéticas es esta racionalidad imaginativa, este hermetismo: porque es sentir o consentir por una síntesis, clara y distinta, la percepción turbia y confusa, la sensación pura' (206–7). Both the process of artistic composition and that of critical elucidation depend consequently on a high degree of intellectual refinement. The tone of Bergamín's reflections on this point tends implicitly to confirm the élitist attitude that Ortega had perceived in the new art. He seems indirectly to defend the notion of an art by and for a cultured minority when he condemns the popularity enjoyed by – or rather forced upon – certain publicly acclaimed artists: 'todos los verdaderos artistas poéticos sufren, tarde o temprano, esta injuriosa y calumniosa difamación del éxito' (208).

There may also be an echo of Ortega's belief that poetry at the time had become impersonal and formulaic – 'el álgebra superior de las metáforas' – in Bergamín's references in his discussion to mathematics and architecture. It is certainly true that the concepts of precision, proportion, and objective form contained in these sciences were entirely in harmony with the poetic ideals held at the time.[25] Defining poetry as 'un estado maravilloso de cosas, de estas cosas imaginativas, independiente, autónomo,' Bergamín comments 'su delimitación precisa se la dan las matemáticas y la arquitectura: las dos ciencias universales de la construcción, las que determinan sus fronteras' (210–11). If he recognizes that when poetry reaches 'esos extremos de la pura racionalidad' (212) it shares certain affinities with these sciences, he cannot resist the temptation of inverting the terms in a kind of conceptual chiasmus that is reminiscent of his aphorisms. With a characteristically paradoxical volte-face, therefore, he argues that both mathematics and architecture are essentially poetic; since they involve graphic or symbolic representation of abstract concepts, they have an unquestionable aesthetic dimension. What poetry, mathematics, and architecture have in common, in the extreme circumstances in which Bergamín deliberately chooses to locate them, is the function of exteriorizing a formless, inner perception that he would regard as a hesitant spiritual impulse.

It is predictably in this context that Bergamín touches on the idea of deshumanización. The allusion is brief, however, and at first sight appears to be a refutation of Ortega's approach to the subject: 'el arte poético no se deshumaniza (como se ha dicho), sino que se desvive; se desvive por la razón, por la verdad: por la poesía' (215). The comment suggests Bergamín's resolve to be original at all costs, subtly revising a formula with which he is essentially in agreement. The echo here is from one of his earlier propositions – art rejecting life in favour of a truth rooted in reason – but the 'correction' of Ortega is more linguistic than ideological. Bergamín seems more interested in the semantic ambivalence of the verb desvivirse than in the apparently conflicting opinion of Ortega. That ambivalence is ideally suited to the form of his argument and so he exploits it to the full.[26]

Clearly, the very title that Bergamín chose to give this essay, together with the interpretation of Hermes which underpins it, are indicative of a particular view of poetry, and of art in general, as a kind of intellectual puzzle. As I have already suggested, this coincided with the general feelings of the period. The notion of an hermetic art, difficult of access, elusive and enigmatic, was certainly current at the time. 'El pensamiento hermético de las artes' can be viewed fundamentally as an elaborate exposition of this idea. If the essay displays certain oddities of style and presentation it is because this basic idea that it contains has been refracted through Bergamín's rather unconventional mind and temperament, thus acquiring a series of unusual characteristics in the process. The specific value he attaches to hermetism in poetry is most clearly explained towards the end of the essay when he writes: 'la obra poética, *artefacto* imaginativo, es una cerradura que pone la razón al pensamiento: y el pensamiento escapa, divinamente, como Hermes, por el ojo de la llave de la cerradura que quería impedirlo' (220).[27] Bergamín's prose is never easy to paraphrase in English, especially in a case like this where a number of central concepts that have been systematically defined are condensed into a deceptively straightforward formula; but perhaps the image he uses here is striking enough to convey the basic idea. The point of departure – the 'space' to be enclosed – is 'el pensamiento,' which Bergamín would argue is of divine origin. When 'la razón' intervenes, it subjugates and controls, giving a rigorous form and substance to this initial perception. This form, however, still allows the elusive escape or expression of that original 'pensamiento' or 'sensación pura' around or against which the poetic artefact has been constructed. This is Bergamín's personal way of describing the nature of artistic creation in general, and more particularly, of defining the principles that guided the best new art and poetry of the twenties.

Bergamín's 'Notas para unos prolegómenos ... ' are of special historical interest, since they made up the text of the lecture he gave in the Seville Ateneo during the famous trip there in 1927. They are consequently related to the pro-Góngora initiatives of that year, although Bergamín made the poet only a point of reference in a wider argument that embraced more general aesthetic principles. Unfortunately, only extracts of the 'Notas ... ' were published so that the sequential development and overall scope of the arguments are difficult to judge. However, on the basis of the fragments available, it is possible to isolate the main areas of concern to the writer and to establish their connection with the ideas set out in 'El pensamiento hermético de las artes.'

Bergamín begins by outlining the sense of the contemporary approach to art: 'el arte – dice la estética reciente – es intuición, imaginación, fantasía: representación poética y no práctica ni conceptual.' Preferring, predictably, the original formula to the conventionally logical one, he subverts the contemporary concept of an anti-mimetic art and argues that the new poetry of the twenties is in fact an imitation of nature, but in a precisely defined sense:

El poeta depura la expresión, la forma de su pensamiento, hasta hacerlo, de nuevo, naturaleza, reduciéndolo a pura imaginación, a sólo forma ... La invención poética de la prosa es un proceso de depuración artística del lenguaje: el arte poético consiste en esta imitación natural, en esta re-creación pura del verbo.

In other words, if writing involves the creation of a separate poetic reality out of the distilled essence of language, then the poet is indeed imitating nature. The analogy rests on the similarity between the mechanisms of creation rather than between the end products.[28] The references in the passage quoted to 'depuración' and the insistence on poetry as quintessential form echo the prime concerns of the decade. Bergamín includes prose as well as verse in this 'arte poético'; I shall return to this point in some detail in the next chapter in order to suggest a connection between his own prose and the predominant stylistic interests of the time.

Bergamín goes on to illuminate several of the aesthetic ideals of the period, giving them a precision and authority that they lack in the writings of other critics. He explains exactly, for example, the relationship between form and substance in the type of poetry he is discussing from a theoretical point of view. He argues that the substance – 'el asunto' – of a poem cannot be separated from its form, that what a poem has to 'say' is inextricably linked to what it 'is': 'el asunto, en la obra poética, es, necesariamente, la forma ... el poema es el propio asunto poético.' It is not that the poem is explicitly 'about' poetry, but that what the poet writes, being a separate reality in itself, does not need to respect any other criterion than that of self-affirmation. The creative process he describes is basically the same as the one outlined in 'El pensamiento hermético de las artes,' though here the emphasis is placed on the substantive form, which the initial inspiration ultimately assumes. Rather than constituting a mould into which that inspiration is poured, the poem is viewed as nothing more – nor less – than that very mould: 'el poeta reproduce la representación imaginativa – la origina, espontáneamente, en su espíritu – y piensa la forma al imaginar el asunto, unificando el proceso expresivo artístico en una sola realidad formal que es la obra poética.' The insistence on the formal, objective, autonomous reality created by the poet corresponds once again to the importance attached to this point at the time: 'la forma poética – arte poético, prosa y verso, poesía pura – es el *poema*, y existe, fuera de toda otra realidad, por sí misma – y para sí misma – por sí sola. La sola realidad poética es la poesía.' Such remarks as these establish a direct link with the kind of self-generated, self-governing artistic reality described in 'El pensamiento hermético de las artes.'

Clearly the historical interest of these two texts lies in the way they formulate on a meditative, theoretical level those basic aesthetic concerns that gave momentum and a specific creative orientation to the major poets of the twenties. In addition, it is important to realize – not only from a historical viewpoint but also for an understanding of the overall coherence and thrust of Bergamín's prose writings – that there is a close relationship between these two texts and many of the aphorisms that he wrote at the time. It was in fact while examining a series of Bergamín's aphorisms that Cano Ballesta remarked on their 'extraordinario interés para conocer el pensamiento de esta generación en torno al fenómeno lírico' (their extraordinary interest for an understanding of this generation's ideas on poetry).[29] What this comment quite rightly suggests is that the discursive articulation of his ideas on aesthetics in 'El pensamiento hermético ... ' and the 'Notas ... ' was complemented by the axiomatic expression of similar views in the aphorisms he published in those years.[30] The two prose styles may seem very different on the surface but from the point of view of content they are often intimately linked. Indeed the problems of interpretation posed by the extreme condensation of thought in the aphorisms can at times only be fully resolved by reading the corresponding essays, since these provide the sequential elaboration and the complete logic that have been eliminated from the aphorisms.[31] This relationship is particularly clear in the case of those aphorisms dating from the mid-twenties and touching on aesthetics.

The correspondence between aphorism and essay will be immediately clear from the following examples concerning hermetism in poetry. Although it is uncertain whether they stem from or, alternatively, contribute towards the lengthy reasoning of 'El pensamiento hermético de las artes,' the connection between the two is clear:

El principio de las soledades es enigma. La poesía tiene su principio – y su fin – en la evidencia, sola, del enigma.

El poema es, siempre, criatura enigmática.

¿Qué eres, cuándo eres, si no eres enigma?

La poesía es hermética, como el dios griego: reciennacido inmortal.

(Carmen)[32]

The insistence on the hermetic qualities of poetry is evident elsewhere, establishing an exact parallel with the arguments of 'El pensamiento hermético':

Lo hermético no es el cierre seguro, sino el ojo de la cerradura por donde el dios breve sabía escapar.

(Hermes)

La poesía es un arte hermético – porque es divina. El arte de entrar y salir por el ojo de la llave.

(Martirio)

The idea that difficulty is a distinct virtue of poetry, both for poet and reader, is alluded to in various aphorisms. It is elliptically expressed, for example, in the following observation:

Es una verdad como un templo. Mala verdad.

(Aforústica)

The implication here is that a less easily perceptible truth, one requiring a greater intellectual effort on the part of the reader or writer, is preferable to the truth that is obvious, immediately discernible. The same idea appears in the following comment, which stresses how the complex problems of elucidation posed by 'el nuevo arte poético' constitute a positive value:

¡Cuidado! Comerse una manzana es más fácil que comerse una naranja o una granada, y comerse una naranja o granada, más fácil que comerse un cangrejo cocido. La obra artística puede ser manzana, naranja, granada o cangrejo cocido, y no hay que añadir que, en éste último caso, necesita un mayor esfuerzo de entendimiento: sin contar con que ya es un buen síntoma para el arte el que no haya por donde cogerlo.

(Transparencia)

Bergamín goes on to defend the principle of difficulty in poetry viewing it as a kind of absolute ideal and implying that those criteria of rational understanding presented in 'El pensamiento hermético' are quite capable of perceiving the luminous, intelligent clarity of an apparently obscure poet:

Lo oscuro no es lo dificultoso; ni lo claro, fácil o lógico o razonable.

Poeta: no le tengas miedo a la oscuridad. Mientras más oscuro es el poeta, más clara es su poesía.

La luz más profunda sólo se entrega a la más profunda oscuridad.

Si quieres expresar la luz, hazte cámara oscura.

(Transparencia)

The reflections on depersonalized, substantive poetry, and on poetry as pure aesthetic creation, are similarly in harmony with the ideas set out in the two long texts of 1927. With his customary originality, Bergamín contradicts, in the following example, the general opinion that 'el estilo es el hombre' and emphasizes the objective nature of the reality that the poem, rendered in an extra-personal style, creates:

El estilo no es personal, sino real: el estilo no es el hombre mismo, sino la cosa misma (objetivo y no subjetivo), la realización de la obra artística: cosa ideal o realidad pura.

(Transparencia)

In 'El pensamiento hermético' Bergamín uses the phrase 'verificación poética' to describe the process whereby the poem comes into being, affirming itself and forging a separate, exterior poetic reality. The same process is graphically described in the following aphorism:

La independencia y pureza, la existencia y realidad de la obra poética, es su mismo origen o situación, su darse a luz o salir fuera: su nacimiento. Y nace porque se desentraña de lo humano en voluntad formal – emotiva – de ser o de estar, de existir – fuera – situándose.

(Transparencia)

Predictably, he also draws attention to the contribution that reason and refined intelligence make towards the creation of the poetic artefact. In a dialogue that characteristically implies far more than it says, he writes:

–¿Por qué – decís – pensamiento poético?
– Porque el pensamiento solo es poético.

(Aforística persistente)

The remark implicitly draws upon these arguments in which Bergamín has described the role played in poetry by unadulterated thought. There is something of Juan Ramón Jiménez's sensuality in the sublime when the idea resurfaces elsewhere:

He mirado a mi pensamiento, y he visto, desnuda, su belleza.

(Transparencia)

It is remarkable that practically without exception, these aphoristic reflections on poetry operate in a kind of vacuum. No attempt is made to illustrate or justify them with reference to particular poets who could be said to exemplify the 'arte poético' under consideration. It would have been natural, for example, to use Góngora as a specific point of comparison with the poetic ideals being promoted in those years. To be fair to Bergamín, however, Góngora is the subject of some discussion in the 'Notas ... ' and figures prominently in another essay, also written in 1927, which is worth mentioning. This is his suggestively entitled 'Patos del aguachirle castellana.'[33] It is mainly a sweeping denunciation of all those critics who failed to appreciate the absolute 'arte poético' of the time, but it also establishes a clear connection between what was sought after in the twenties and the achievement of Góngora himself. The analogy rests, according to Bergamín, not on the superficial and misleading similarities between the kind of poetry written by Góngora and the young poets of the twenties, but on the coincidence of motivation and ambition:

El arte poético de Góngora vale, hoy, para los nuevos, porque es arte y porque es poético; nada más; otros paralelismos no existen; si no es el de la verdadera intención estética que anima, como a Góngora, a los poetas del nuevo renacimiento lírico.

It is not, therefore, that Góngora constitutes a model that the poets of Bergamín's generation are slavishly imitating, but that the latter share his goal of creating a pure, poetic reality beyond the subjective, founded in the exclusively aesthetic. It is striking here that for Bergamín, an appreciation of Góngora is nothing special in itself. The *Polifemo* and the *Soledades* are simply examples, enjoying an exceptional notoriety in 1927, of an approach to poetry that has an absolute validity above and beyond the identity of the individual poet: 'Góngora existe, y eso es todo: como Petrarca, Dante, Goethe o Baudelaire.' It is the principle rather than the specific case that concerns Bergamín, since a capacity to appreciate Góngora's work proves not the wisdom of a partial allegiance but rather the reader's 'entendimiento y gusto de persona humana.'

Bergamín's role as 'gusano de luz' or 'conciencia pasiva' of the poets of his generation did, however, prompt him to write a series of essays between 1926 and 1929 on contemporary Spanish poetry. In these essays there is a clearly discernible relationship between the 'arte poético' outlined in his aphorisms and lectures of the time and the work of specific writers. The interest of these texts stems partly from the way in which, as I have suggested, they were written from within the framework of concerns that engrossed the writers of the day. This is what places Bergamín in the same category as, say, Gerardo Diego, and sets him apart from Ortega. Bergamín clearly had a much more intimate and committed relationship with the poets and poetry of the twenties than did Ortega, despite the latter's interest and generosity as a publisher. This difference is reflected in their work: whereas Ortega, out of intellectual curiosity more than anything, extracted and specified the principles he judged to be implicit in what he saw and read, Bergamín applied his critical familiarity with the aesthetic imperatives of the decade to the works that his friends published, measuring the degree to which they exemplified in their writing the 'arte poético' that he had described on a general, theoretical level.

The best example of this critical monitoring of theory and practice is Bergamín's response to Alberti's *Cal y canto*. In order to appreciate the authority that Bergamín's views had in this area, it is worth bearing in mind that Alberti entitled his collection of poems *Cal y canto* in accordance with a suggestion by Bergamín.[34] Being a loaded reorientation of a fragment of a popular saying, this title bears the hallmark of Bergamín's style and recalls not only the characteristic techniques of his aphorisms, but also the way in which many of the titles of his own books function.[35] The opening paragraph of his essay 'El canto y la cal en la poesía de Rafael Alberti' demonstrates how the title he had suggested was designed to capture the sense of the rational, unsentimental approach to poetry dominant at the time and which Alberti had adopted:

'Entre santa y santo, pared de cal y canto.' Entre el poeta y la poesía no hay relación viva: no hay sombra de pasión, de enamoramiento. No hay erotismo sensual, ni sentimental. Se levanta un muro, una pared infranqueable: de imperativa, limpia, pura castidad. Pared de cal y canto. La obra poética absoluta.[36]

It is precisely the renunciation of the subjective, of the prosaic and effusive 'relación viva' between poet and poetry that gives Alberti's work, according to Bergamín, its absolute strength. Alberti's outlook clearly conformed to the ideals of an anti-vitalist art set out in 'El pensamiento hermético de las artes.' Bergamín registers in *Cal y canto* 'el ansia de pureza, de la desnudez poética ... esa andaluza pasión por la exactitud, por la inteligencia' and emphasizes how the kind of poetic process that has taken place has been one of conscious, rational craftsmanship:

Para que el pensamiento, poéticamente puro, *se transmute en sueño* – como Dante decía – hay que cerrar los ojos y apretar las manos: pero es porque, antes, los ojos y las manos (la inteligencia) estuvieron abiertos a todo, para coger y apresar las cosas: porque sólo apresándolas de ese modo inteligente, podrán luego darse a la luz de nuevo: expresarse, hacerse formas de creación o invención poética. Sin inteligencia no ha habido ni puede haber poesía, arte poético. Sin razón, poética, de ser, no hay nada.

The echoes here from previous theoretical remarks will be immediately apparent and require no commentary. What Bergamín is doing is to insist on the importance of these general aesthetic principles and to underline the way in which Alberti has responded to them in his work:

... cuando con un rigor matemático de precisión, su pasión ardiente (inteligencia) encuentra y mide en su poema las más exactas – y por eso las más admirables, maravillosas – relaciones imaginativas.

Alberti's poetry also provides Bergamín with an example of the basic distinction between the 'realism' of an unimaginative mimetic art and the absolute, self-justifying 'reality' that is the product of the 'arte poético' of the time. He dismisses 'el realismo realístico' and argues with characteristic ingenuity:

El realismo puro no es otra cosa que eso: una cosa poética; cosa de imágenes, de ideas, de pensamientos: es cosa de pensar. En definitiva, cosa de juego. (Cosa de verdad.) De juego limpio y exclusivamente formal: no hay nada más formal que el juego. Toda forma o formación, real no formalismo, es eso sólo: un juego (hermético, enigmático). Cosa poética sin más ni menos. Ni más ni menos que poesía.

The masterly enactment in *Cal y canto* of the abstract ideals of 'el arte poético' explains the enthusiasm Bergamín felt for Alberti's work as it passed through this exacting phase. The poet's 'hambre hermética, pura, exclusiva, de realidad: de razón poética' indicates, for Bergamín, the successful establishment of a link between theory and practice.

Similarly, the Guillén of *Cántico* was praised by Bergamín as a kind of exemplary embodiment of the ideals he had sketched in his theoretical writings: 'En Jorge Guillén vino a realizarse, con perfección incomparable, con maestría superada, el ideal del poeta puro – puramente formal.'[37] He began his review of *Cántico* with an emphatic declaration that gave great satisfaction to Guillén and considerable offence to Jiménez: 'Ni Valéry. Ni Góngora. Ni Juan Ramón Jiménez.'[38] The point to bear in mind, however, concerns the critical concept behind this blunt statement. Bergamín's rejection of 'similarities' or personal 'influences' was not simply a comment on the singularity of *Cántico*, but also a reaffirmation of the criteria set out in 'El pensamiento hermético de las artes' and in some of his aphorisms. Since historical and psychological perspectives have been shown to be ineffective as means of just evaluation, the 'situación crítica,' as Bergamín calls it, of a work of art can only be perceived in rational, aesthetic terms. Merely to isolate personal affinities is to fall into the trap set by the 'criterio vitalista' and to fail to do justice to the uniqueness of the poetic artefact that every writer, like Guillén, creates: 'La poesía es arte hecho (*arte facto* de los escolásticos): cosa y no persona: realidad espiritual (no hay otra): imaginativa' ('La poética de Jorge Guillén').

Bergamín goes on in the same review to describe Guillén's poetry as 'hermética como la razón: presa en la sorpresa,' and to praise its 'substantividad poética'. These comments only make complete sense when they are read in the light of his more generalized reflections on the guiding principles of art and poetry where the value attached to particular terms and ideas is clearly explained. This is also true of the articles and reviews he devoted at the time to works by writers like Cernuda, Salinas, and Espina, for example, where it is evident that their writing is judged partly in terms of its fidelity to certain aesthetic norms that he has specified in his own work on the subject. *Perfil del aire*, therefore, is described as a 'librito esencial y puramente poético' ('El idealismo andaluz'). The main virtue of Espina's style is its 'máxima voluptuosidad de la precisión.'[39] The poetry of Salinas is seen in the following terms: 'Cuando la emoción humana le vence es ya como un fantasma, un espectro que se filtra por las paredes verticales, desnudas, de sus versos.'[40] The sense of Bergamín's judgments in such cases as these depends on an accumulation of critical logic that the reader unfamiliar with 'El pensamiento hermético ... ' and the 'Notas ... ' will not have access to. This is why, ideally, Bergamín's writings on the theory of poetry should be read in conjunction with his essays on the practice of poetry in the same years. His formulation of an abstract 'arte poético' is complemented by an assessment of that art in action.[41]

* * *

Bergamín's critical writings of the period, however, go a good deal further than these comparisons. He was also interested in charting the general developments in Spanish poetry at the time, in acknowledging the appearance of new talent, in establishing the place that individual writers and works occupied on the literary stage, in indicating their particular merits. This clarifies the sense of Alberti's comment in his memoirs on Bergamín's activities as a critic: 'Nadie como Pepe comenzaba a escribir con más fervoroso entusiasmo de la poesía española, convirtiéndose a la larga en el mejor comentarista de la nuestra, ya casi perfilada por aquellos años' (Nobody began to write with such fervent enthusiasm about Spanish poetry as Pepe. He gradually emerged as the best commentator of the poetry of our generation which by that time was practically fully sketched out).[42] This means that when looked at in their entirety, Bergamín's reviews and essays can be seen to constitute a fairly comprehensive assessment of the poetry of the pre-war period. Especially significant about this assessment is that it was made *at the time*, by someone who was intimately associated with all the initiatives of the major poets of the day, who was an acutely perceptive reader of their work, and who took upon himself – in his role as *gusano de luz* – the responsibility of explaining and defining it to the reading public.

It might be legitimate, therefore, to look on Bergamín as the first critical historian of the so-called Generation of 1927. Indeed, there are a number of noteworthy signs that this was precisely how he was perceived at the time. For example, when Valbuena Prat published his brief study *La poesía española contemporánea* in Madrid in 1930, the sources he used to document and support his judgments were almost exclusively the articles Bergamín had published in the previous five or six years. It was an implicit recognition that by that year (1930), Bergamín had become established as the most informed and authoritative critic of the poetry of the twenties. This was made explicit in the following year when a group of disgruntled young writers launched a journal entitled *Extremos a que ha llegado la poesía española*. The first issue opened with an unsigned article – 'Poesía sin historia' ('Poetry without history') – expressing dismay at the absence of any systematic attempt to evaluate critically the ways in which Spanish poetry had evolved in the previous decade. Bergamín was singled out as the only critic who had provided a perspective of any kind on the subject:

Seguramente no por falta de estímulos ha permanecido en España la poesía de hoy, la actual, sin que nadie haya intentado hacer su historia, recogerla y perseguir su situación – poética más que histórica. Tan sólo José Bergamín, en algunas ocasiones dispersas ... ha querido poner sus puntos sobre las íes y proceder a la catalogación ... [43]

(Although there has been no shortage of stimulus, Spanish poetry of today has not yet inspired anyone to attempt to write its history, to see it as a whole and to define its situation – more poetic than historical. Only José Bergamín, on a few disparate occasions ... has taken the trouble to give some order to the subject and to propose a catalogue ...)

The reason why this perspective of Bergamín's seems to have escaped the attention of almost all later critics of the period may well be that, as I have mentioned before, his writings were never collected in book form. The 'ocasiones dispersas' on which he did formulate an overall view of the topic may simply have been lost sight of because they never became the basis of a systematically developed appraisal. It is a pity that he did not follow through with his plan, outlined to Unamuno in 1924, to write a complete history of contemporary Spanish literature. This would obviously have made his role as critic and literary historian much easier to appreciate in subsequent decades. The shape and thrust of his approach to Spanish writers of the twenties and thirties are discernible in some of the most informative articles of the time on this subject.

The most important of these articles is undoubtedly 'Literatura y brújula' (1929).[44] By examining it in some detail, incorporating references from other texts that complement the ideas expressed in it, it is possible to reconstruct Bergamín's overview. Ostensibly, the article is a review of Salinas's *Seguro azar*, just published; but this is only a pretext. As the title indicates, Bergamín is concerned more to help his readers navigate through a situation that, because of critical neglect or insensitivity, has become chaotic. The kind of clarification he provides is useful even for the reader and critic of today, since the data and emphases that he chooses to give serve as a reminder of how the scene was perceived at the time, without the distortions and simplifications of subsequent critical practice. He begins, for example, by drawing attention to the historical emergence of the young writers of the twenties, giving a full account of the names of those who had gained some kind of eminence:

Al grupo de escritores siguiente a la generación que sucedía a la llamada del 98, grupo o generación eclipsada por un solo nombre: el de Ramón Gómez de la Serna, seguía el de los pudieran situarse históricamente, al menos en gran parte, por su aparición en la significativa revista *Indice*, y hacia las postrimerías de la revista *España* (1921–1923).

   Provisionalmente, la revista literaria francesa *Intentions* adelantaba en 1924 una rápida antología con el título de *La joven literatura española*. La presentaba: Valéry Larbaud. La formábamos: Dámaso Alonso, Rogelio Buendía, Juan Chabás, Gerardo Diego, Antonio Espina, Jorge Guillén, Federico García Lorca, Alonso Quesada, Adolfo Salazar, Pedro Salinas, Fernando Vela, Antonio Marichalar y yo. Si a estos nombres añadimos los de: Melchor Fernández Almagro, Benjamín Jarnés, Ernesto Giménez Caballero, Vicente Aleixandre, Emilio Prados, Juan Larrea, Fernando Villalón, y los más jóvenes: Rafael Alberti, Luis Cernuda, José María Hinojosa, Manuel Altolaguirre ... (no quisiera olvidar ninguno), tendríamos designados personalmente, como debe hacerse, a los responsables, en parte o en todo, del movimiento literario motejado de *joven* o *nueva literatura*, y también, por algunos, más confusamente (y hasta estúpidamente) de *vanguardismo*.

It is interesting that Bergamín should place emphasis on the historical *origins* of these writers, drawing attention to the importance of certain literary journals in making their work known. Generally speaking, this has not been the approach taken by later critics, despite the advantage that it offers of suggesting how and where the initial literary momentum of the decade was generated. The writers that were anthologized in *Intentions* and the other list of names that Bergamín gives also testify to an aspect of the decade that critics have tended to overlook: the breadth and variety of talent. Bergamín's inventory is not limited to the major poets of the decade – those that have come to be known as the 'generation' or 'grupo poético' of 1927 – but also includes eminent critics like Vela, Salazar, and Marichalar, and prose writers like Jarnés and Giménez Caballero, who clearly formed a substantial part of the literary reality of the time. The same is true of poets like Chabás, Larrea, and Hinojosa who, as critical criteria became subsequently narrower, have almost invariably been deprived of an eminence that they obviously enjoyed in the twenties. The panoramic view that Bergamín offers here, therefore, has the virtues of retrieving something of the wealth of activity that characterized the decade.

Bergamín's hostility to the label *vanguardismo* is indicative of his opposition as a critic to any attempt to reduce the sense of this wealth of activity to a single common initiative, imposing upon it a convenient but misleading descriptive tag:

Es muy fácil eludir las diferenciaciones críticas que el examen de la obra, o intentos, de las personalidades literarias significa (por separado o conjuntamente en sus relaciones históricas y poéticas) admitiendo o rechazando la totalidad por una denominación sin sentido ni significación alguna. Con referirse a una etiqueta se justifica la ignorancia y despreocupación literaria, habitual en España en todos y especialmente en los medios etiquetados, a su vez, de intelectuales. Si a esto se agrega la acostumbrada utilidad pública que del río revuelto de toda inquietud espiritual sacan los pescadores del éxito, los merodeadores y contrabandistas de la ocasión (sobre todo si no es pintada ni calva y hallan algún pelo de donde cogerla) se comprenderá el estado ya casi caótico que en pocos años – seis o siete – se ha formado alrededor de la motejada *nueva literatura*.

Hay en todo movimiento literario relaciones comunes que permiten trazar sus límites – sus fronteras y vecindades – con relativa generalidad. Pero no conviene olvidar que al hacerlo abstraemos y, por lo tanto, desvirtuamos las tendencias mismas, inseparables de las personalidades, individualidades concretas que las verifican. Y si es así, aun cuando los diferentes escritores se unan voluntariamente en un mismo intento (cuestión de técnica, o escuela, o de programa: Romanticismo, Parnasianismo, Simbolismo, Unanimismo, Suprarrealismo, etc. ...) ¿cómo no ha de serlo cuando estas previas intenciones falten? ¿Cuando el escritor no comparte propósitos previos, porque no parte de principios dados, de ningún propuesto o supuesto común?

The lesson in literary history and critical procedure that Bergamín offers here is particularly interesting. He would argue that in general labels or *isms* can be useful as broad definitions when a group of writers share declared intentions, but still cannot adequately account for the use that each individual writer makes of those intentions. Significantly, he underlines the absence of any common literary program uniting the writers of the twenties. Evidently, unlike so many critics of later decades, he did not consider the Góngora celebrations of 1927 to be a genuine 'common literary program,' precisely, I suspect, because it represented only a passing, surface manifestation of an attitude towards writing in general that went beyond a specific sectarian allegiance. Such an attitude, though shared by different writers, still allowed for *individual* expression, and imposed none of the constraints of an explicit program of intent. In his opinion, the absence of such a program only underlined the need to concentrate on the *singularity* of the work of each notable writer of the twenties. This is a point strongly developed in his other articles of the period.

Bergamín then proceeds to identify and comment on the general trends that have surfaced in contemporary Spanish poetry. He argues, perhaps too categorically, that none of the prominent *isms* of the opening decades of the twentieth century made any noteworthy impact on what he describes as 'el auténtico lirismo tradicional.' While *modernismo* did have a collective significance, it represented only an unproductive detour for poets like Jiménez and Machado. His criticisms of 'el esteticismo impresionista post-romántico' are voiced at length in one of his most polemical articles of the pre-war period, 'Poesía de verdad,' where the pretext is, again, the publication of a volume of poetry by Salinas.[45] In 'Literatura y brújula,' *ultraísmo* and *suprarrealismo* are seen as isolated and derivative and their influence in Spain as marginal and not particularly memorable. In his prologue of 1930 to Vallejo's *Trilce*, Bergamín referred in some detail to *creacionismo* and to the more substantial role that it played in Spanish poetry of the twenties, though he considers its main principles to be 'en aparente oposición, si no contradicción, con la tendencia de la nuevamente radical poesía española que definían individualmente, Pedro Salinas, Jorge Guillén, Federico García Lorca, Dámaso Alonso, Rafael Alberti ... '[46]

Within these tendencies and movements, however, Bergamín recognizes the individual forces that he considers to be the main 'frontiers' that contain or define the literary initiatives of the twenties:

Conviene no olvidar que la transcendencia poética de la obra imaginativa de Ramón Gómez de la Serna desvirtúa por contraste con su genial autenticidad otras vecindades, otras sugerencias. La influencia poética de la literatura de Ramón Gómez de la Serna es, por sí sola, tan extensa y poderosa, que casi a Ramón solo podría considerársele como un fenómeno literario colectivo. En cierto modo, los escritores siguientes hubieran debido ponerse de acuerdo para vencer su fuerza torrencial: prefirieron reconocerla – y agradecerla – al desviarse, como no tenía más remedio que suceder, de ella. El nombre – la obra monstruosa – de Ramón Gómez de la Serna es una frontera común de los nuevos intentos poéticos. Otra, frontera movidiza, la de la personalidad poética más aún que la obra misma (*obra en marcha: forma del huir*) del poeta *andaluz universal* Juan Ramón Jiménez. La más aguda, fina, ardiente inteligencia: la que ha polarizado más direcciones caprichosas de las brújular por su norte.

His attitude towards Gómez de la Serna is interesting if somewhat ambivalent. He suggests on the one hand that the writers of his own generation, anxious to assert their independence, side-stepped the temptations that Gómez de la Serna's work represented. On the other hand, however, Bergamín acknowledges the strength of the example that he set. What at least emerges from this apparent contradiction is the overwhelming *presence* of Gómez de la Serna in the literary world, to which the younger writers of the time could not remain indifferent. Only Cernuda, of the critics of Bergamín's generation, would take up this idea and demonstrate how the poets of the twenties became indebted to the techniques of the *greguería*.[47] In other later critical assessments of the period, Gómez de la Serna – precisely, perhaps, because he did not fit comfortably into the schematizations proposed – would tend to be mentioned only in passing.[48] The traces of the *greguería* style in Bergamín's aphorisms, together with the essays that he devoted to Gómez de la Serna's work during these years,[49] serve as a useful reminder of how, in any comprehensive account of the literary realities of the period, room needs to be found for this individual 'fenómeno literario colectivo.'

The importance attached to Jiménez as another driving force in the literary world has become something of a critical commonplace, and Bergamín's remarks simply confirm it. He had already alluded to it in his important article of 1927, 'El idealismo andaluz,' where he had suggested that the true inspiration for the new art of the twenties came from the south, in the shape of Jiménez, Falla, and Picasso:

La transcendencia estética universal de Andalucía que se ha afirmado, idealmente, por la poesía de Juan Ramón Jiménez, la música de Falla y la pintura de Picasso, ha tenido, sobre todo el resto de la actividad artística española última, una influencia radical y decisiva. Este 'andalucismo universal' ha influído tanto en poetas, músicos y pintores nuevos – andaluces o no – que es fácil reconocer su huella en cualquier caso, y de todos es muy reconocida la trinidad andaluza a que me refiero, y aceptada, en su plena significación ideal, como la única herencia positiva, quizás, del pasado artístico español más reciente.

The remark is suggestive because once again Bergamín's approach to the period is a wider one than critics have generally adopted, and encompasses music and painting, as well as poetry. His idea of the overall thrust given to artistic activity in general in Spain in the twenties by this 'trinidad andaluza' stresses how so much of that activity, while embodying local strengths, achieved at the same time a notable international or universal status. From the literary point of view, however, the importance of Jiménez is of prime concern and Bergamín goes on, in 'El idealismo andaluz,' to state unequivocally: 'La obra poética de Juan Ramón Jiménez – unida, como en Mallarmé, a su ejemplaridad personal – ha señalado el momento inicial de la nueva evolución lírica en España.'

What is important here is not so much that Bergamín establishes the primacy of Jiménez's influence over the poets of the time – a point of view reiterated by countless critics subsequently – but that his views on this subject are very carefully worded and amount to an attempt to define that influence more precisely than has generally been done. Whereas critics writing about the work of writers like Guillén, Salinas, and Cernuda have been quick to isolate the specific literary debts (of conception and articulation) that these poets owed Jiménez, Bergamín prefers to emphasize the relevance of Jiménez's *personal* example and his role as an initial *guide*. His point of view is evident in a comment he makes on Guillén in the same essay of 1927:

El 'clasicismo vivo' de Jorge Guillén, traspasado de idealidad andaluza y reminiscente de recuerdos clásicos de España y Francia su empeño ético-estético (que es la verdadera influencia ejercida en él como en todo lo nuevo mejor, en todo lo joven, por Juan Ramón Jiménez; influencia más personal, directa – y directriz – viva, que literaria) le han situado, por la clarividencia artística y consciente de su maestría, en vecindad constante de toda la joven poesía nueva …

Bergamín's attempts to qualify in this way the sense of Jiménez's influence over the poets of the twenties were to provoke an extremely hostile reaction from Jiménez himself and ultimately to lead to the breakdown of the relationship between Bergamín's generation and their poetic mentor.[50]

There was nothing malicious – at first, at least – about Bergamín's handling of this subject. It was entirely consistent with the distinction that he always drew between personal affinities and literary differences, and the emphasis he placed on the *individuality* of the work of each poet he wrote about. The point is made, for example, in 'Literatura y brújula' where, having called into question the usefulness of generic labels and underlined the absence of any common program in the literature of the twenties, he goes on to say:

No hay entre la diversidad de las nuevas tendencias literarias otro propósito o dirección común que la de ser exclusivamente literarias, autónomas, independientes. Es inútil que la tontería de cualquier edad, la tontería crónica o anacrónica del cronista periódico puro – o impuro o mixto – periodista profesional, se esfuerce en reducir a un calificativo genérico, absolutamente vacío, esta variedad, multiplicidad de intentos y resultados. Cada uno de los nuevos escritores tiene su mundo aparte. Y esto no es novedad. Siempre y en todo movimiento literario, aun en los agrupados poéticamente en banderías, ha sucedido lo mismo. Es condición del arte literario esta separación e independencia, esta pura individuación.

Bergamín showed no interest in pursuing what he believed to be the false critical ideal of establishing exhaustively what writers had in common, grouping them together by documenting the similarities between their work. What his essays of the period reveal is his respect for this concept of 'pura individuación,' and he was to remain faithful to the principle he condensed into a memorable aphorism: 'La verdadera crítica no dice "*se parece a* ... " sino "*se diferencia de* ... "' (True criticism does not say '*this seems like* ... ' but '*this is different from* ... ').[51]

Bergamín's opinion, voiced in 'Literatura y brújula,' that literature in general, and more particularly Spanish literature of the twenties, was at best a 'coincidencia de contrastes' reappears constantly in his essays of the period. He refuted, for example, the notion current in the late twenties that the Cernuda of *Perfil del aire* was merely a disciple or echo of Guillén:

En las cristalizaciones poéticas que un platónico amor andalucista han favorecido en Jorge Guillén, encuentra, precisamente, el sevillano Cernuda – diciéndolo vulgarmente – 'la horma de su zapato'; una crítica falsa – la de los parecidos – se complace en subrayar la semajanza; pero la verdadera crítica debe hacer todo lo contrario: evidenciar la diferencia; sobre todo, porque no se debe fijar en la horma – o norma – ni tampoco, siquiera, en el zapato, sino en el pie desnudo. La poesía de Luis Cernuda, desnuda de todo parecido externo, es originalísima ...

('El idealismo andaluz')

He did exactly the same in the case of Alberti and Lorca whom he describes as

los dos poetas que la crítica *parecidista* ha insistido tanto en aproximar falsamente, cuando sólo pueden tocarse por extremos, por antagónicos, por absoluta y totalmente opuestos y contrarios; como sus paisajes natales – Granada y Cádiz – divergen sus direcciones estéticas: Lorca viene de lo popular, naturalmente, como un resultado, como un fruto; Alberti va a lo popular, con intención artística, para realizarlo ...

('El idealismo andaluz')

What interests him in a writer like Guillén are the distinctions between a work like *Cántico* and the writers who stand at the frontiers around it:

Estos nombres: Poe, Mallarmé, son vecindades poéticas del libro *Cántico*. Relaciones para definirlo por diferenciación, por distancia: distancias no salvadas porque no se pueden perder. La pérdida de la distinción poética racional es la de sus imitadores o falsificadores engañosos: de los que materializan la relación poética y confunden la forma, medida espiritual, con el molde vacío (cualquier métrica o sistematización hueca, restos mortales de distintas poesías) ...

('La poética de Jorge Guillén')

Elsewhere he drew these kinds of distinction between Altolaguirre and Prados, for example, and between Antonio Espina and the figures with whom he was constantly compared: Larra, Solana, Gómez de la Serna.[52]

Bergamín's critical essays of the pre-war period do seem, therefore, to constitute an illuminating overview of the major literature of the time. If the full potential of this overview was never realized in a systematic survey of any kind, the main outlines of his arguments are still clearly visible. In his published work he examined in some detail books by writers like Salinas (from *Presagios* and *Víspera del gozo* to *Seguro azar* and *La voz a ti debida*), Alberti (from *Marinero en tierra* and *La amante* to *Sobre los ángeles* and *Yo era un tonto* ...), Guillén (*Cántico*), Cernuda (*Perfil del aire*), and Lorca (*Poeta en Nueva York*), and referred to others by Gerardo Diego (*Manual de espumas*), Altolaguirre (*Las islas invitadas*), Espina (*Signario*), and more generally to Gómez de la Serna, Larrea, and Dámaso Alonso.[53] Read against the backcloth provided by his writings on wider questions of aesthetics and poetic theory, it becomes possible to gauge more fully the status Bergamín enjoyed at the time as an informed and enthusiastic commentator on the poetry of the period.

At the beginning of his essay on Guillén of 1929, Bergamín reflected on the general relationship between poetry and criticism:

... toda poesía determinada implica una poética determinante, que, a su vez, explica esta poesía. Sin choque con su propia conciencia crítica, la obra poética no existe. La crítica es consecuencia de la poesía, se deduce de ella y la corrobora; la afirma, negativamente, como el Mefistófoles goethiano la creación divina; tiene la virtud de una línea; subraya con su trazo la sombra que proyecta toda luminosa creación poética: la define por su misma generación, relativamente espontánea, limitándola, terminándola, determinándola.

('La poética de Jorge Guillén')

This comment provides an insight not only into the inextricably linked activities of creation and criticism but also into the nature of Bergamín's relationship with the poets of his generation. While it is true that some of these poets – most notably Guillén, but also Cernuda and Salinas – would later articulate themselves that implicit critical awareness that lay behind their activities as poets, it would still be fair to say that Bergamín's function, as their work appeared in print, was to assume the responsibility of completing, so to say, the 'cycle of affirmation.' It may well have been a secondary function, a more modest one in comparison with that of the poet himself, as Gerardo Diego suggested when he described Bergamín as 'iluminador ... de la poesía ajena'; but it was still an indispensable procedure for throwing into relief the nature of the achievement of the individual poet. To return to the imagery of one of his aphorisms, it was as if Bergamín's critical writings were *márgenes al resplandor*, a kind of darkroom in which the luminosity of his friends' work could most fully be brought out.

4

'Trofeos de la sutileza':
The Stylist

In his discussions of 'el arte poético' Bergamín draws no distinction between verse and prose. The poet, in his view, is not distinguished by any particular typographical layout but rather by his use of language, by his refinement of the raw materials at his disposal, and his ultimate creation of a separate, artistic reality. He believes that 'la prosa, como el verso, de los poetas, se afirma por un esfuerzo – triunfante – de depuración, que es voluntad de forma' ('Notas ... ' 1927). This rejection of any *essential* difference between verse and prose when they embody a *voluntad de forma* produces an interesting shift in the way the best of Spanish literature of the twenties can be, and perhaps should be, read. It eliminates, for example, that superficial distance that separates, say, the Alberti of *Cal y canto* or the Guillén of *Cántico* from the Jiménez of *Platero y yo* and *Españoles de tres mundos.*[1] More important, in the context of this study, it provides the incentive for reconsidering certain aspects of Bergamín's own prose style. The purpose of such a reconsideration would not only be to draw attention to the 'poetic' qualities of some of his writings of the period (though this is an important topic in itself), but also to show how his own *voluntad de forma* locates his work within the same overall framework of aesthetic ideals that inspired the poets of his generation. The purpose, in other words, is to suggest something that critics have almost entirely overlooked: that as a prose stylist Bergamín functioned as a unique and fascinating counterpart to those gifted writers of verse.

When Ramón Gaya remarked that Bergamín's prose of the 1920s could be read as an 'indecisa forma de versificación' (hesitant form of versification), he was referring specifically to his aphorisms. It is certainly true that many of them, by virtue of the perception they contain and the way in which that perception is expressed, could legitimately be viewed as isolated poetic fragments. Cernuda's definition of the *greguería* – 'un minúsculo poema en prosa' (a minuscule prose poem) – could equally well be applied to those aphorisms that operate on the basis of an ingenious metaphor or a lyrical interpretation of some prosaic aspect of reality.[2] Consider this aphorism, quoted earlier:

El cohete es una caña que piensa con brillantez.[3]

Its status as poetry can best be appreciated by comparing it with some of the lines that Cernuda refers to when documenting his idea of the *greguería*'s impact on the techniques dominant among poets in the twenties. He quotes Gerardo Diego, for example:

La guitarra es un pozo
con viento en vez de agua

(The guitar is a well
full of wind instead of water)

and Salinas:

La rosa ... la prometida del viento (176)

(The rose ... the wind's fiancée)

What these lines have in common with the *greguería* and by extension, with the metaphors of Bergamín's aphorisms, is that they function as lyrical definitions, recasting some object (which may or may not be considered intrinsically 'poetic') in a new, more imaginative and sugges- tive mould. How the idea is arranged on the page – run on in prose or divided up into lines of more or less equal length – is of little consequence. If Diego's description of the guitar was simply written in one sentence as prose, it might be mistaken for a *greguería* but it would not forfeit its status as poetry, as poetic fragment. Similarly, the fact that Bergamín chose not to divide up his aphorisms, avoiding the temptation of giving them the formal appearance of verse, has no bearing on the essential poetic qualities of many of the insights themselves.

The effect of the variety of moods and ideas expressed in *El cohete y la estrella* and *La cabeza a pájaros* is to disguise and practically conceal the basic lyrical instinct that underpins a considerable number of the aphorisms.

The reader browsing through the section of *La cabeza a pájaros* devoted to music may easily overlook the sense of comments, such as the following, casually included among the solemn and playful opinions on composers, performers, and instruments:

El número es la prisión silenciosa de la música. (142)

Debajo del mar, el silencio es claro, denso, cuajado, transparente, luminoso: como la inmovilidad aparente de los astros. Música de estrellas. (142)

These are memorable not as the insights of a critic but as the imaginative, deftly worded perceptions of a poet.

This tendency in Bergamín to shift from the moral or sententious to the suggestively poetic is more evident in some places than in others. In a section of *La cabeza a pájaros* like 'El grito en el cielo,' for example, the writer's powers of lyrical interpretation are given freer rein and consequently stand out more clearly against the other attitudes and poses he adopts:

El gallo es un reclamo divino: anuncio luminoso de la creación. (158)

La disparatada gritería de las veletas en los aires clama al cielo. (160)

La veleta es reloj de viento: el gallo en la veleta canta, y cuenta, la eternidad. (160)

La veleta es alegre corazón del viento. (161)

Here, the cock and the weathervane provide the stimulus for the elaboration of a series of striking metaphors. The question of their formal disposition on the page is marginal to an understanding of the nature of the insights themselves. If they happen to be separated by an asterisk or by a blank space, this does not alter the fact that they could just as easily have been joined and rearranged into a single sequential interpretation – in verse – of a subject summarized in a heading such as 'La veleta' or 'El gallo' or 'El grito en el cielo.' Bergamín clearly has the requisite qualities of the poet – as far as perception and expression are concerned – but simply chooses not to use them in a way that is conventionally, i.e. formally 'poetic.' What Cernuda says of the relationship between Gómez de la Serna's *greguerías* and the poets of the twenties is equally valid for the relationship between their work and many of Bergamín's aphorisms: 'Que

Gómez de la Serna escriba sólo prosa y los otros escribieran verso, no es obstáculo al parentesco' (174). (The fact that Gómez de la Serna wrote only prose while the others wrote verse does not invalidate the similarity.) Obviously, to associate poetry only with the traditional metrics of verse is an unacceptable simplification.

There is one interesting sign in Bergamín's work that supports the idea that in many respects the form in which the aphorism is rendered is immaterial. By the fifties and sixties Bergamín had ceased to feel constrained by his own self-consciousness about writing verse. At that stage in his life, the idea of 'competing' with the poets of his generation had ceased to be relevant and he was able to acknowledge in his published work that his true vocation as a writer led him naturally towards poetry. In 1963, for example, he published a book entitled *Duendecitos y coplas.*[4] It contains many short verse compositions that bear a marked resemblance to his aphorisms. The similarity is clearest in those cases in which the specific idea contained in certain aphorisms of *La cabeza a pájaros* is reformulated in verse. The aphoristic dialogue of 1934:

– No tengo sobre qué caerme merto.
– Por eso estás vivo (137)

becomes

Me dices que nunca tienes
en donde caerte muerto:
por eso estás vivo siempre. (76)

Similarly, the aphorism that runs

Más sabe el Diablo por viejo que por Diablo. Lo mismo da. Porque cuando empezó a ser Diablo empezó a saber: y empezó a envejecer (114)

is essentially reproduced in the following lines:

'Más sabe el Diablo por viejo
que por Diablo.' Es igual.
Porque el Diablo envejece
por saberlo todo mal. (160)

It is not that the original aphorisms themselves – in what they say or even how they say it – are especially lyrical in these cases, but that they can equally well be presented in verse as in prose. If Bergamín's *coplas* are read as poetry (as a particular type of poetry: philosophical, meditative, etc.), it is only because they are printed on the page as poetry and therefore invoke a convention of reader response. There is, however, nothing *essentially* different between the aphorism and the *copla*. It could well be that in Bergamín's case, Unamuno's belief that 'no se piensa más que en aforismos' (we think only in aphorisms) is entirely true: the form that those aphoristic thoughts are given is of secondary importance.[5]

Bergamín's aphorisms may also be considered 'poetic' in another sense which ties in with the emphasis placed in the 'Notas ... ' of 1927 on *depuración* as a creative principle of 'el arte poético' in both prose and verse. That is, the aphorism is, by its own nature, the product of the distillation of thought, the quintessential formulation of an idea. The aphorist refines the process of reasoning and elaboration until he is left with the pure concentrated substance of what he wants to say. His procedures are akin to those of the most rigorous poet – in verse. This is most convincingly conveyed in Bergamín's case in the relationship between his aphorisms and discursive essays, a topic that has already been touched on. It is evident that in an aphorism such as the following:

La poesía es hermética, como el dios griego: reciennacido inmortal

(Carmen)

he has condensed and streamlined all the complex and perhaps ungainly insights that he worked out at length in 'El pensamiento hermético de las artes.' Similarly, the twenty-five pages of 'La decadencia del analfabetis-mo' are essentially – quintessentially – summarized in the aphorism that reads, 'Bienaventurados los que no saben leer ni escribir porque ellos serán llamados analfabetos' (*La cabeza a pájaros*, 110).[6]

This principle of *depuración*, however, and the 'rigor del análisis' of creative writing that it implies are much more clearly discernible in Bergamín's *Caracteres*.[7] This book has an odd historical distinction since it was the only prose work to appear in the famous collection of supplements of the journal *Litoral*, a collection which to all intents and purposes was devoted exclusively to poetry. The series opened with Lorca's *Canciones* and Alberti's *La amante* and went on to include works (in verse) of all the major poets of the decade: Cernuda, Prados, Aleixandre,

Altolaguirre, Villalón, Hinojosa ... It took up where the Biblioteca de Indice had left off and promoted those talents associated at the time with 'la joven literatura' and later with the 'Generation of 1927.'

Bergamín's *Caracteres* was the third supplement to appear and its inclusion in the series bears witness not only to the writer's prestige and his close association with the activities of his friends, but also to the way in which this particular book was read and understood. The coherence of the series was by no means marred by the inclusion in it of a collection of prose texts, since their style was seen to embody the same creative ideals, the same commitment to poetry, to 'el arte poético,' that were manifest in the work of Lorca, Alberti, Cernuda, and the rest. The formal differences between their writing and Bergamín's were not viewed as a reason to consider him as a case apart.[8]

Bergamín may well have been inspired to write his *Caracteres* by the example set by Jiménez in his 'caricaturas líricas.' It is certainly arguable, for example, that the techniques of emphasis and evocation used by both writers are basically similar; but there are important differences of intention. Whereas Jiménez deliberately set out to capture, by means of lyrical exaggeration and interpretation, some aspect of an identified writer or cultural figure, Bergamín was more concerned with sketching profiles of human archetypes. The titles that he gave his texts – 'El temeroso,' 'El torturado,' 'El trasnochado,' and so on – draw attention to the way he attempted to eliminate the connection between the sketch itself and the individual on whom it was based. That he did not always insist on this separation is evident in the way he allowed his first portrait – 'El alegre' – which was modelled on Alberti, to be used as a kind of lyrical prologue to *La amante*; but in general his technique was to submit his subject to a process of poetic abstraction, or 'derealization,' in the sense that Ortega gives this term in *La deshumanización del arte*.[9]

The only satisfactory way of demonstrating the poetic status of the texts contained in *Caracteres* is to analyse a number of examples, explaining their meticulous formal organization and the style and techniques used in them. A good example to begin with would be 'El incandescente'(14), which happens to be modelled on Vicente Aleixandre:

No sé porqué, debajo de la incipiente calva de su cabeza, creía yo que ardía una brasa incandescente.

Todo él estaba ardiendo desde hacía mucho tiempo en un secreto incendio interior, consumiéndose poco a poco, muy lentamente, en una combustión de siglos.

No me atrevía, casi, a aproximar a él mis dedos, para no quemarme. Y cuando salíamos al aire libre, temía que el viento le avivase, prendiéndole en una sola llama que le consumiera en un instante.

Pero cuando en un recogido interior, el leve soplo de sus labios, formulaba rítmicamente su pensamiento, yo sentía – ¡oh Shelley! – animarse la pura brasa en ascua viva y me acercaba al calor y a la luz tenue y sagrada del sublime rescoldo.

The general mechanics of the portrait here, as elsewhere, are fairly straightforward. Bergamín begins by taking a single physical feature, and using it as a base or platform, builds up a more detailed picture in which abstract qualities or ideas are highlighted. The description moves immediately from the denotative (the 'incipiente calva de su cabeza') to the connotative (the 'brasa incandescente'). The associations suggested by this move are then elaborated upon in the rest of the text. In 'El incandescente,' this shift of direction or emphasis – from physical likeness to metaphorical interpretation – is underlined in the second paragraph where the initial insight ('Todo él estaba ardiendo desde hacía mucho tiempo') is suddenly tightened and intensified ('combustión de siglos').

By moving through a series of interrelated images or metaphors, continually working and reworking the basic idea he is proposing, Bergamín maintains a strict overall coherence within the text. In this example, for instance, all the textual items closely complement each other: the nouns *brasa, incendio, combustión, llama, ascua, rescoldo, calor, luz,* and the verbs *arder, consumir(se), quemar, avivar,* and *prender.* All revolve around the central equivalence established at the outset between *calva* and *brasa,* and prepare the ground for the lyrical hyperbole that the text exploits: the speaker's 'fear' of burning his fingers on this inner fire, the apparent 'risk' of the subject bursting into flames when exposed to the outside air.

Language is used throughout with great sensitivity and precision. This is especially evident at the phonic and rhythmic levels at which the text functions. The second paragraph, for example, is structured around a stressed vowel (*é*) which marks the pace at which the sentence advances and the stages through which it passes: from *él, ardiéndo, secréto, incéndio* to *consumiéndose* and *léntaménte.* The rhythmic balance and internal harmony of the paragraph is emphasized in the positions of the gerunds *ardiendo* and *consumiéndose,* the second registering and then intensifying – through both sound and meaning – the resonances set up by the first. This kind of balance is noticeable, too, in the final paragraph where at the end of the sentence the *pura brasa* moves delicately into the *ascua viva.* The two items seem to mirror each other or hold each other in check with their symmetrical noun/adjective and adjective/noun pattern, with all four words having the same number of syllables. It could be argued, in addition, that these carefully controlled structures and relationships are not simply values in themselves, but also correspond to the idea that the text finally frames: the subject's rhythmic formulation of thought in poetry.

That the text as a whole can legitimately be read as poetry is suggested, for example, by its overall structure, which is reminiscent of that of a sonnet. Although the analogy need not be taken too far, there is a degree of similarity in the rigorous organization of the different parts of the text. It begins by establishing the essential theme and then carefully unfolds as that theme is explored and shaped, each paragraph having its distinctive function. But the text's poetic qualities can perhaps be most graphically conveyed by the simple device of rendering a sentence into verse:

Y cuando salíamos al aire libre,
temía que el viento le avivase,
prendiéndole en una sola llama
que le consumiera en un instante.

Even if the lines do not scan exactly, the effect is still quite remarkable. It clarifies the point that Jiménez, for example, used to make implicitly when transcribing one of his poems as prose, or alternatively when copying out one of his prose texts as verse: the character of the language itself and the perceptions communicated in the texts remain unchanged. Hence the categories that Jiménez used to establish – poesía en verso and poesía en prosa – were simply formal clarifications. In the case of the sentence from 'El incandescente' copied above as verse, the effect is to enable the reader to recognize more easily what is already implicitly evident in the prose form: the writer's ear for rhythm and his concern for harmonious structure. For example, the internal echoes (salíamos/temía; viento/ prendiéndole) are more readily discernible, as is the disposition of accentuated vowels that establish the sentence's rhythm. The fact that the second and fourth lines in this rearrangement have an assonant rhyme (avivAsE, instAntE) may be fortuitous, but it does conveniently help to question yet again the usefulness, in cases like these, of the formal distinctions between verse and prose. It is only because these distinctions have tended to be rigidly adhered to that critics have been dissuaded from viewing Bergamín's writing in a work like Caracteres as a natural extension of or complement to the practice of 'el arte poético' of the nineteen twenties.

It is worth making one final remark about 'El incandescente.' The text moves from the specifically physical to the lyrically abstract in two ways: by shifting immediately from *calva* to *brasa*, as has been mentioned, but also by extending the idea of the figurative *brasa* itself. Bergamín enriches the metaphorical language of fire by using a series of suggestive connotative adjectives: the *brasa* is *pura*, the *luz* is *sagrada*, the *rescoldo* is *sublime*. Coming at the end of the text, these adjectives naturally signal the climax of the entire interpretation it has proposed. This can be read at an anecdotal level: Aleixandre has finally realized his own poetic potential. Having silently tended his lyrical instinct for many years, he now brings it to life in the poems that will appear in *Ambito*, his first book. But this attachment to the circumstances of an identified or identifiable individual is not Bergamín's prime concern. To return to the point he made in his 'Notas ... ': 'La forma poética – arte poético, prosa y verso, poesía pura – es el poema, y existe, fuera de toda otra realidad, por sí misma – y para sí misma – por sí sola.' This suggests that an appropriate way to respond to a text like 'El incandescente' is to set aside the possible or probable connection with an experienced reality and to consider it as a self-enclosed, self-referential whole. At this higher level, therefore, the text can be read as linguistic artefact, as pure artistic reality. And the interpretation it offers in this way is, appropriately, one that concerns only poetry itself. It portrays 'the poet,' rather than any specific poet, who contains within him the ageless energy ('combustión de siglos') that is freed in the act of composing or reciting ('al leve soplo de sus labios, formulaba rítmicamente su pensamiento'). The text becomes finally both statement about and exemplification of the 'luz tenue y sagrada del sublime rescoldo' of poetry itself.

'El incandescente' suggests as a whole that Bergamín was endowed not just with the ability to spawn poetic fragments of the type that appear, in isolation, in his aphorisms, but also with the technical skills to create something more substantial and systematic out of a particular perception. He clearly had the capacity to transform the prosaic (in this case, even the most prosaic of bald patches) into a delicate and refined lyrical evocation in which every textual element is made to perform a definite function, whether it be semantic, phonic, or rhythmic. Other portraits from *Caracteres* merely confirm the presence of these skills, but in order not to give the impression that 'El incandescente,' because it is *about* poetry, is an exception within the collection, one additional example would not be out of place. His sketch of 'El pródigo' reads as follows:

Lo primero que llegaba de él, en el recuerdo, era su risa: una risa clara, atronadora y caudalosa como un río; una risa torrencial, desbordante; una inundación de risa fertilizadora.

Vivía del caudal inextinguible de su risa – o, mejor dicho, vivían los demás – porque él la desparramaba a su alrededor, la arrojaba a todos, generosamente, como si tirase monedas de oro por la ventana.

Iba y venía la marea incesante de su risa, sobre él; le traía y le llevaba, ante sí, sobre sí – dentro y fuera – como un mar secreto, acariciando el suave contorno femenino de la playa de su melancolía; y en su playa solía estarse escondido entre la arena o pegado a una roca como un molusco, haciéndose un caparazón de su amargura.

¡No se reía debajo de la cáscara amarga de sus pensamientos! Pero había que romperla para encontrar lo tierno del corazón – la pulpa dulce o agridulce – la melancólica alegría, distante de la de su risa, tal vez, pero más blanda y conmovida. (17)

The same fundamental techniques mentioned in connection with 'El incandescente' are evident here. Bergamín's point of departure is the initial equivalence between *risa* and *río*. This establishes the conceptual, figurative framework within which the total coherence of the text is maintained. The elaboration of this opening simile within the limits it sets is clearly marked: from river (torrent, flood) to tide, sea, beach, sand, rock, and mollusc. The focus gradually narrows as Bergamín approaches the particular quality that interests him. By exploiting the double meaning of *caudal(oso)*, he is able to forge a link between the idea of water and the notion of abundance and wealth implicit in the subject's laugh. This, in turn, is developed and made explicit with the incorporation of the *monedas de oro* thrown through the window, suggesting not just generosity but disinterested generosity: the subject does not knowingly distribute alms but simply allows others to derive sustenance from his natural, spontaneous gestures.

There is once more a precise, calculated use of language. In the opening paragraph, for example, each adjective used suggestively defines a different aspect of the *risa/río*: *clara* has a visual sense but also evokes purity; *atronadora* renders the sound, but also, like *torrencial*, suggests strength and intensity; *desbordante*, in turn, develops the idea of this uncontainable energy, using the notion of volume. The essential thrust of these adjectives is complemented and intensified in *fertilizadora*: the *risa/río* overflows, its waters generating new life on this flood plain where others can proceed to find nourishment. The verbs used in the opening two paragraphs are also harnessed to serve this idea, each one capturing the generous, outgoing movement: *desparramar, arrojar, tirar*, with the implied *desbordar* and *inundar*.

In the organization of its individual sentences and paragraphs, this text also displays the same concern for rhythmic structure. At the beginning, for example, the tertiary rhythm of the opening description (*clara, atronadora, caudalosa*) is magnified in the triple version of the laugh itself: *una risa clara ... ; una risa torrencial ... ; una inundación de risa*. The structure of the sentence is not fortuitous. These waves of description, the accumulation of adjectives, evoke in themselves the gushing, overwhelming nature of the subject's laugh. Once more, form complements and illuminates substance. This is made even clearer in the way in which the third paragraph is structured. Here, the form which the description assumes mirrors in its own rhythms and patterns the movement of the tide. Words ebb and flow like the water itself: *iba y venía; le traía y le llevaba; dentro y fuera*. It is a perfect example of the kind of technique used by the craftsman of language: surface organization supplies the design in and through which the shapeless idea is most effectively fixed and conveyed.

This oscillatory movement of the tide, evoked in this series of quick, intense binary combinations, establishes another structural principle on which the text operates. There is a range of dualities within the text: the shift from water to wealth, engineered by the ambivalente *caudal*; the change of focus from laughter to river and from river to sea; the penetration from outer to inner. These concentrate attention on the climax of the interpretation which in itself depends upon the idea of duplicity – the *mar secreto*. The text is, as it were, funnelled towards the final paragraph in which these combinations of distinctions and opposites are condensed into the single image of the mollusc with its hard shell and soft inside. The image summarizes the contradiction between external feature and internal identity. The duality of the character portrayed is then shown to be present even within this figurative form: his *melancólica alegría* is contained within its *pulpa ... agridulce*.

Like 'El incandescente,' 'El pródigo' has only the thinnest veneer of narrative. The first-person speaker, discreetly present in the former, disappears from 'El pródigo' where the text functions more directly as absolute, objectified, artistic description. But in both cases it is the *voluntad de forma* that sustains and organizes language and idea. Like all the other portraits, each is a lyrical, metaphorical interpretation, spinning out of what at first sight appears to be unpromising raw material a finely structured evocation. If only for phrases like 'la luz tenue y sagrada del sublime rescoldo' and 'acariciando el suave contorno femenino de la playa de su melancolía,' their status as prose poems – as 'poetry' irrespective of formal arrangement – is assured.

*   *   *

These remarks on Bergamín's aphorisms and the portraits of *Caracteres* stress his acute awareness of the effects that language could produce and his concern as a prose writer with tightly controlled textual organization and the relationship between content and expression. Discussion of Bergamín as stylist, however, needs to be taken further in order to provide some account of his essays. These long discursive texts display a series of features that go beyond the overtly 'poetic' and point to the other dimension of his writing at this time that won him distinction. The best way to approach the task of specifiying these features and to see how this aspect of the topic leads on from what has already been argued in this chapter, is to refer back to 'El pensamiento hermético de las artes' and consider a passage like the following:

1   La razón de que sean poéticas las artes es su novedad, su nueva edad eterna de inmortales; porque su razón de ser es hermética: es la del pensamiento eternamente recién nacido inmortal de la razón divina: Hermes, el que nace, y se hace, de nuevas, sorprendido: el que es parte y parte de la razón; el que

5   partiendo de la razón divina, partiéndose de ella, sale huyendo como disparado o disparatado, por lo que se dijo: *rápido como el pensamiento*. Y eso son las artes poéticas: artes del pensamiento: artes de disparar la razón, de disparatarla. Y por eso son verdaderas: porque son herméticas; porque disparan o se disparan contra la vida: la obra poética se dispara contra la vida porque

10   está cargada de razón. ¡Qué cosa más disparatada! – suele exclamar el irracional, creyéndose muy razonable ante la obra poética, y enuncia, sin saberlo, una exacta definición; la obra poética puede definirse, exactamente, con matemática exactitud, por su propia ley generadora, como lo que es: una cosa disparatada. No cabe cosa más disparatada, en efecto, que lo que es,

15   porque lo es, exclusivamente, puramente racional: poético. (218–19)

The most appropriate response to a passage like this is to realize that it has to be read not only in terms of its *content*, but also in terms of its *form*.

The principal historical interest of 'El pensamiento hermético' may well lie in *what* it has to say about a subject of major concern in the twenties, but this should not obscure the importance of *how* those ideas are articulated. What distinguishes Bergamín from Ortega – and indeed from all the other intellectuals who wrote on literature and aesthetics in this period – is above all his style. The refinement and the ingenious hermetic elusiveness of his longer essays of the twenties and thirties reveal a commitment to the very ideas he formulated in texts like 'El pensamiento hermético.' This commitment may have been conveyed indirectly – through form and expression – but it still constituted an unconditional creative allegiance to the ideals championed by the major writers of the day. In other words, the passage quoted above shows how Bergamín was *practising* 'el arte poético' at the same time as he was *theorizing* on it. This connection is a crucial one for an understanding of his eminence as a prose stylist; it needs to be justified by a more detailed analysis.

The texture and flow of the extract from the essay I have chosen are entirely characteristic of the writer. The deliberately precise punctuation guides the reader through the different stages at which ideas have taken shape and been developed. Thought does not advance lineally but rather in an intricate spiral in which ideas spin off one another. Their route is marked not by conventional logic so much as by related sounds, parallel structures, associated and dissociated meanings. In its total exploitation of the resources of language, the passage – like the essay as a whole – is a stylistic tour de force. Its refined difficulty and the intellectual challenge it throws out are precisely those encountered in the most 'hermetic' poetry of the twenties and thirties: the difficulty of 'tuning in' rationally to the writer, of being able to register, with an effort of the intellect, the procedures that have made the final polished statement possible.[10]

Some of these procedures need to be catalogued in order to appreciate the mechanics of the writer's style. The exploitation of surface resonances, for example, sometimes irrespective of their semantic connection, is typical. In the opening part of the first sentence, Bergamín focuses on the relationship between *novedad, nueva edad*, and *de nuevas*. But the association is made at the level of sound rather than meaning. The ambivalence of the word *nuevas* is used to forge a link between *nacer sorprendido* and *hacerse de nuevas*, which both express the element of surprise. *Nace*, as pure sound, ties up with *hace*. *Parte* then appears as both noun and verb, preparing for the subsequent gerund echoes in *partiendo* and *partiéndose*, which are then picked up again in *huyendo*. Attention shifts, perhaps by way of the *par-* sound in the initial parts of the sentence, to another cluster of words in which sound and meaning intermingle: *disparado, disparatado(a), disparar, disparatar(la), disparan, se dispara(n)*. These open the way for the rest of the proposed argument.

It becomes clear that all textual items are being subsumed into complex patterns of sounds and meanings, all carefully controlled by the writer. At the same time, these patterns produce distinctive rhythmic effects. The rhythms are often tertiary, as in the heavily ornamented portraits of *Caracteres*, and reveal how the text is thickened and made denser by insistently repeating a structure or variants of a basic idea. The definitions of Hermes, for example, in lines 3–5, move in this way: *el que nace* ... , *el que es parte* ... , *el que partiendo* ... Ideas are painstakingly shaded and rounded out, as in lines 7–8: *artes poéticas* ... , *artes del pensamiento* ... , *artes de disparar la razón* ... This technique also serves the purpose of rhetorical emphasis, as in lines 12–13: the *exacta definición* ... *puede definirse, exactamente* ... *con matemática exactitud* ... This essential repetition, involving discreet changes of grammatical function, constantly reappears.

As in *Caracteres*, the coherence of the passage as a whole is guaranteed by the clearly defined framework within which the argument is developed. At the conceptual level, the text operates here on the interplay or apparent conflict between reason and unreason. The words *razón* and *disparate* mark the extreme limits between which the writer's mind moves. It is important to notice that the conventional relationship between these two terms is gradually broken down so that Bergamín is able to produce a final definition of the work of art that defies logic: *la obra poética* is *una cosa disparatada* and at the same time *puramente racional* (lines 12–15). It is in this way that content and expression become so inextricably linked as to become indistinguishable, since the subversion of these meanings is only made possible by the subversion of language. All Bergamín's ingenuity is channelled towards undermining the traditional status of words and the sense they communicate. This is immediately evident in the word-plays – the dual value attached to *parte* and *nuevas*, for example – but it goes further than this. Ideas that to all intents and purposes are incompatible are gradually brought nearer to each other by means of subtle and opportunistic leaps. No concept is seen as univalent: *la razón*, for example, is not just logic or rationality, but also explanation, justification, origin, and cause. The term appears as both subject and object, as noun and adjective, alone and with its opposite, casually and intentionally. Similarly, the notion of speed as sudden movement is used in a variety of senses, from the alarmed birth of Hermes and the bullet leaving the gun to the trajectory of thought and the launching of reason against life. Within the context of this tortuous if imaginative reasoning, *lo dispar(at)ado* becomes the definition of *lo racional*. The substance of the idea is faithfully reflected in the procedures by which it has been produced. The conclusion that can and should be drawn from this brief example was formulated by Angel del Río who described Bergamín the essayist as 'el representante máximo en la prosa contemporánea del neobarroquismo, por el que enlaza con la tradición de los conceptistas españoles del siglo xvii, Quevedo y Gracián, en relación paralela y semejante a la que los poetas tienen con Góngora' (The outstanding representative among contemporary prose-writers of the neo-Baroque tendency. In this way he links up with the tradition of the Spanish *conceptistas* of the seventeenth century – Quevedo and Gracián – and establishes with them a relationship that is analogous to the one that the poets have with Góngora).[11] This remark coincides exactly with what I have already suggested, namely that as a stylist Bergamín functioned *parallel to* the poets of his generation. If the sense of this parallel is partly evident in the poetic elements of *Caracteres* and his aphorisms, it is more fully illuminated by viewing essays like 'El pensamiento hermético de las artes' as representations in prose of what Alberti, Guillén, Diego, and the rest were seeking to achieve in poetry. This is how best to understand the complementary role that Bergamín as stylist played within the boundaries that have conventionally contained the 'Generation of 1927.' What remains to be clarified is the exact meaning of tags like *neobarroquismo* and *conceptista* when applied to Bergamín and their usefulness for a more complete understanding of his writing.

*　　*　　*

In his judgment on Bergamín's prose style, Angel del Río both confirmed an opinion that had been voiced earlier in Spain and established the type of standard critical response that Bergamín would elicit subsequently. From the thirties to the eighties, in fact, attention has consistently been drawn to the presence in Bergamín's essays of stylistic tendencies related to seventeenth-century Spanish literature and usually termed 'baroque' or *conceptista*. The insight originally came from Salinas who proclaimed enthusiastically in 1934: 'José Bergamín es un estilista que habrá que poner al lado de los mejores maestros del arte conceptista del siglo xvii' (José Bergamín is a stylist who should be placed alongside the best exponents of *conceptista* art of the seventeenth century).[12] This was later taken up by Luis Felipe Vivanco who wrote that 'Bergamín barroquiza intelectualmente su prosa. En ella alcanza plenitud de forma el conceptismo latente de su pensamiento' (By virtue of his intellectual procedures, Bergamín gives a baroque flavour to his prose. The latent *conceptismo* of his thought reaches its fullest expression in his prose writings).[13] The idea reappears in Max Aub's comment that Bergamín 'frente a lo gongorino general de la época, representa el conceptismo' (In opposition to the general gongorine tendencies of the age, he represents *conceptismo*).[14] The examples could be multiplied,[15] but these are enough to suggest that if there is one firmly entrenched commonplace in the rather limited field of Bergamín studies, it is this notion of a stylistic allegiance to the seventeenth century. What all the critics who have referred to this notion have in common, however, is their reluctance to justify or illustrate at any length what they mean by the labels they unanimously agree are the most appropriate ones to pin on Bergamín. The initial problem, therefore, is one of definition and terminology.

The word *barroquismo* or *neobarroquismo* is something of a nightmare for the literary critic.[16] Whatever precise value the term may have had when first coined has since been eroded by indiscriminate use and the usual opportunistic pillage practised by critics working in a variety of different fields. Full sympathy should be offered to the critic who, after much scholarly reflection, concluded that if used with sufficient caprice or intransigence, the term 'baroque' could mean anything or nothing.[17] The value of an exhaustive chronological survey like the one undertaken by René Wellek is that it stresses not merely how unwieldy the adjective 'baroque' can be, but also how great the distances have been that have separated the various interpretations proposed.[18] When Wellek confesses that 'in using such a term as baroque, we have to realize that it has the meaning which its users have decided to give it' (86), he underlines the degree of purely subjective preference that has always prevented the word from being standardized in any way. Despite Helmut Hatzfeld's valiant if at time impenetrable attempts, the '*comparatiste* of genius' that Odette de Mourgues hoped would one day be able to resolve all divergent interpretations in a single, all-embracing vision, has not yet appeared.[19]

In view of this situation, the only viable approach to the problem at hand is to formulate a practical working definition for the purpose of testing its usefulness in describing Bergamín's prose. What may be lost in scope will hopefully be gained in precision. It should be borne in mind that my concern is above all with a *style* rather than with a general world view or a historical modus operandi that can be viewed as extending into such unlikely realms as politics.[20] I am therefore consciously side-stepping the problems posed by the existence of an 'espíritu barroco,' despite the fact that these problems are relevant for an understanding of certain aspects of Bergamín's outlook.

At the level of style, there is a general consensus on the meaning that can be given the word 'baroque.' Even critics working in different fields (music, architecture, painting, and so on) generally agree that the term denotes dense exuberance and richness, extreme ornamentation and floridity. Spanish critics in particular have constantly drawn attention to these features. Emilio Orozco Díaz, for example, writes of a 'recargamiento ornamental y decorativo' (ornamental and decorative overloading).[21] Ortega made the same point when referring to Góngora: 'lo mejor de Góngora ... tiene un carácter de exuberancia incomfortable para todo el que sea medianamente psicólogo. Recuerda la escultura de la India, que en formas intrincadas, frenéticas y locas, cubre a lo mejor la ladera de un monte' (For anyone with an average degree of psychological insight, what is best in Góngora has an uncomfortably exuberant nature. His work recalls Indian sculpture which in its frenzied complications is capable of covering the side of a hill).[22] Juan Ramón Jiménez confirms the importance of this basic idea: 'Por barroco entiendo: esencialmente: cargazón, exuberancia, frondosidad, retorcimiento' (By Baroque I understand, essentially: dead weight, exuberance, lushness, distortion).[23] Remarks such as these provide the means by which the initial part of the problem concerning the 'baroque' nature of Bergamín's prose style can be satisfactorily solved.

In Bergamín's essays, the clean lines and sharp contours of the ideas he is intent on conveying are often overrun by an abundance of textual ornamentation. Developing the architectural analogy suggested by Ortega, it could be said that upon the pure lines of the column/idea are superimposed intricate designs and patterns which, though closely related to the essential structure itself, expand and complicate its proportions. The simplicity of the straight line remains the basis of the whole construction, just as the aphorism remains the basis of many of Bergamín's most heavily loaded and misshapen paragraphs; but it is encased in a complex mould. Just as the architectural elaboration is both a value in itself and a complementary expansion of the main structure, so the verbal flourishes and parenthetical repetitions and variations of Bergamín's discursive prose are designed both to amplify the sense of the fundamental thought in which they are rooted, and at the same time to stimulate the reader through their own ingenuity and subtlety. The parallel between Bergamín's essays and the kind of *neogongorista* poetry that some of his companions wrote in the twenties can again be grasped by considering the architectural analogy Dámaso Alonso himself used when explaining the baroque elements of Góngora's *Soledades*:

> Volviendo al concepto estrictamente arquitectónico, así como en el barroco las superficies libres del clasicismo renacentista se cubren de decoración, de flores, de hojas, de frutos, de las más variadas formas arrancadas directamente a la naturaleza, o tomadas de la tradición arquitectónica de la antigüedad, así también en las *Soledades*, la estructura renacentista del verso italiano se sobrecarga de elementos visuales y auditivos, de múltiples formas naturales y de supervivencias de la literatura clásica que no tienen ya un valor lógico – no un simple valor lógico – sino un valor estético decorativo.[24]

(If we return to the concept in its strictly architectural sense, we find that just as in the baroque period the free surfaces of the classical Renaissance become covered with decoration, with flowers, leaves, fruits, with a wide variety of forms taken directly from nature or from the architectural traditions of antiquity, so also in the *Soledades* the Renaissance structure of Italian verse becomes loaded down with visual and auditory elements, with multiple natural forms and with vestiges of classical literature which no longer have a logical function – a straightforward logical function – but rather play a decorative, aesthetic role.)

It is precisely the presence in Bergamín's prose of these often self-justifying aesthetic or decorative elements that gives it its baroque dimension and which requires exemplification.

Instances of this baroque floridity could be taken from practically any part of Bergamín's work, corresponding to any historical period. This is significant since it underlines the permanence of this aspect of his style and differentiates it from the temporary allegiance to the ideals of *gongorismo* declared by the poets of his generation. What for the latter was a provisional affiliation – which soon became a constraint – was for Bergamín a lasting and constantly renewed commitment. In order to give this discussion a specific focus, however, only one book will be used to clarify these arguments: *Mangas y capirotes*, published in 1933,[25] This book represented his major achievement as an essayist in the years before 1936 when he began to collect his work systematically in his *Disparadero español*.[26] *Mangas y capirotes* also happens to be the book which produced the comments on his baroque, *conceptista* style from Salinas and Vivanco, and so is ideally suited to this purpose.

Consider the following passage:

1   La comedia española, 'esfera del pensamiento', como la elegante figuración
    geométrica de Tirso de Molina nos la representa, gira por su racional
    movimiento revolucionario sobre su propio conocimiento generador, 'con toda
    la alegría de su soledad circular', como diría el griego: con esa plenitud
5   alegre de su propia determinación poética en el espacio y en el tiempo, de su
    rumbo y destino eterno; y así se proyecta en el cielo de la fe, de la fe en lo
    divino, por cuyo amor se mueve, o a cuyo amor se mueve, revolucionariamente
    en definitiva, al igual del 'sol y de las otras estrellas'. Esta es su razón y su
    sentido: lo que la ha popularizado por su propio conocimiento tan rotunda-
10 mente. Esta es la razón y el sentido popular de todo este teatro; la gloriosa luz
    de eternidad que su cristalina esfera de pensar transparenta: la fe católica de
    Cristo. La razón y el sentido popular de la fe católica en España: como la razón
    y el sentido popular español del catolicismo. La 'esfera del pensamiento' es
    esta comedia española inventada por Lope de Vega para el pueblo y por él, en
15 la que verdaderamente se entera España de sí misma, porque, entera y
    verdaderamente, se populariza por ella; popularizándose, en efecto, por un
    teatro entero y verdadero: entera y verdaderamente popular; porque se entera
    y verifica poéticamente por la fe católica en la viva popularidad que lo
    determina. (28)

The actual substance of the argument here is minimal. In the preceding
five paragraphs (pp. 25–7), Bergamín has already clearly established his
interpretation of the subject, namely that Golden Age theatre in Spain
was defined and generated by its own popularity, by its representation of
the nation's Catholic faith that, conversely, enabled the people or public
to define and know itself through the theatre. Read in this context,
therefore, the passage quoted above is merely a rephrasing or confirmation of a point already made. It can be viewed as a variation on a simple
though ingeniously argued theme, and as such, is an ornamental flourish.
The writer has moved, in other words, from logical exposition to
self-referential – perhaps self-indulgent – rhetorical re-elaboration.
    Within this extract, however, the same near-repetition and delicate
reshaping and filling out of ideas are evident. It is this fullness and
luxuriance of expression in Bergamín's writing that produce its baroque
physiognomy, and a closer analysis of how thought and language operate
in the example given will clarify this point.
    The heavy punctuation, for example, recalls the passage quoted earlier
from 'El pensamiento hermético de las artes.' The reliance upon colons

and semi-colons indicates the indefinite, self-renewing structure of Bergamín's sentences. Ideas are neither conceived nor expressed in the simple terms of a beginning, a middle, and an end. An initial thought generates a series of complementary reflections, which explore and exhaust its implications. There is, consequently, a sense of expansion and growth in his prose. This principle is particularly clear in the final sentence of the extract (lines 13–19) where the long opening phrase ending in a semi-colon leads on to an afterthought to which, by means of the colon in line 17, is added a complementary yet amplificatory comment. This, in turn, is judged to be incomplete and, as if to sum up what has gone before, the writer appends a concluding explanation. It is this kind of concentrated use of punctuation – not only commas, semi-colons, and colons, but also parentheses and dashes – that help to give Bergamín's writing its characteristic expansiveness.

This effect is also produced by the continual incorporation into the text of references to or quotations from other writers. The 'delicia perenne de alusiones' (constant pleasure of allusion), to use Salinas's phrase, produces an element of ornamentation in Bergamín's essays, as in lines 1, 3–4, and 8 of the example quoted. It may even be legitimate to suggest that these constant allusions, the source of which is not always given, function in an analogous way to the references (mythological, astrological, and so on) that are characteristic of *gongorismo* in verse. Viewed from a certain angle, the insistent evocation of parallels, of echoes and resonances from other texts, from a whole series of national literatures and historical periods, often provides the same kind of intellectual challenge and textual infrastructure that can be found in the most heavily loaded gongorine or neo-gongorine poetry.

The texture of Bergamín's prose is also thickened by the abundance of asides, additional explanatory comments that are worked into the text. These seem to repeat some point already made, but by slightly rewording it, they inflate it so that its dimensions change fractionally. In lines 6–7 of the passage above, the repetition seems to be almost verbatim, but the way in which 'de la fe en lo divino' is added to 'en el cielo de la fe,' and in which 'a cuyo amor' delicately redirects the sense of 'por cuyo amor' has the effect of piling shades of meaning and intention on top of each other, making both thought and language denser and more intricate. There is also one example in the passage quoted of how an idea is respun and rephrased to a remarkable degree. The raw materials are essentially the same in each case, but the pattern produced each time is always unique. The difference between the three sentences (lines 8–13) beginning 'Esta es su razón y su sentido ...', 'Esta es la razón y el sentido popular ... ,' and 'La razón y el sentido popular ... ' is apparently minimal. They use almost identical formulae and their content is substantially the same. Bergamín deliberately accumulates words and phrases in order to strengthen and ornament what he is saying. His 'verbosity' is composed of subtle variations in which words are added or subtracted, phrases are almost imperceptibly rearranged, for the purpose of building up out of the multitude of complementary, interrelated details, a total, richly elaborate kaleidoscopic vision. It is precisely this stylistic constant that can be related to the repetitive echo style of the baroque, described with memorable simplicity by Dámaso Alonso as 'repetición constante, constante variación.'[27]

This principle of repetition and variation is strikingly evident in the final sentence of the paragraph quoted, where the elaboration of a limited number of sounds and meanings produces the characteristic effect of dense textual ornamentation. The adverb *verdadera(mente)* is repeated three times, and the root adjective *verdadero* and the related verb *verificarse* each once. The verb *enterarse* is used twice and echoes both the adverbial *entera*, used twice, and the adjectival *entero*, used once. Similarly, *el pueblo* leads on to *se populariza*, which in turn connects with *popularizándose*, *popular*, and *popularidad*. This reveals the careful way in which the grammatical function of words with the same root is changed, and sounds are made to play upon each other, creating a complex pattern of words and meanings, all inextricably linked. All this is held within an overall figurative context of absolute coherence: the image of the sky (*cielo*, *espacio*) through which the heavenly bodies (*esfera*, *sol*, *estrellas*, *luz*) harmoniously move (*girar*, *rumbo*, *circular*, *revolución*).

Since these principles of expression operate throughout *Mangas y capirotes*, any further detailed examples would be superfluous. Each paragraph read as an individual unit, each group of paragraphs read as a sequence, each of the three essays that make up the book, and the book itself taken as a whole display these same characteristics of formal organization: repetition and variation, constant growth and elaboration, density of language, thickness of texture, intricate patterns of sounds, words, and ideas. These are the features of the text that generate its ornate floridity, and it is in this sense that the term 'baroque' can be applied as a useful critical description.

*   *   *

If only because of the frequency with which it has been used to define

Bergamín's prose style, the word *conceptista* has an undeniable potential as an equally illuminating description. Like 'baroque,' however, the term poses a series of problems of definition. The nature and mechanics of *conceptismo* have been the subject of considerable debate ever since Gracián attempted his ambitious survey in 1642.[28] Since my concern is simply to gauge the relevance of the general principles of *conceptismo* for an understanding of Bergamín's writing, I shall avoid the more controversial and involved aspects of the subject and instead concentrate on the essential meanings that Gracián and subsequent interpreters have put forward.

Fundamentally, the conceit is concerned with correspondence, with the perception of a relationship between two ostensibly dissimilar terms, objects, or ideas. In Coleridge's words, it aims at the 'balance or reconciliation of opposite or discordant qualities.'[29] Gracián's own definition refers to the same notion of an ingeniously superimposed harmony and symmetry. He defined the conceit as 'un acto del entendimiento que exprime la correspondencia que se halla entre los objetos. La misma consonancia, o correlación artificiosa exprimida, es la sutileza objetiva.'[30] The faculty of wit plays a central role in formulating the conceit. For Gracián, wit was the supreme intellectual power that discovered these unsuspected correspondences and concealed harmonies, and in articulating them stimulated the intellect in a surprising but pleasant way. The process of establishing the different kinds of 'correlación artificiosa' also had a clearly defined aesthetic function, namely to neaten and polish the form of the insight so that it was as delightful to the ear and eye as it was to the understanding: 'no se contenta al ingenio con sólo la verdad, como el juicio, sino que aspira a la hermosura.'[31]

In order to avoid giving a simple catalogue of the different forms that Bergamín's *conceptismo* takes, I would like to concentrate on one particular type of verbal ingenuity. This concerns the use he makes in *Mangas y capirotes* (as in all his essays of the period) of the fixed formulae of popular speech. There are a number of good reasons for proceeding in this way beyond the obvious one of wishing to make this discussion more cohesive. The first is that by focusing on this aspect of the style of Bergamín's discursive prose, the similarity with the mechanics of many of his aphorisms can be established. In this way, what is said about *Mangas y capirotes* here can be viewed as extending some of the remarks made in chapter 2. The second reason is more important, since it links up directly with what has been said above concerning the baroque texture of Bergamín's prose. In many cases, the *conceptista* exploitation of the possibilities offered by popular expressions determines the very structure and movement of his writing. The whole flow of his reasoning is often dependent precisely on his technique of exhausting the semantic potential of an idiom of some kind. The tangential commentaries and digressive asides that create the baroque floridity of his essays are frequently a direct consequence of his ingenious dissection and rearrangement of the linguistic items contained in a popular phrase. It is possible to show that the expansiveness of Bergamín's style as an essayist is in large part a product of the way in which the *conceptista* temperament functions.

Clearly, this point cannot adequately be made by referring to brief, self-contained examples of how popular expressions are used in *Mangas y capirotes*, though it should be remembered that these isolated instances occur constantly throughout the text.[32] In order to demonstrate satisfactorily how the reasoning that underpins the text determines its shape and structure, the example has to refer to an entire section of the book. This makes the illustration somewhat lengthy and cumbersome but is the only way of doing full justice to the idea.

In a nine-page section of the essay entitled 'La corrida de los tiempos a las luces claras de la burla,' Bergamín elaborates on his basic argument that Golden Age drama, in the themes it handles and in its spiritual orientation, implicitly responds to the public's desire for immortality. According to the writer, this desire is embodied in Lope's *Arte nuevo de hacer comedias*. As an illustration of this point, and as a eulogy to Lope, Bergamín contrasts – in typical disjunctive fashion – Tirso's *El burlador de Sevilla* and Lope's *La fianza satisfecha*. The section is built up entirely around the idiom *jugar a cara y cruz*. With the associated ideas that lead off from it, with the related images it suggests and the unrelated images to which it is ingeniously linked, the idiom provides the coordinates for a richly elaborate and wide-ranging interpretation. The idiom is dismantled and its parts examined from every conceivable angle. Then it is reassembled in different ways, put to different purposes, its original dimensions continually modified or inflated. Given below are those extracts in which the idiom is exploited by Bergamín's tireless *conceptista* ingenuity:

La nocturna sombra de la temporalidad le arremete al hombre en el teatro, impetuosamente enfurecido, como el toro. Y el hombre, enmascarado de luz, le quiebra o le cruza en la misma cara, como a la muerte. El que 'estuvo tres horas cara a cara' – como dijo Lope – mirando este teatro, mirándose en ese espejismo teatral, sabe que detrás de esa cara que se le ofrece, la cara del espejo, está la cruz de Cristo; y que a esa cara y a esa cruz se lo juega todo ... (95–6)

La especulación racional de lo divino, que en el teatro griego tenía dos caras, una cara de risa y otra de llanto, curvando la línea de su clara superficie especular en cristalina máscara de tragedia o de comedia, en el teatro tragicómico español del xvii tiene cara y cruz, como una moneda al jugarla; por eso fía largamente su propia existencia aparencial a lo divino, como el héroe lopista cuya figura se perpetuó en tantas comedias españolas cuando exclama:

> ¡Que lo pague Dios por mí
> y pídamelo después!

La risa y el llanto están inseparablemente unidas y separadas, porque son las dos caras de la misma moneda. La risa y el llanto se cruzan en una misma cara o por la misma cara. (97)

... lo divino ... que se ha hecho humano por la cruz y no por la cara; cuando el hombre se ha hecho divino negándose por esa cruz que le respalda ... La suerte está echada a lo divino: a cara o cruz. Para ganarlo o perderlo todo. (97)

La cara y la cruz de la moneda del teatro lopista, que Calderón echará al aire para destacar luminosamente sus destellos, tiene su más clara representación, su más honda resonancia espiritual, en la comedia verdaderamente famosa de *El burlador de Sevilla* ... (97–8)

... esta pura cara poética de *El burlador*, la más transparente y cristalina del sentido tragicómico de la burla, esencial en este teatro, está respaldada, efectiva y expresamente, por la Cruz, puesto que el reverso de su figura lo compone una comedia de Lope de Vega que la antecede y complementa ... El reverso de esta contante y sonante moneda teatral de *El burlador de Sevilla*, tan contada y sonada, lo forma la no menos famosa, en su tiempo, comedia de Lope de Vega llamada *La fianza satisfecha*. Vamos a mirar esta moneda teatral por sus dos caras, por sus dos lados ... (98–9)

Echando al aire esta moneda, como para jugarla, veremos que al

> ¡Tan largo me lo fiáis!

del Burlador, responde por el otro lado, por el reverso de esta cara, el héroe lopista de *La fianza satisfecha* exclamando:

> ¡Que lo pague Dios por mí
> y pídamelo después! (99)

Don Juan no da la cara más que al destino; para burlarlo, cruzándose con él limpiamente ... (100)

Don Juan se condena por la cara: por su linda cara. Leonido se salva por la cruz, por su sangrienta cruz. El burlador de la comedia de Lope satisface su larga fianza, al final, pagándole a Dios lo que le debía de su propia moneda, que es su propia sangre: muriendo como Cristo, crucificado. (103)

Al reverso de la maravillosa escenificación dramática de *El burlador de Sevilla* está la estremecedora escenificación de Lope de Vega en *La fianza satisfecha*,que la respalda y la apoya, duplicando su significación burlesca. Este doble juego tragicómico de la burla hallará en el teatro calderoniano su desenvolvimiento integral y definitivo. (103–4)

The passage as a whole is remarkable because its arguments fill out and gather momentum, thanks to the idiom's suggestiveness. Bergamín extracts from the literal and figurative meanings of its parts the material out of which his own ideas on the subject under review are constructed. It is possible to chart the way in which connections are contrived and unusual links forged, thereby illustrating the relationship between exuberant form and conceptual approach. The *cara* part of the idiom at one level leads to *máscara* and *enmascarar* (with their opposites *transparente* and *cristalina*) and to Don Juan's *linda cara*. At another level, it ties up with *mirar(se)*, *apariencia*, *espejismo*, *espejo*, *especular*, *especulación*. At a third level it suggests *lado*, *reverso*, *respaldar*, *duplicar* and allows the development of the idea of a theatrical *moneda*. Simultaneously it justifies the incorporation into the argument of Lope's phrase *cara a cara* and the idiomatic (but delexicalized) *dar la cara*. The *cruz* part of the expression opens up the way for the religious interpretation of the subject. *Cruz* (with or without a capital letter) leads to *cruzar(se)*, *santificarse*, *salvarse*, and to the adverbial phrase *a lo divino*. The literal action of tossing a coin together with the notion of placing a bet – both suggested by the idiom as a whole – explain how the expression *echar la suerte* and the verbs *ganar*, *perder*, *jugar*, *jugárselo* find a place in the argument. The dimensions of the argument sometimes overlap and intersect: the *doble juego*, for example, functions as a bridge between the areas sketched above. Similarly, the presence of a *moneda* – implicit in the idiom and made explicit in the text – establishes the connection with the 'financial' aspect of the argument: *especulación*, the use of the colloquial *con(s)tante y sonante* (which in turn finds its baroque, *conceptista* echo in *contada y sonada)*, the idea of a *fianza*, and the act of *pagar*. And since it is a double-sided coin that is *jugada a cara y cruz*, it provides the conceptual framework within which the two plays by Tirso and Lope are compared and contrasted. Upon what is most unremarkably common is erected an argument impressive not only for its evocative complexity, but also for its billowing network of interlocking relationships. There is no better illustration of the *centro* to which Gracián referred when pondering the mechanism of the conceit: 'ese *centro* de quien reparte el discurso líneas de ponderación y sutileza a las entidades que lo rodean.'[33]

A similar example is furnished in a passage from the essay entitled 'La pura verdad por el arte de vestir al muñeco.' This stretches over some eight pages, and in it the multiple variants and suggested cognates of the popular *ver/no ver* conceit are imaginatively threaded together in order to weave a rich fabric of sounds and words, ideas and insights. Unsurprisingly, the passage resists any attempt to paraphrase it, since the logic and shape of its arguments depend sequentially on the new connections it establishes, as it gathers strength and expands, between seemingly unrelated concepts. Essentially, Bergamín's aim is to contrast the different truths revealed in the theatre to the Greek and the Christian and the different ways in which audiences perceived those truths: 'por la revelación creía en la verdad el griego; por la revelación verifica su fe el cristiano' (29). Whereas the Greek's vision is one of imminence, a revelation of death and the finite sense of life, the Christian's is a transcendent one, seeing beyond what is portrayed on stage, sensing his own immortality in the spectacle of life constantly revived and renewed. Given below are the extracts that demonstrate how the full development of the argument is only made possible by the exploration of the basic contrast contained in the *ver/no ver* conceit:

El griego creía para mirar, para ver lo que miraba, y veía porque creía, o lo que creía: veía lo que creaba o poetizaba en el acto mismo de mirar: *in actu oculi*: 'en un abrir y cerrar de ojos'; en un instante, en un momento. El griego detenía ante las cosas su pensamiento por la mirada para creer en ellas, iluminándolas de racionalidad actual, presente, momentánea ... (29)

El cristiano, por el contrario, ve para creer: para ver más allá de lo que mira; y lo ve y no lo cree, porque ve lo que no ve; porque ve visiones; y así no detiene al pensamiento con la mirada ante las cosas para iluminarlas de racionalidad solamente ... (30)

Por eso hace el cristiano correr y saltar al pensamiento como un loco o enloquecido; en una verdadera enajenación racional; furioso de poesía y entusiasmado por la verdad de su revelación divina; y ve lo que no ve porque ve o porque va más allá de lo que mira: porque va a verlo; va a ver so es verdad, por lo visto, lo que no ha visto – lo que sólo ha oído y entendido por la fe en la palabra divina. Va, por lo que se ve, a lo que no – porque va a que le cumpla Dios su palabra, o a que se cumpla en Dios su palabra. Y es que más allá de lo que ve, de lo que mira; más allá de esa racionalidad, poéticamente humanizada y divinizada por el griego; más allá de ese límite fronterizo de su sombra, ha previsto el cristiano, por la fe, otra luz para sus ojos humanos cegadora: ha previsto, o ha presentido, el cielo ilimitado de una inextinguible luz gloriosa.

Y 'ojos que no ven, corazón que no siente': que no siente porque presiente. Los ojos cegados por la fe ahondan por su misma oscuridad la percepción auditiva, afinándola, agudizándola. 'Se hace todo oídos' el cristiano: como San Pablo al caer herido por la luz divina: como Moisés ante la zarza ardiendo con angélica luz cegadora; 'porque la fe es por el oído y el oído es por la palabra de Dios', según el apóstol. 'Se hace todo oídos', por la fe, que le entraña y le desentraña, laberínticamente, de ese modo, por el oído, la palabra divina: el Verbo de Dios, hecho Hombre ... (30)

Lo que ve el cristiano con sus ojos, cuando se mira en este espejo de su teatro católico español, es lo que no ve mientras más mira; que mientras más mira y menos ve mejor se siente cantar en el corazón de la fe: la música de su sangre; mejor presiente lo que no siente en su corazón, por sus ojos ciegos: la pura corazonada de la fe; el presentimiento divino de lo eterno, la revelación de la verdad, de la luz, de la vida, inmortal, imperecedera.

Los ojos del griego, por el contrario, le hacían sentir la vida, en lo aparente, como velo o vestido o traje de verdad; y en esta forma, la vida se le revelaba, por la muerte, enmascarándose de su mentira: trágicamente. 'Ojos que ven, corazón que siente': que solamente siente por lo que ve y porque lo ve; y no ve más que lo que mira. No se le puede 'quitar el dolorido sentir', el trágico sentir de la vida, al que, 'primero, del todo no le quitan el sentido', este sentido visual, que es de sólo verla como apariencia luminosa, como máscara de la muerte

¿Esto es mirar o morir?

Sentimiento trágico de la vida es éste, como diría Unamuno, por el que se vierte la sangre del corazón como un llanto, efusivamente. Y esta sangre acaba por enturbiar los ojos.

Esta sangre, esta efusión de sangre, apaga la luz racional de esa poesía trágica teatralizada por los griegos para los ojos solamente; haciéndole llorar y sentir al corazón su dolor más profundo: a la vista, a la simple vista, sangrienta, de un fin sombrío, de un infierno sin esperanza, de una verdad que es la certeza dura de la muerte.

Mucho extraña que haya quien
suene la música bien
pudiendo escuchar el llanto.

'Y el llanto sobre el difunto'; porque lo que ha entrado por los ojos, vuelve a salir por ellos, llorando; por las lágrimas, por la música trágica de los lloros. Que por eso la música de esta sangre no es la de la fe: la del oído, la de la palabra divina; sino la de la razón, que era una pasión para el griego, la de los ojos por el llanto, la de la luz apresada y expresada por la sombra: la del cuerpo humano, silencioso, cuando danza. La embriaguez oscura de Dyonisos. La zarabanda de la muerte.

los ojos que dan enojos
al ver y mirar en ellos,
más valiera no tenellos.
Pero bueno es tener ojos.

Al enojado por lo que ve, por lo que mira, más le valiera no tener ojos; pero bueno es que los tenga para sentir, para sentirlo; porque los ojos que ven la vida de este modo mortal, perecedero, le hacen sentir al corazón, llorando, su trágica borrachera crepuscular de luz y de sombra, su macabra danza. Trágico modo de purgar el hombre, por la sangre, su delito mayor: el de haber nacido. Así llevaba a su corazón el griego por lo que veía, por lo que lloraba, la mayor desdicha según su filósofo: una idea confusa de lo divino; y hasta una trágica difusión, o profusión sangrienta y llorona, de sus mismos dioses. (31–2)

Por eso era el teatro, para los griegos, por principio, en su origen como en su finalidad, causa o cosa de ver y, sobre todo, de mirar; y muy de mirar, porque ver sin mirar le tenía al griego sin cuidado.

Ver que es ver y no cuidar.
Mirar que es cuidar y ver

dirá Calderón. El *actu oculi* de los griegos abre y cierra los ojos cuidadosamente como un diafragma: entrañando en la oscura cámara del pensamiento para concebirlo, para poderlo concebir, todo un mundo imaginativo que, al darse a luz, al revelarse luminosamente, al verificarse en el teatro o por el teatro, al escenificarse, al salir afuera se expresa en inmovilidad, en éxtasis: en instantáneas determinaciones o definiciones estáticas de la vida, de un modo, por así decirlo, fotográfico. El *actu oculi*, el abrir y cerrar de ojos del teatro, al cristianizarse, se convierte en una sucesión rapidísima de actos de ver; sucesión en el tiempo en vez de simultaneidad o coexistencia en el espacio; es el espacio el que se encadena por el tiempo, de esta manera, como una cinta de cinematógrafo. No se mira a la vida en este teatro sin parpadear, fijamente, para aprehenderla o apresarla por el pensamiento de una vez para siempre, como se hace en el teatro de los griegos, sino que se la mira y no se la ve, a fuerza de mirarla tanto; mientras más se la mira, menos se la ve: para olvidarla; olvidándose el haberla visto para poderla ver sucesivamente de nuevo: proyectándola como sucesión, como movimiento en el espacio, como tiempo. Este mecanismo teatral del teatro católico ve y no ve la vida, efectivamente, en su abrir y cerrar de ojos, por su vivísimo parpadeo, porque es como si no la viera, en efecto; porque si la ha visto no se acuerda; no se quiere acordar, para verla siempre de nuevo; para creerla o crearla en el tiempo y no en el espacio; para recrearla y recrearse dinámicamente por ella en un teatro humanamente temporalizado: ejecutado virtualmente por el tiempo, por virtud cardinal dramática de tiempo. (34–5)

La luz de la fe, que rapidiza temporalizando al pensamiento, hizo del arte poético teatral de Lope de Vega un arte entero y verdaderamente nuevo; nuevo y nunca visto, por 'visto y no visto': por milagroso; el 'arte de birlibirloque' teatral, que es, sencillamente, el arte de teatralizar la fe, de popularizarla por el teatro, por la poesía. (37)

It is such writing as this that makes Bergamín's prose so distinctive and inimitable. As a sustained piece of *conceptista* exposition, it would be impossible to find anything to match it in the field of contemporary Spanish literature. It serves a useful purpose in identifying briefly the ways in which relationships are established and the extremes to which they are taken as they are made to develop ideas remote from the original point of departure. Texture is again derived from procedure, and the elaborate organic whole is created out of multiple, unlike, internally conflictive ingredients.

The starting point is the question of perception, which is interpreted in three distinct but interrelated ways. The principle of seeing engenders on the one hand *mirar* and *mirada* (linking up with the *espejo* of the theatre), and on the other, the verbs *ver* and *prever*, the adjectives *visual* and *aparente*, the nouns *apariencia*, and *máscara*. All these converge, in turn, on *parpadeo* and *parpadear*. The principle of hearing is specified in *oír*, *entender*, and *cantar*, and suggests various associations like *palabra* and *Verbo*, *música* and *musicalizar*. The idea of feeling, expressed basically in the verb *sentir*, spirals off in a number of different directions: *sentido*, *sentimiento*, *presentir*; *corazón*, *corazonada*; *sangre*, *verter(se)*, *llanto*, *llorar*, *lágrimas*, *lloros*. Predictably, because of the *conceptista* interpretation to which they are subjected, these forms of perception frequently intersect. Hence, the *música de la sangre*, for example, refers back to the sensitized hearing (and feeling) caused by blindness and at the same time forward to the *lágrimas* that express the *música trágica de los lloros*.

The characteristically *conceptista* use of contrast and antithesis is constantly in evidence in the passages quoted. It generates the kind of literal and figurative *claroscuro* in Bergamín's writing that is reminiscent in many ways of seventeenth-century expression in the arts. The act of seeing, for example, inevitably invites its opposite, and blindness is duly registered in the words *cegar* and *cegador*. Bergamín goes further, however, and balances the entire series of terms denoting light and clarity of vision – *luz*, *iluminar*, *luminoso*, *encender* – with their opposites: *sombra*, *sombrío*, *oscuridad*, *apagar*. At the same time, the argument is expanded by attaching figurative associations to this contrast between *luz* and *sombra*: on the one hand, *vida*, *esperanza*, *fe*, *inmortalidad*, and on the other, *muerte*, *infierno*, *difunto*, *mortal*, *perecedero*. The most ingenious exploitation of this *claroscuro* idea comes, perhaps, towards the end of the piece in a characteristically tangential series of associations. Maintaining the literal and figurative distinctions between light and shadow, Bergamín employs a range of photographic images (*abrir/cerrar*, *diafragma*, *darse a luz*, *revelarse*, *cámara oscura*) to refer back to his original contention concerning the revelation of faith, the registering of truth, in the Christian theatre.

If it is remarkable that, as in the case of *jugar a cara y cruz*, an elaborate argument is spun out of the relatively simple *ver/no ver* conceit, it is equally remarkable how a number of other popular expressions are worked into the text. Though remotely related to the principle of perception by virtue of the literal sense of the words they contain, these expressions are made to tie up with the ideas of seeing and feeling being explored in the argument as a whole by the familiar process of delexicalization. Hence an entire family of proverbs, colloquialisms, and popular expressions is ingeniously made to complement what the writer is saying: *en un abrir y cerrar de ojos*, *hacerse todo oídos*, *quien más mira menos ve*, *ojos que no ven corazón que no siente* (and its opposite, a typically Gracianesque conceit of revision), *si te he visto no me acuerdo*, *ver visiones*, *visto y no visto*, *por lo visto*, *por lo que se ve*, and *a la vista*. To incorporate all these into the text is quite an achievement in itself, since it requires imposing a logic, arguing a connection, that is apparently, 'at first sight,' untenable. However, the achievement is made even more noteworthy by the fact that simultaneously Bergamín makes use of a series of learned, literary references. These come from a number of different sources and are handled in such a way that they, too, balancing and complementing popular language, become links in the writer's reasoning, adding to the overall texture of the passage. The sources of some of these references are openly acknowledged: 'la fe es por el oído y el oído es por la palabra de Dios' (St Paul); 'la música de la sangre' (Calderón); 'ver que es ver y no cuidar' (Calderón). Other references of this kind are simply indicated by quotation marks and it is presumed that the reader will be able to identify the source: '¿Esto es mirar o morir?' (Mira de Amescua); 'los ojos que dan enojos' (Calderón), and so on.

Despite their rather tedious length, these two examples do perform the useful function of suggesting how the external features of Bergamín's essay style – the floridity and expansiveness – are determined by the reasoning procedures and the attitudes to language that characterize the writer. The momentum for this spiralling and seemingly self-generating prose stems from the recognition – perculiar to the *conceptista* mind – of what could be termed the 'indefinite' nature of language and ideas. As he encounters certain words, Bergamín realizes that because of their ambivalence or multivalency (double meanings, lexicalized and delexicalised functions, associated concepts, etc.), their sense is not static but leads off into several different directions. It is as if he sees a challenge in them. He follows each path they open up, not simply to see where they lead (though this is a sure sign of his indefatigable curiosity), but also to see if he can incorporate each discovery they yield, each new idea they generate, into the central line of reasoning from which he has temporarily strayed. The result is, as I have suggested before, that this clear central line is overrun with associations and almost obscured by each fresh design and suggestion that is attached to it. This is why, in a general sense, the 'baroque' and the *conceptista* elements of Bergamín's prose style are essentially interdependent, and explain two related levels at which his writing operates.[34]

*   *   *

This discussion can be rounded off by indicating how *Mangas y capirotes* on a smaller scale displays the kinds of *conceptista* features evident in the style and construction of some of Bergamín's aphorisms. The tendency, for example, to confront differing ideas, responses, attitudes, and interpretations in balanced symmetrical form is constantly in evidence:

Y ese cuerpo desnudo que para el griego era una respuesta, para el cristiano fue una interrogación. (48)

... el sueño blando de la muerte, el duro sueño de la vida. (84)

Mientras que los hombres, para vivir, se hacen ideales, las mujeres se hacen ilusiones. (101)

This type of elegant structure becomes more recognizably *conceptista* by the incorporation of some type of word-play into the statement:

El teatro nacional de Lope se hace nocional en Calderón. (21)

... el paso de la muerte, el peso de lo muerto ... (63)

... como un móvil de eternidad y no como una eternidad inmóvil; como inquietud de vida y no como quietud de muerte ... (36)

As in the aphorisms, the structure becomes even more emphatically symmetrical through the use of the chiasmus:

... España, soñándose en Historia, como en Lope de Vega, e historiándose en sueño, como en Calderón ... (22)

The basic contrast between Lope and Calderón is intensified by this mirror effect. The same kind of scheme of interlocking, geometrically complementary relationships is evident in this comment:

Un pueblo se conoce cuando se verifica definiéndose por el teatro: cuando se teatraliza. Un teatro se verifica cuando se define conociéndose por su populari-dad: cuando se populariza. (25)

The whole range of possible changes of grammatical function is used. The shift can be of adjective and verb as in this case:

... era España tan popularmente infantil o puerilmente popular ... (86)

or between verb and noun as in the following:

Todas se historiaban en poesía o se poetizaban en historia. (87)

Often the chiasmus contributes little to the substance of what is being argued, but its formal ingenuity adds an aesthetic elegance to the rhetoric used. Consider these examples:

... el sentido de su razón y la razón de su sentido ... (61)

... el engaño de la verdad y la verdad del engaño ... (136)

... cuando su historia se hace teatro como cuando su teatro se hace historia ... (26)

... en una poesía que se teatraliza en una historia como en una historia que se teatraliza en poesía ... (22)

At a linguistic level, Bergamín's *conceptista* style in *Mangas y capirotes* shows in his constant manipulation of phonic and potential semantic relationships between words unconnected in a conventional sense. Paragraphs are often structured around clusters of words that have similar sounds but which do not always have a common root or which would not normally converge in such an insistent way: *entrándonos/enterándonos/integrándonos* (16); *generadora/generación/engendradora* (26); *especulativo/especular/espectacular* (47); *puntualizándolo/apuntándolo/puntia-gudizándolo* (94). Pairs of words, with or without an etymological kinship, are brought together and made to pursue a single line of reasoning: *circular/circulatorio* (27); *ejercicio/ejecución* (44); *personalizan/personifican* (58); *realidad/realeza* (77); *caricatura/caracterización* (130). Also particularly frequent in this connection is the play upon pairs of words that have the same root but a different prefix, or where the prefix is present in only one half of the pair: *desvela/revela* (36); *enterrar/desterrar* (42–3); *fundir/confundir* (59); *pende/depende* (61); *templándose/contemplándose* (83); *pasar/traspasar* (84). Clearly, it is a question of exploiting a phonic or remote etymological link and of placing both words at the service of an argument to which they would not normally be expected to contribute simultaneously. There are also a number of cases of what could be called 'false pairs,' where a link is forged between an apparent common root and the use of what could be misconstrued as a prefix – as in *mística/tomística* (36 and 114) – or where two apparently unrelated concepts – *zarza/zarzuela* (117), for example – are brought together by a purely coincidental phonic similarity and by what might be called an 'invented suffix.' Elsewhere, there is a constant exploitation of phonic parallels and semantic dissonances: *burlar/birlar* (88,92,93); *burladores/burladeros* (95); *príncipe/principio* (84); *asunción/ascensión* (82); *paso/peso* (62), and so on. It will already be evident that in Bergamín's prose the relationship between form and content is so intimate that any conventional distinction between language and ideas ceases to be relevant. It might, however, be useful to stress that *Mangas y capirotes* is shot through with paradoxical interpretations of the subjects it covers. When presenting his ideas, Bergamín makes constant use of the 'agudeza paradoja' that fascinated Gracián.[35] The most standard notions on Golden Age theatre – perhaps precisely because they are commonplace – are constantly reversed, reformulated, redirected. By virtue of the elasticity of his logic, Bergamín is able to confront the reader with a stream of strikingly unusual interpretations. The frequent killings in Golden Age plays, for example, occur 'por razón de estado' and not for any amorous reason (70). Don Juan's principal virtue is his chastity (107) and he is shown to have no interest in deceiving women (100). If such ideas as these are read against the incidental paradoxes that litter Bergamín's prose – ending is the same as beginning (34), seeing is not seeing (35), a wish to die is a wish to live (68), and so on – the provocative *conceptista* tenor of his general method of arguing can be gauged.

* * *

Mangas y capirotes provides an illuminating point of access to Bergamín's prose as a whole, since its methods of conception and articulation are to be found throughout his longer essays of the twenties and thirties and indeed in many of those written in the post-war period, too. The procedures adopted in this particular book explain why the adjectives 'baroque' and '*conceptista*' have consistently occurred to critics seeking to describe the writer's style, and my examination of the forms and structures used, the deployment of language in general, will, I hope, have assigned specific values to these umbrella terms. These affiliations, looked at in conjunction with the more poetic modes of expression evident in certain series of aphorisms and in the texts of *Caracteres*, draw attention to the unusual position Bergamín occupied as a prose stylist in the literature of those decades.

5

'Entre tablas y diablas': The Dramatist

Es peligroso asomarse al interior.

J.B.

When *Caracteres* appeared in 1927, Bergamín included in it a list of the works he had written up to that time. Of the two that had been published, one – *Tres escenas en ángulo recto* – was made up of a series of dramatic sketches.[1] Of the thirteen other titles he gave (all of unpublished material), eight were of plays,[2] giving some idea, at least in a quantitative sense, of the energy he channelled into the theatre during this period. And yet Bergamín's work as a dramatist is probably the least known aspect of his literary career. Even in the most comprehensive surveys of Spanish drama before the Civil War, it is rare to find a reference to the plays he published in the twenties.[3] This is not to suggest that critics have somehow contrived to ignore a playwright of major stature, but simply that any assessment of this writer is incomplete without some discussion of those plays. They in fact deserve special attention since, in their form and content, they turn out to be central to an understanding of Bergamín's work as a whole during the years covered by this study.

There are a number of factors that explain why Bergamín's plays have been neglected for so long. The fact that they were never performed, for example, undoubtedly blunted their impact.[4] In addition, only a small number of his plays from the pre-war period have survived, so that his reputation – if that is the right word – as a dramatist rests on the fragile foundation of *Tres escenas en ángulo recto*, the sketches of *Enemigo que huye*, and the text of *Los filólogos*, which dates from 1925 but which has only recently been discovered and published.[5] But it is above all the extreme elusiveness of Bergamín's writing as a dramatist that has made the critic's traditional task of 'situating' and 'explaining' his plays particularly difficult.

Bergamín's dialogues are often constructed around a rapid parry and riposte of epigram and paradox, the sense of which remains tantalizingly incomplete. His texts tend to operate on shifting and conflicting planes of meaning, made even more impenetrable by his frequent reminders to his reader that the entire construct is merely an illusion: the texts reveal their status as literary texts just as the characters are conscious of being manipulated fictions. Consider as an example the following exchange between *El Señor* and *La figura de Arlequín* in the opening scene of *Tres escenas en ángulo recto*:

s. Eres una lección de geometría.
a. De geometría comparada.
s. ¿Comparada con qué?
a. Comparada con la verdad.
s. Si el hábito no hace al monje, ¿qué es la verdad?
a. La verdad fue un monje deshabitado.
s. ¿Qué le llevó a marcharse de sí?
a. La hartura de sí mismo.
s. Harto de fraile a la carne quiso volver.
a. No fue eso.
s. ¿El qué entonces?
a. Huir del desierto.
s. ¿Para qué?
a. Para que lo fuera; desierto de verdad.
s. ¿Y qué hizo el solitario?
a. Se enfureció.
s. ¿Cómo?
a. Poniéndose fuera de sí.
s. ¿Y su soledad?
a. La dejó dentro.
s. ¿Dónde?
a. En el hueco que quedaba; para que su voz se oyera en el desierto.
s. ¿Cómo?
a. Ahuecándola.
s. Y ese portavoz, ¿qué decía?
a. Decía: no.
s. La soledad sin ti, ¿por qué te importa?
a. Porque soy temeroso de Dios.
s. Y del Diablo aprendiste a engañarle.
a. Cuidado con el escotillón.

s. ¿Dónde está?
a. Debajo de mí.
s. ¿Quién tira de ti?
a. Respóndete tú mismo. (14–15)[6]

The text assumes the air of a juggling act. The writer's ideas, promising though they might seem, never actually materialize. The reader is likely to end up bewildered and empty-handed, reluctant to even guess at what it might all mean. All Bergamín's plays, in one way or another, pose similar problems of approach and interpretation. In view of this, it is helpful, initially, to stand back from the texts themselves and to consider two aspects of Bergamín's outlook as a writer and critic that, taken in conjunction, provide a point of access to them. The first aspect concerns his belief, voiced on a number of occasions in the twenties, that literature should perform a specifically religious function. The second involves his understanding of how the theatre, in general, works.

In a letter to Unamuno at the beginning of 1928, Bergamín wrote: 'Para mí el arte – literario – todo arte, es adjetivo: arte de ... Y ahora están en el arte *para* el arte – que es morderse la cola. Peor que el arte *por* el arte. Todavía peor. Para mí el arte debe ser, en definitiva, ni más ni menos que una propaganda religiosa. Y nunca "demasiado humano." Propaganda o propagación espiritual.'[7] It is an interesting comment in the importance it attaches to the obligation of literature to posit problems of religious belief. Although not all Bergamín's writing conforms to this scheme, it is none the less true that he consistently devotes attention to problems of faith. If this is already evident from my discussion of his aphorisms, it will become even clearer from this examination of his plays. The remarks made in this letter are also revealing in the way they underline the notion of personal reticence. The 'demasiado humano' is an oblique reference to Ortega's *La deshumanización del arte* – via Nietzsche, of course – in which the idea of aesthetically objectifying emotion and response by eliminating the 'elementos humanos, demasiado humanos' is argued at some length. Bergamín evidently shared the concern, current in the twenties, to avoid making purely personal circumstances the substance of any literary text. Naturally, this concern results only in a *tendency* towards objectivization or derealization, since any preoccupation, particularly a religious one, is bound to be anchored in personal feelings. The overall tenor of these reflections is worth bearing in mind, however, since it stresses Bergamín's anti-confessional instincts: his general reluctance to speak too openly in the first person. This kind of outlook partly determines, for example, the enigmatic, elusive style of his plays and also explains the approaches adopted elsewhere, especially in his journal *Cruz y Raya*.

Bergamín did not only make this point privately in this incidental observation to Unamuno. It reappears, for example, in an essay he published later in 1928 entitled 'Ni arte ni parte.' This is essentially an attack on the *opportunistic* use of religion for political or artistic purposes. Bergamín argues that for the genuine Catholic, faith cannot be compartmentalized or manipulated for the sake of convenience in this way, since it is what gives a total coherence and meaning to all his activities:

El camino real de Roma – catolicismo – que es el único camino *real*, es ruta celeste y no tiene derecha ni izquierda determinada por una exigua economía espacial. Las relaciones son distintas, siderales, de proporciones astronómicas. ¿Derecha o izquierda de qué?, cuando estamos, no en *parte* – ni en *arte* – sino en *todo*, en el Universo – catolicismo – en la Iglesia (natural y sobrenatural, visible e invisible), católica, apostólica, romana: en la universalidad. Yo, que soy católico de nacimiento, como todo el mundo – católico de nacimiento, como es natural, y de renacimiento, como es sobrenatural – no conozco, naturalmente – ni sobrenaturalmente – ninguna otra universalidad.[8]

This all-embracing spiritual commitment would encompass in Bergamín, therefore, both personal reflection and literary invention. It would also account for the radical nature of a number of works he wrote in the twenties and the kinds of activities he became involved in during the thirties. As far as his theatre is concerned, this belief in a spiritual universality explains why most of his plays take as their subject the searching questions that Bergamín, struggling with his own religious anxieties, was asking himself at the time. Presumably, he considered them worthy of being presented in dramatic form – as 'propaganda o propagación espiritual' – to other, possibly like-minded Catholics.

Bergamín's most comprehensive essay on the theatre was published soon after the Civil War and bears the elaborate title: 'Musarañas del teatro. Poesía a voz en grito. Tablas y diablas no son más que imaginación.'[9] It is not very well known because it has never been reprinted in an accessible volume of essays, but it is particularly useful here as a preamble to an examination of Bergamín's own plays. In this essay, he argues that the prime virtue of the theatre in general is that it enables the playwright to depict the activity of the mind. Consciousness and the whole process of introspection can be given a dramatic form on stage:

Sobre las tablas del teatro y entre sus diablas celestes, el hombre se visibiliza por entero – por entero y verdadero – : aparentando vanamente hasta lo más secreto y hondo de su ser; porque la figuración escénica le refleja en la intimidad de su conciencia humana, visibilizándole o aparentándole de este modo escénico. (10–11)

In some ways this recalls Unamuno's idea of the kind of stark inner reality that can be portrayed on stage or in the novel and which has little to do with the conventions of realism: plot, situation, character development. It is significant that Bergamín, in fact, quotes one of Unamuno's definitions of the theatre when considering the poetic resonance that words acquire when spoken on stage:

Lo que hace el teatro con la palabra es darle a su realidad imaginativa o fantástica resonancia poética total; ampliando por la voz su alcance humano; o por el espectáculo, para los ojos, ese mismo alcance; y por la figuración y forma teatralizada, por la fábula o asunto imaginado, también esa amplitud, ese ímpetu. Que por eso decía nuestro Unamuno que el teatro es siempre grito. O sea, voz en grito. (11)

In other words, no matter how hushed or intimate the self-revelation may be that takes place on stage, it is communicated to the audience at full volume: 'el teatro no es un confesionario discreto; la confesión en el teatro se hace con altavoz' (12).

What Bergamín says in this essay can be seen as having a direct bearing on what he himself set out to do, in his own fashion, in his theatre of the twenties. It would be wrong to think that 'Musarañas del teatro' provides (some twenty years after the event) the theory that supports the practice of *Tres escenas* and *Enemigo que huye*; but there is a complementary relationship between the essay and the plays. A good many of Bergamín's ideas must have been based, perhaps unconsciously, on his own creative experiments with the genre in the twenties and in this way shed light on what he, as a young man, intuitively envisaged to be the main potential of the theatre. Even if, in the case of his own plays, this potential was never fully realized in public performances, the guiding imperatives, voiced with authority and confidence in 1943, are still present in his work of the twenties, albeit in an embryonic, hesitant form.

Bergamín's basic arguments – that the theatre provides access to the inner depths of the mind and that literature in general should respond to certain spiritual directives – are summed up more succinctly in the following observations in 'Musarañas del teatro':

Una verdadera poesía teatral es la que vuelca ... ante nuestros ojos lo más hondo, secreto y entrañable de la conciencia humana. Aunque lo haga brutalmente, o sin formas literarias, al parecer. El hecho poético de la teatralidad es éste, religioso, de comunicación o comunión humana. (16)

Todo teatro, o teatralidad verdadera, parece religión o religiosidad: como, a su vez, toda religión o religiosidad, cuando se comunica o hace también común, nos parece que se teatraliza. Teatro y religión coinciden, natural y sobrenaturalmente, en hacerse, por la poesía, expresión y comunicación, o comunión, de la conciencia humana. (24)

In the light of these remarks it becomes easier to appreciate that what *Tres escenas en ángulo recto* and the sketches of *Enemigo que huye* have in common is their presentation of problems relating to religious faith. It is possible to go even further and say that the pivotal point of each play is the moment at which the central character plumbs the depths of his consciousness in order to resolve conflicts created by unfulfilled spiritual aspirations. The main difficulty for the reader lies in identifying and interpreting correctly these moments of introspective communion or communication, a difficulty that often stems from the unconventional way they are shown on stage.

Towards the end of the first act of *Tres escenas*, for example, the two characters – *El Monje* and *El Señor* – debate with bewildering sophistry the possible ways of achieving salvation. *El Señor* then descends ceremoniously through a trap-door in the stage. This is to be viewed as a climax to his search for a 'método de perfección,' and the whole of the second act is devoted to his prayers and meditations while 'underground.' Indeed, the descent of *El Señor* is designed to be seen as a kind of figurative death: a descent into hell, into the self, in the hope that subsequent resurrection will stand as a guarantee of discovered faith. *El Monje*, for example, generously throws down his habit after his disappearing companion and explains:

Ten. Cuando se baja a la tierra es bueno este sudario; muchos lo piden en su testamento. Ahí te lo envío. (18)

In the same spirit, *El Señor* reflects once he is alone and in darkness:

No hay cielo para mí. Todo es interno. Y es peligroso asomarse al exterior – y al interior. ¿A qué infinito abismo? No le hay. Estoy en su fondo. No cabe más profundidad. ¡Infierno sin llamas! ... ¿Qué soy? ¿Dónde estoy? (21)

This self-consciously histrionic withdrawal into the self finds a parallel in Bergamín's exploration of the Hamlet theme in 'Variación y fuga de un fantasma' in *Enemigo que huye*. Hamlet first appears on stage with a copy of Pascal's *Pensées* in his hand and his opening soliloquy begins:

'El silencio eterno de los espacios infinitos me espanta' ... ¿Me espanta o no me espanta? Esta es la cuestión. (49)

Hamlet is characterized throughout the play, like *El Señor* of *Tres escenas*, by his anguished doubt and self-questioning. The scene in which the *cómicos* appear is designed, just as Bergamín would later imply in 'Musarañas del teatro,' to give a strident dramatic form to his innermost misgivings and mournful reflections. His words to the actor who prepared to act out in the *mise en abîme* the role of Hamlet make this point explicitly:

Lo que tú haces es postizo; por eso eres actor; pero tú haces lo que yo no hago, lo que no puedo hacer; tu acción es pasión viva, y mi pasión, ¡ya ves!, ahora, es un suceso muerto. Monta un escenario, una plataforma desde donde gritar, y tendrás conciencia. Eso quiero: mostraros lo que es una conciencia viva. Así gritaréis vosotros, y yo tendré la culpa de todo – las culpas de todos. ¡Qué solemne peso! Pero mi escenario es el vuestro, el escenario de mi historia: la conciencia especular de la culpa. ¡Un escenario dentro de un escenario! ¡Sublime empresa! (60)

Here one of the central paradoxes of Bergamín's style and attitude as a writer becomes clear: it is only by means of the histrionic pose that what is most genuinely felt can be communicated. The *persona dramática* acts as the faithful, visible representation of the concealed inner consciousness of the *persona real*.

The use of specifically theatrical devices to represent 'lo más hondo, secreto y entrañable de la conciencia humana' is modified in the second sketch of *Enemigo que huye*, entitled 'Variación y fuga de una sombra,' devoted to the Don Juan theme. Here the central character's introspection is given a cinematographic and in some senses a surrealistic dimension. Like *El Señor* in *Tres escenas*, Don Juan experiences a kind of death. In his case, this is produced by the adverse effects of the radical 'desentrañamiento' proposed by Faust, his doctor, as a cure for his spiritual and existential malaise. Don Juan makes the mistake of drinking too quickly the potion that is prepared for him – a potion made up of the enormous white hand of 'un magnífico comendador de escayola' (82) dissolved in water. Faust reflects on the result:

Se ha blanqueado como un sepulcro, sólo que al revés; se ha endurecido de un golpe; no sé si ha muerto. (87)

The whole of the second act of 'Variación y fuga de una sombra,' like the central movement of *Tres escenas*, is devoted to the central character's experiences while in a death-like trance. It is subtitled 'Don Juan en sueños' and, in its haphazard sequences and in its mixture of outlandish extravaganza and allusions to the cinema, is characterized by a kind of cinematic surrealism. It soon becomes clear that in this state Don Juan is acting out fragments of his own personal drama, episodes in his struggle with his conscience. He is assisted in this by the semi-malevolent but therapeutic companionship of the Devil, who at one stage, for example, organizes a nocturnal celebration in his honour:

D. Aquí estarás bien colocado para presentar el espectáculo.
D.J. ¿Qué espectáculo?
D. Una gran fiesta que doy en tu honor esta noche.
D.J. ¿Aquí?
D. Este es el teatro de la naturaleza, o sea, el escenario de Dios; pero el Señor me lo cede, amablemente, esta noche, para que yo haga mi festival. (109)

Again it is a question of the staging of self-analysis, of opening up 'entre tablas y diablas,' the inner recesses of the character's consciousness. This is made explicit by the Devil who reassures the defensive Don Juan:

D.J. ¿Qué tengo yo que ver contigo?
D. Todo; tienes que verlo todo; por eso estamos juntos.
D.J. No me fío de ti.
D. Y haces muy bien.
D.J. ¿Por qué?
D. Porque el hombre no debe fiarse ni de su sombra, y yo lo soy.
D.J. ¿El qué?
D. Tu sombra. La sombra de una sombra. Eso soy: la sombra de las sombras.
D.J. ¿Y quieres asombrarme con tu fiesta?
D. O ensombrecerte.
D.J. ¿Más todavía?
D. ¡Sombría burla!
D. La de la oscuridad: la negra noche del espíritu que nos envuelve.
D.J. Nada veo.
D. Así ahondarás en tu sentimiento.

D.J. ¿Para qué?
D. Para expresarlo; para decirlo; para serlo. (110)

Each of Bergamín's main characters is, in a sense, enveloped at one point or another in this 'negra noche del espíritu' in which they strive to find a solution to their most deep-rooted anxieties. In the 'Coloquio espiritual del pelotari con sus demonios' with which *Enemigo que huye* ends, it is again diabolic intervention that, despite its accompanying traumas, signals the roundabout route to salvation. The spiritual anguish and self-torture of the central character is evident in his name: *Eautontimorumenos*. He questions the demons who taunt him with their sophistry:

E. ¿Qué buscáis en mí?
DEMONIO FÍSICO. Tu perdición.
E. ¿Para qué?
DEMONIO METAFÍSICO. Para encontrarte luego. (147)

The whole process by which *Eautontimorumenos* is able to come to grips with his spiritual torment is engineered, therefore, by these demonic companions. It is they who give graphic form on stage to his conscience or consciousness, supervising the move towards self-awareness to which Bergamín's demented characters invariably aspire.

The remarkable scene in which the conscience of *Eautontimorumenos* is actually examined is important because it typifies the unusual way in which the serious business of depicting an anguished mind is handled by Bergamín. The often grotesquely humorous devices he uses are precisely those that can mislead viewers into thinking that the scenes they are witnessing are inconsequential, the products of an over-active, unhinged mind. In the case of *Eautontimorumenos*, the first change that occurs on stage to indicate that the examination is about to take place involves the pelota score-board. This suddenly becomes 'un contador de bolitas de diversos colores, que irán encendiéndose poco a poco, respondiendo al diálogo; lo forman siete espacios iguales, encabezados por una letra mayúscula luminosa' (148–9). Bergamín is making the character act out the method of penance devised by Saint Ignatius that allowed for the sins of each day of the week to be dutifully recorded. The Demons begin to interrogate *Eautontimorumenos*, aggressively repeating the question '¿Cuántas veces has hecho ESTO?' (149). As the subject replies, the seven different coloured lights become illuminated, thereby recording the range and gravity of his errors.

The amazement of *Eautontimorumenos*, the serious purpose of the whole exercise, and its relationship with the ideas set out in 'Musarañas del teatro' become clear in the exchange that follows:

E. ¿Qué es esto? ¿Qué quiere decir ESTO?
D.F. Lo que no es lo otro.
D.M. Ni lo de más allá.
E. ¿El qué?
D.F. Tu conciencia.
E. Visible.
D.M. Por tus pecados.
E. ¿Mi conciencia es pecado?
D.F. No; tus pecados son conciencia.
E. ¿De qué?
D.M. De tu juego.
E. ¿Y qué pretendéis?
D.F. Examinarlo.
E. ¿Para qué?
D.M. Para que sea limpio.
E. Y yo, ¿qué haré?
D.F. Sufrir nuestro examen.
E. No quiero sufrir.
D.M. Entonces, espera.
D.F. Y desespera. (150)

The despair of *Eautontimorumenos* reaches such a point that he goes through the elaborate ritualistic motions of committing suicide. Like Don Juan and *El Señor*, therefore, he comes to experience a kind of death. His subsequent resurrection and the greater lucidity he derives from it complete the cycle of intense self-questioning that Bergamín's characters are drawn into and that corresponds to the process of 'conscience communion,' which the writer believed to be the major function of the theatre.

*   *   *

The use Bergamín makes in the 'Coloquio espiritual del pelotari con sus demonios' of material provided by St Ignatius draws attention to a strategy he adopts in almost all his dramatic works. He takes formulae that are already given and reworks them, rethinks them, and reorchestrates them in accordance with his own needs and interests. It is the same procedure that he uses when handling popular language, the fixed values of which are continually subjected to imaginative revision. That this technique lies at the heart of his drama may already be evident in the names of characters like Don Juan, Hamlet, and Faust, while even *Eautontimorumenos* has his literary precedents.[10] It turns out, however, that all his plays from the post-war period are also fundamentally 'theatre upon theatre.'[11] Works like *La muerte burlada* (1944), *La hija de Dios* (1945), *Medea la encantadora* (1954), and *Los tejados de Madrid* (1961) are all derived from previous texts, from situations already given.[12] Bergamín's role as a dramatist has in general been to re-examine these texts and situations, amplifying and enriching them by developing certain of their ideas. It could be said that he has 're-written' them in the light of his own personal concerns, exploiting the reader's supposed familiarity with them in order to emphasize his own individual preoccupations.

In his plays of the twenties, the sources to which Bergamín felt drawn give an idea of the general direction in which his spiritual and philosophical interests moved. The sources themselves are not difficult to identify: Shakespeare's *Hamlet* in 'Variación y fuga de un fantasma'; Goethe's *Faust* and the Don Juan tradition in 'Variación y fuga de una sombra.' In the 'Coloquio espiritual ... ' the debts to the *Ejercicios* of St Ignatius may be less explicit but they are basically no less difficult to discern. In *Tres escenas*, the fundamental borrowing is from the early harlequinesque tradition.[13]

The reasons for Bergamín's fascination with these archetypal or historical figures are largely self-evident. In one way or another, in their original or subsequent versions, they focus dramatically on certain elemental tensions or ambitions in man. For Bergamín, the restless sceptic, they must have evoked the problems of identity and self-knowledge with which he wrestled as a young man: the search for substantiality and salvation, the struggle with doubt and faith. He sought to elaborate upon these problems in accordance with the specific nuances of his own innermost concerns and in obedience to the stylistic imperatives peculiar to his temperament. However, a fundamental problem is posed by the fact that the basic themes and situations traditionally associated with the figures of Faust, Hamlet, and Don Juan are not always readily recognizable in the *variations* that Bergamín composed around them. The example of 'Variación y fuga de una sombra' will serve to illustrate this process of artistic metamorphosis whereby allusion sometimes becomes enigma.

Bergamín adds a good deal of eccentricity to the erudition of Goethe's Faust, but retains the somewhat sycophantic attentiveness of Wagner, his companion and aid. Don Juan consults the learned doctor complaining of an acute personality disorder, but the unorthodox treatment he receives brings him so close to death that his problems are almost solved for good. When Don Juan slips unceremoniously into unconsciousness, he is transformed into a kind of phantasmagoric literary 'misplaced person' and proceeds to stumble through a series of adventures that are essentially distorted resonances of episodes from the life of Goethe's Faust, now himself transformed into Don Juan's physician and analyst.

The entire second act, therefore, of 'Variación y fuga de una sombra' stands as an oblique parody of the situations encountered by Faust in the first part of Goethe's play. For example, just as Faust meets a 'jet-black hound / of poodle breed,'[14] which follows him into his study and mysteriously balloons into Mephistopheles, so Don Juan is accompanied in his dreams by 'un perrito callejero negro y sucio' (91), who is later magically transformed into the Devil. While Faust soars away on Mephisto's cloak, Don Juan is transported on a flying carpet piloted by the Devil. Whereas the former land in Auerbach's cellar in Leipzig, the latter's destination – perhaps unintentional – turns out to be a Chinese cabaret in New York city. Faust's original encounter with Margareta as she leaves confession becomes Don Juan's meeting with a girl named Margaritina as she heads for home after a visit to the cinema. It is significant that the film she has seen is entitled 'Los héroes del mar,' since the torrential rain that falls throughout the scene eventually floods the street in which the girl lives and to which Don Juan has gallantly escorted her. If in Goethe's Faust Mephistopheles sings his risqué song beneath Margareta's window, in Bergamín's version the Devil's playfully malicious serenade is delivered from a moored gondola. Goethe's Walpurgis Night is strangely echoed in Bergamín's 'Fuga de los animales del arca,' and the lyrical intermezzo of the Golden Wedding of Oberon and Titania is the precedent for the 'festival místico' of the 'Bodas de Puck y la damita de la media almendra.'

The parallels are constant, if rather warped and misleading at times. It is only as these parallels accumulate that the reader is likely to realize that 'Don Juan en sueños' is a recreative disfigurement of the original trajectory of Goethe's Faust. The situation is made even more mystifying, however, by Bergamín's simultaneous use of other devices and allusions. When Don Juan and the Devil, for example, take flight in their gondola, they are pursued by a horde of irate policemen in a scene worthy of the most memorable chases of the silent screen. There are biblical allusions, too: the naked Don Juan, for example, acts out the role of Adam, and by accepting an apple offered to him by a fruit-seller evokes man's fall from grace. These are balanced by a number of echoes from Spanish folklore: *El Sapo* (104), the *Brujas* (108), and *El Escarabajo* (117) all sing songs that come directly from oral tradition, while 'la damita de la media almendra' has her origins in the popular phrase used to describe a very shy or bashful young girl. Other details are composed of purely private recollections. Take, for example, the names of the three voices that combine in a *cantata* to evoke, as the scene indicates, 'El rumor del mar': *Ligia Oceánica, Diógenes Pugilator,* and *Asterias Glacialis.* These are simply names that Bergamín came across by chance in a book devoted to creatures of the sea and which, because of their sonority, he committed to memory.

This illustration of Bergamín's method of reshaping given situations and characters helps to explain some of the more outlandish moments in the plays that at first sight may simply appear unintelligible. The wide, eclectic framework of reference is part of an overall strategy that both focuses and distorts. Bergamín toys with the reader's credulity and his familiarity with certain ostensibly fixed data, but at the same time strives to lead him towards the serious issues at stake, the new emphases that he is arguing. In order to appreciate the motives behind this recreative technique, attention now needs to be directed at those issues that he raises.

Instead of taking each text separately and grappling with its individual peculiarities, it is more fruitful to identify the broad concerns voiced in the plays as a whole. All Bergamín's main characters are afflicted by a feeling of disorientation, of being contingent wanderers, like *Eautontimorumenos*: 'sin camino ni guía' (154). In different ways, they share the basic anxiety felt by the demented Hamlet who reflects: 'Yo no sé adónde voy a parar' (68). Their sense of aimlessness, of anguished unknowing, is qualified by the kind of 'aspiración infinita' expressed by the *Arlequín* of *Tres escenas* (31). Faced with an unending series of unanswered or unanswerable questions – exemplified in the insistently interrogative tone of Hamlet's and Faust's soliloquies – the characters seek some kind of permanence and stability beyond the precarious present. The *temporal* dimension of the anguish felt by *Eautontimorumenos* is typical: '¡Ay de mí! Quiero la eternidad que pasa y no pasar a la eternidad' (148). The uncertainty of ever possessing that eternity explains their sense of fear and abandonment. Hamlet, for example, finds in Pascal a kindred spirit who has trembled, as he does, before 'el silencio de la eternidad' (49), while Don Juan mourns the fact of 'la ausencia divina' (125).

Obviously, such hopes and misgivings revolve around a specific spiritual theme. The absent guide, the potential guarantor of eternity, is clearly God himself, and Bergamín's plays basically depict the struggle involved in encountering this deity and securing salvation. God's apparent indifference is the immediate source of the characters' suffering, and Hamlet's despairing question '¿Soy o estoy, perdido en la noche, en las tinieblas sin entrañas?' (53) is symptomatic of the elemental doubt that assaults them all. Don Juan, for example, consults Faust in the hope that the latter's learning will resolve his misgivings about his own identity and explain 'si me he inventado o me han inventado' (81). The depression felt by a *Eautontimorumenos* – 'sufro en cuerpo y alma de esta fatiga' (148) – is comparable with that of the Devil himself, whose complaint concerning the effect of God's abandonment is like that of any other of Bergamín's characters: '[Dios] me dejó a oscuras; me quitó la bella luz, que era mi nombre bello' (124).

The preoccupation with this sense of futility and loneliness justifies the attention paid by these characters, in varying degrees, to the problem of gaining or regaining faith, of finding the right path to follow in order to achieve salvation. The central question, debated with such refined sophistry in *Tres escenas*, is that of how to 'ganar el cielo' (30). Various answers are proposed. On the one hand, for example, practice and habit – the ambivalent 'hábito del monje' – are shown to be not only convenient but also quite effective. On the other hand, it is suggested that for some only divine intervention, grace itself, is an adequate solution. Bergamín tends to mistrust any mechanical means of sustaining faith. The 'excelencias del método' extolled ironically by the *Arlequín* are shown to depend on the acrobatic skill with which his companion climbs a rope-ladder in order to reach heaven. The rigorous demands of St Ignatius's exercises are not favourably portrayed in the scene in which *Eautontimorumenos* is interrogated by the two *demonios*. Indeed, it is only this tormented character's encounter with a young girl – a conventional but none the less moving personification of innocence and grace – that seems to kindle any kind of hope within him. Similarly, Hamlet seems to be temporarily uplifted only by his meeting with Ophelia (63).

Hamlet is an example of a more radical 'método de perfección' proposed by Bergamín in order to resolve the conflicts that seem to dog his characters. His mental derangement stands as the extreme antithesis to the kind of calculating rationality that elsewhere poses as a means of securing salvation. Hamlet's madness is made to represent the kind of folly that, perhaps following Pascal's recommendation that 'il faut s'abêtir,' Bergamín describes elsewhere in his work as an indispensable condition for communing with God. The link here between the plays and the aphorisms is direct. When Hamlet confesses, 'Si me pongo fuera de mí es porque quiero entrar dentro de Dios' (73), he touches on the theme of the abdication of reason that is fully developed in *El cohete y la estrella* and *La cabeza a pájaros*. In the latter collection, for example, there are two revealing aphorisms that clarify the sense of Hamlet's confession and make explicit his formula for salvation:

METODO DE PERFECCION. – Lo primero es enfurecerse: ponerse uno fuera de sí. Lo segundo es entusiasmarse: entrar dentro de Dios.

Para entusiasmarse hay que enfurecerse, y para poder enfurecerse – ponerse fuera, salir afuera – había que haber entrado primero. Hay que morirse antes si se quiere resucitar después. (106)

In the second of the two aphorisms quoted above, Bergamín establishes a parallel between the progression from *enfurecerse* to *entusiasmarse* and that from death to resurrection. This underlines the similarity between the destinies of the characters that appear in the plays and argues the presence of an overall unifying theme in them. Just as Hamlet moves from insanity to proximity to God, so *El Señor*, Don Juan, and *Eautontimorum-enos* are, as it were, resurrected – or at least primed for resurrection – following the figurative deaths they experience as they descend into their unconsciousness. *El Señor*, for example, following his bout of painful introspection, is able in the final act to climb nimbly up to heaven on a rope-ladder. In answer to the *Arlequín's* question '¿Cuándo te has hecho equilibrista?' he replies 'Cuando aprendí a resucitar' (31). Faust's final diagnosis of Don Juan's condition, following the treatment prescribed for his disorder, is summed up in the sign that he orders Wagner to place around his patient's neck; it reads: 'Disponible para resucitar' (139). Despite the multiple sins registered against him and his subsequent suicide, *Eautontimorumenos* is revived at the end of his 'Coloquio espiritual' and invited to begin the game with the score-board fairly balanced at zero-zero. Each of Bergamín's main characters traces this kind of trajectory, moving clumsily, comically, or poignantly from doubt and despair towards some surer ground from which their conquest of faith or ascent to heaven is likely to be more successful.

This optimistic interpretation seems to be qualified, however, by the curiously phantasmagoric status of the characters that appear in Bergamín's plays. The reader cannot fail to be struck by the fact that the texts are peopled by *sombras*, *fantasmas*, and *esqueletos*. This requires some clarification. It clearly reflects, at first sight, the writer's mournfully obsessive view of the human condition and corresponds to his concern with problems of identity and substantiality. The exact value attached to each of the macabre forms assumed by his characters is never unequivocally asserted, but some general remarks on their significance – valid in the wider context of the kinds of issues Bergamín raised during this period – can be made.

One essential defining feature of man, in Bergamín's view, is his vulnerability, largely a consequence of the overwhelming sensation of his own contingency and mortality. The image he uses to express this condition – a kind of *ser para la muerte* – is the simple one of the naked human body. When *El Señor* declares to his companion in *Tres escenas*, 'Aunque te metas en un saco siempre serás un cuerpo desnudo' (13), he implies this fundamental lack of protection against those forces of time and death that gather to annihilate him. By having a 'muñeco sin vestir, desnudo esqueleto de fantoche' (32) fall from heaven and grotesquely imitate each move made by the *Arlequín*, Bergamín draws attention to this inescapable fact of man's condition. The same idea reappears in an aphorism of *La cabeza a pájaros* where his stark definition of the image of death is couched precisely in these terms: '*Imagen espantosa de la muerte*: un muñeco desnudo.'[15]

Nakedness, in other words, depicts human frailty, the irreversible advance towards death. A complementary notion is conveyed by representing man as a shadow. The vague, contingent insubstantiality of Don Juan, for example, is specified in Faust's description of him as a 'sombra sin nombre.' Since a shadow is a product of some source of light, however, this also implies the nature of the bond that links man to God. It is a consolation to Bergamín's characters to realize that such a bond must in fact exist, since it invites speculation as to some ultimate union with that source of light. But the problem, as has been suggested already, is that of locating and identifying a God who remains forever unseen. Bergamín's Hamlet, for example, gropes towards an awareness that his existence, however shadowy and tenuous, is at least derived from some superior authority and not solely from his ghostly father:

Si yo soy su sombra – una sombra, la sombra de un fantasma –: ¿de dónde proyecta su luz en mí? ¿Qué luz, qué divino fuego la enciende? (57)

Of the possible solutions proposed by Bergamín to the problems of man's underlying impermanence, a seemingly promising one is the protection offered by the Church. The practice of religion appears to provide a means of covering the naked body with the monk's habit. *El Señor* in *Tres escenas*, for example, considers this pragmatic way out but dismisses it ultimately as an unworthy 'estratagema' and comments on the potential consequences:

Si sales muerto, serás un esqueleto; si te escapas vivo, un cuerpo desnudo como eras. (13)

The allusion here to man's transformation into a skeleton is an interesting one since, surprisingly, it turns out to be Bergamín's most optimistic though not unironic view of man's capacity to resolve his own inherent weakness and to transcend death. Although in the iconography of the Middle Ages and the seventeenth century, the skeleton tended to symbolize the constant presence of death, reminding man of his precarious status on earth, this proves not to be the case in Bergamín's work. He totally revises the value attached traditionally to the image and makes of the skeleton the representation of what is eternal, even of what is divine, in man. Bergamín would argue that while human flesh is eminently perishable, a body's bones are, ironically, the one permanent attribute that survives after death. When he wrote in *La cabeza a pájaros*, 'Lo último que forma el cuerpo vivo son los huesos: que se hacen duros para durar' (120), he implied that man's skeleton is his only guarantee of any kind of lasting substantiality. The positive value it possesses is also suggested in the following comment in the same book:

La momia perpetúa de un modo abstracto la expresión concreta de la muerte. El esqueleto perpetúa de un modo concreto la expresión abstracta de la vida. (103)

This basic if somewhat idiosyncratic revision of the meaning associated with the skeleton plays an important role in *Enemigo que huye*. The operative phrase, drawing attention to this idea, is Faust's reassuring comment to Wagner. The latter is alarmed at seeing Don Juan transformed, thanks to the potion of dissolved plaster that he has drunk, into a living skeleton:

w. ¿No se espanta?
f. ¿De qué? Lo mejor que le puede pasar a un cuerpo desnudo es convertirse en esqueleto. (138)

If Wagner's anxiety is perfectly understandable from a conventional viewpoint, Faust's unruffled confidence in the final outcome of his treatment of Don Juan is equally acceptable, given the new values attached to both the *cuerpo desnudo* and the *esqueleto*. As Faust reflects at the end of 'Variación y fuga de una sombra,' it is not so much that Don Juan has undergone a process of transformation, but rather that he has finally encountered his true nature: 'Al fin aprendió a ser lo que era: una sombra hecha huesos inmortales' (138). This recognition dramatizes Bergamín's thoughts on the human condition: that no matter how desolating the sensation of human transience, there still exists the possibility of substantiality. And, as has already been mentioned, it is around the neck of Don Juan the skeleton that the encouraging sign 'Disponible para resucitar' is hung at the end of the play.

The kind of relationship in this play between the *sombra* and the *esqueleto* can also be found in 'Variación y fuga de un fantasma.' There is an obvious analogy between the shadow and the ghost as expressions of man's lack of substance. Just as Don Juan acts out the role of a *sombra* because of his uncertainty over his identity, so Hamlet, alone and unsure of his status and identity, aware only of his father's ghostly reappearances, concludes that he is merely 'el nombre de un fantasma – el nombre vano, el nombre y el hombre – el fantasma que es sólo sombra; fantasma, hijo de fantasma' (52). Once again it is suggested that within this evanescent existence, the one possible consoling attribute is the skeleton, since it alone is capable of affirming some kind of solidity and permanence. When Hamlet finally confronts his father, for example, he asks: '¿Y tú qué eres o qué has sido? ¿Dónde están tus huesos?' (53). His father's bones would, as it were, be tangible proof of his existence, a sign that beyond the mystery of death there is something solid and graspable that survives.

Hamlet's search for proof of this kind as an answer to his own self-questioning reappears in his final outburst of despair when he seeks evidence of God's existence, putting the same question to this elusive deity as he did to his father:

¿Dónde están tus huesos, Señor, si no eres fantasma, un fantasma sin nombre? (73)

When nothing is revealed to him, Hamlet concludes bitterly: 'Dios es un fantasma; una burla; una blasfemia' (73). Clearly, the best thing that could happen to any ghost – human or divine – and not just to a *cuerpo desnudo* or even to a *sombra*, would be for it to become transformed into a skeleton, this macabre source of comfort and reassurance in Bergamín's world. These remarks on the positive value given to the skeleton help to explain why in 1973 Bergamín chose to republish both *Tres escenas* and *Enemigo que huye* under the title *La risa en los huesos*. Predictably, the title harks back to a colloquial phrase – 'tener la risa en los huesos' – but is reorchestrated in accordance with the writer's established technique and made to suggest some of the underlying intentions that went into the composition of the plays. Attention is drawn first to the humorous and irreverent elements that are present in them, underlining the ironic and tongue-in-cheek way Bergamín has subverted given ideas, situations, and characters. The mention of bones then evokes the specific nature of the resolution to the drama of man's condition that the writer argues. These bones, as I have pointed out, constitute the one unchanging, indestructible form that is ever present within man and which he finally assumes following death. *La risa en los huesos* is, however, only the latest generic title that these plays have been given. By returning to the other title that Bergamín had first thought of using, it is possible to formulate another overall interpretation with a different emphasis.

It was Bergamín's original intention to bring together the two *variaciones* and the 'Coloquio espiritual' under the title *El clave mal temperado*.[16] In one sense, this title would have openly acknowledged the discordant notes continually produced in works in which many disparate elements have somewhat awkwardly been combined. As I have already suggested, the reader may easily be mystified by the mixture of mythological, religious, literary, scientific, cinematic, folkloric, and private allusions on which the plays draw. In another sense, the specifically musical connotations that this first provisional title had link up with the *variación y fuga* form that Bergamín gave to two of the plays. It appears that Manuel de Falla once commented to Bergamín that he was more of a musician than a writer, since he tended naturally to write fugues.[17] This is interesting, since it suggests that the musical analogy is as helpful as the achitectural one used in the previous chapter to explain the form and structure of the longer essays.[18] Indeed, the construction of any baroque fugue – with its central theme and tireless variations – recalls the way ideas are formulated and strung together in a work like *Mangas y capirotes*.[19] The same principle could apply to some of Bergamín's dramatic works in which there is a constant reworking and reshaping of a basic idea.

The two *variaciones* were eventually brought together, within *Enemigo que huye*, under the title *Polifumo*. This was Bergamín's way of paying playful homage to Góngora, though no mention has ever been made of this in discussions of the literary tributes paid to the poet in the mid-twenties in Spain. Bergamín eventually found inspiration for the title he needed for all three plays in the proverb 'a enemigo que huye, puente de plata.' The sense of the proverb, as defined by the Academy *Diccionario de la lengua española*, is that it 'enseña que en ciertas ocasiones conviene facilitar la huida al enemigo, o el desistimiento de quien nos estorba.' Since its applicability to this group of plays may not be immediately apparent, some clarification is needed.

Bergamín had at first thought of using only the second part of the proverb – *puente de plata* – partly because for him it continued to have the musical associations expressed more directly in *El clave mal temperado*. The reader may recall that the section of *La cabeza a pájaros* devoted to music is entitled 'Puente de plata.' One of the aphorisms in this section actually reads: 'La música es el *puente de plata* del pensamiento' (139), and suggests how in the writer's view, forms of music provide ways of putting thought to flight. Just as the enemy could be encouraged to flee by the provision of a *puente de plata*, so his own thoughts, whimsical yet disturbing, could be channelled away along paths that were more musical than theatrical. Indeed, it is notable that in the plays that have been discussed, consistent use is made of incantatory choruses and elusive sonorous images. To return to the idea of Bergamín's reluctance to spell out the sense of the insights and anxieties that concerned him, it is as if the sound patterns of the *cantatas* and serenades, the purely phonic texture of the tongue-twisters and pseudo-prayers, offer a kind of escape route for the overt self-expression that the writer preferred to avoid.

It appears, however, that Juan Ramón Jiménez, whose judgment on such matters the young Bergamín was unlikely to ignore, found the image of the *puente de plata* too demanding for the eclecticism and lightheartedness of some of the plays' contents. It was on his recommendation, then, that the less exacting first part of the proverb was used as the title. At least *Enemigo que huye*, as a title, implicitly retained the musical connotations that he felt the plays had. At the same time, it exploited in characteristic fashion the ambivalence of the word *fuga*, applicable not only to the form that the writer chose to give his ideas, but also to their restless and self-conscious evasiveness.

*   *   *

All except one of the considerable number of plays listed as unpublished in 1927 were lost during the Civil War when Bergamín's house in Madrid was sacked. Bergamín's attitude to these missing texts is predictably ironic and ambivalent. On the one hand, he has expressed a lack of regret at their disappearance, declaring it to be a positive asset both to himself and to Spanish theatre in general.[20] On the other hand, he has sometimes taken delight in teasing interested critics, stating that these texts were certainly his masterpieces of the period and that only their recovery – manifestly inconceivable since he was convinced that they had been destroyed during the Civil War – could give a true impression of his literary stature.[21]

It appears, however, that during the war Bergamín had given some of his papers for safekeeping to his friend Antonio Rodríguez-Moñino. Among these papers was found, in 1977, the manuscript of *La farsa de los filólogos*.[22] Its publication in 1978 may have been justifiable for some solely on the grounds that it was a previously unknown text by one of the most active and original writers of the pre-war period, and yet the interest of *Los filólogos* (the title under which it eventually appeared) is considerably wider. Although the play is thematically distant from the other published works that have been discussed, it does still represent Bergamín's activity as a dramatist in the twenties, and since it touches upon certain consistently defended beliefs, it deserves some attention.

There is an obvious surface point of contact between *Los filólogos* and the plays of *La risa en los huesos* and this is one of tone. When Bergamín wrote in *El cohete y la estrella*, 'Aunque cambie de nombre y se llame como se quiera, la *farsa* es el teatro mismo' (50), he voiced a conviction that he later exemplified in certain scenes and situations in *Tres escenas* and *Enemigo que huye*. Although he was later to describe himself as a 'humorista fracasado,'[23] it is none the less true that in his early drama his taste for the comic and calamitous – despite its underlying seriousness – was fully indulged. *Los filólogos* is defined in its subtitle as a *comedia*, and categorized in its closing scene as a *farsa aristofanesca* (77).[24] These descriptions give a faithful indication of the mood the writer adopts as he systematically deflates and ridicules the solemn self-importance of the scholars who appear in the play. The irreverence with which Bergamín treats these defenders of the academic faith is made even more noteworthy – and potentially scandalous – by the fact that they are clearly modelled on certain people living at the time. It requires little effort to figure out who Bergamín had in mind when he created characters like *El Doctor Americus* and *El Profesor Tomás Doble*. Few of the eminent minds of the time escape his scorn for their pomposity and self-righteousness. *El*

Insigne Ortega, Cazador Furtivo, for example, makes his entrance with a sign pinned to him which says MADE IN GERMANY. *El Maestro Inefable Don Ramón Menéndez* appears out of a trunk, wrapped like a mummy:

Poco a poco empieza a mostrarse en el envoltorio una especie de momia cubierta de riquísimas telas y velos sutilísimos, hasta que, al fin, aparece un brazo; luego, otro; después, un pie, una pierna; etcétera, y últimamente se descubre, en la postura habitual de los bailarines en estos casos, la figura del Maestro inefable Don Ramón Menéndez, que se mueve rítmicamente y conservando en todo lo posible la línea recta y el perfil. (23)

The institution with which the academics that appear in the play are identified also comes under fire. The *joven desconocido* who interrupts their research innocently asks 'Pero, ¿dónde estoy?' and the subsequent exchange is designed to mock the arrogant self-centredness of the mandarins of the Centro de Estudios Históricos:

PROF. DOBLE
Estás en el Centro.
DESCONOCIDO
¿En qué centro?
DR. AMERICUS (solemnemente)
En el Centro de todo. (24–5)

Bergamín's indignation, however, is not directed solely against this kind of pretentiousness but also against the discipline to which these high-minded academics dedicate themselves. His contention is that their fanatical devotion to philology has two regrettable effects. In the first place, it deprives them of all human sensibility. *El Profesor Tomás Doble*, for example, is indifferent to the complaints of hunger and fatigue voiced by the *joven desconocido* and yet is totally absorbed by his pronunciation of certain sounds and by the possibility of improving it. In the second place, their scientific zeal corrodes the spontaneity and the vital creative energies of language in general. That is, the task the *filólogos* have undertaken and which Bergamín finds so objectionable is precisely that of reducing the *natural* poetic anarchy of language to an orderly series of systematized but ultimately inexpressive sounds. The warped evangelical mission of the *Centro* is summed up in a speech by the *Maestro Inefable* whose grandiose cause appears as an impertinent crusade against nature itself. Surrounded by his fawning disciples – represented significantly by a *Coro de Monos* – he holds forth:

Estoy satisfecho de vosotros. Nunca encontraré discípulos mejores. Con vuestro auxilio cumpliré hasta el fin mi destino, y de esta misteriosa selva sagrada saldrá una nueva vida para la humanidad, una nueva era en que el bárbaro lenguaje humano, absurdo tejido de ımaginaciones poéticas, desaparecerá ante la fuerza radiante de la universal lengua filológica. Todo en esta selva será pura filología, y es preciso para ello someternos a nuestra científica disciplina, a la más alta voluntad del bosque, a los pájaros que hoy viven en el libertinaje y la anarquía, en la más desordenada y divertida vida poética. (61–2)

Bergamín is describing, essentially, a conflict between two opposing concepts of language. On the one hand, there is the commitment of the *filólogos* to the ideas of scientific order and precision. Their mascot is the *cacatúa* – 'símbolo de la omnipotente sabiduría filológica' (57) – and their disciples are a *Coro de Monos*. On the other hand, there is an allegiance to the elusive vitality of language, which has nothing to do with academic analysis. It is obvious where Bergamín's sympathies lie and he duly develops his criticisms. Into this second category of what could be called *'anti-filólogos'* fall a number of writers whose wisdom is embodied in the *Lechuza* (Miguel de Unamuno) and whose reverence for poetry is represented by the *Ruiseñor* (Juan Ramón Jiménez). Against the collective bombast of the *Centro*, these characters defend the uniqueness of the creative writer's idiolect. *El Espíritu de Valle-Inclán*, for example, appears at one point as the appointed representative of Unamuno and voices the latter's opposition to the ideal of a systematized universal philological language, denouncing the pompous claims of the *filólogos*:

Miguel me envía para protestar. No hay más centro que el de uno mismo. Yo soy un centro ... Yo soy un centro ... (25)

Unamuno himself later appears to express his indignation – and Bergamín's – at the insensitivity of the distinguished scholars of the day:

¡Farsantes! ¡Hipócritas! ¡Fariseos! ¿Qué sabéis vosotros de la palabra? De la palabra viva, sangre y cuerpo de nuestra alma. De la fe, del amor, de la poesía, ¿qué sabéis vosotros? ¡Id a engañar a los tontos con vuestras mercancías, ya que no sabéis descubrir la vida, como los aurispices, en las entrañas palpitantes del idioma! (28–9)

Given Bergamín's respect and admiration for both Unamuno and Jiménez, it is natural that they should be given the role of leading the opposition to the campaign launched by the *Maestro Inefable*. It is into their mouths that Bergamín placed his own contempt for the philologist as an unnatural species of the human race. The *Lechuza's* definition of the *filólogo* as 'un hombre que, sin dejar de ser hombre, ya no es hombre' (68) is matched only by the *Ruiseñor's* less subtle but more categorically dismissive version: 'la cosa más estúpida de todo el universo' (69–70). The *cacatúa* and the attitudes it represents have no defence against such attacks as these. The parrot's gift of speech is seen more as an indication of treachery and capitulation than as an unusual attribute and it meets an untimely end.

Bergamín evidently felt that the *filólogo* represented a denial of all those elusively unscientific qualities that make up each creative writer's capacity for self-expression. Such a capacity was, in his opinion, defiled by an attempt to explain it or to reduce it to a mere set of grammatical rules. The *filólogo*, therefore, is the antithesis of everything that is natural in man. Indeed, his devotion to his discipline demands the sacrifice of nothing less than his own humanity, and it is this notion that is conveyed in one of the final allusions in the play to the *Maestro Inefable*:

Ved cómo jamás en su figura aparece nada que sea humano. ¿Le habéis visto llorar, reírse, moverse humanamente? El hombre ha muerto del todo en él, para que el filólogo viva. (73)

This makes it perfectly natural for Bergamín to argue that the best *filólogos* are in fact monkeys, since they represent ideally the sycophantic, unthinking devotees of a dehumanizing profession.

Los filólogos is not just an example of youthful iconoclasm, though it does undoubtedly reflect Bergamín's uneasy attitude to all established authority and his tendency to poke fun at it. The play is also something of a declaration of faith in that it signals particular attitudes to language and learning to which he remained loyal throughout his life. His suspicion of learning, for example, which appears fragmentarily in his aphorisms, is (as I have suggested before) developed in his essay 'La decadencia del analfabetismo.' There he launches a systematic attack on literacy as a false goal, lamenting the negative effect it has of undermining precisely those spontaneous creative qualities of language and outlook he defends in *Los filólogos*. His condemnation of the *Misiones Pedagógicas* of the Republican period was considered a scandal at the time, but it was entirely consistent with his views on the damage that could be done by unimaginative teachers.[25] His entire career as a critic and university professor was characterized by a mistrust of the academic exegesis of literature. His literary criticism shows great knowledge and sensitivity, but it also displays an allergy to pedantry. He has always been reluctant to reduce, schematize, and annotate when writing about literature and this is largely why his essays have not come to stand alongside those of his more scholarly contemporaries – Dámaso Alonso, Guillén, and Salinas, for example – as instances of the literary insights and tastes of his age. His activities during the years he spent teaching in universities in South America, though often an inspiration to his pupils, were largely a source of despair to his colleagues. His animosity towards everything that their profession stands for may account for his exclusion from the official world of the academies of Spain. It certainly helps to explain why so many professional literary critics, realizing Bergamín's views on the tasks they traditionally set themselves, have preferred not to become involved in an academic assessment of his work. His writing is full of warnings of the dangers they are likely to encounter:

> Poeta, tu razón de ser
> no es ser de razón engendro;
> Dios no inventó un diccionario
> cuando creó el universo;
> ni para nombrar las cosas
> utilizó un alfabeto;
> ni consultó la gramática
> cuando empezó por el Verbo.

(*Duendecitos y coplas*, 20–1)

6

'Ni más ni menos':
Bergamín and Cruz Y Raya

No hay cruz sin raya para el hombre.

J.B.

The publication in 1927 of the first number or the journal *Carmen*, edited by Gerardo Diego, was acknowledged by *La Gaceta Literaria* in an anonymous poem that began: 'Cada maestrillo, su librillo. / Cada poeta, su revista' (Each little master has his little book. / And each poet, his journal).[1] Despite their playful irony these lines accurately diagnosed what appears to have been one of the driving, almost obsessive ambitions of so many writers of the pre-war period, namely to direct a literary journal. The extraordinary abundance of publications of this kind in the twenties and thirties bears witness not only to the wealth of literary and artistic talent at the time, but also to the seemingly inexhaustible initiatives of writers who, undaunted by their often precarious financial backing or by the strength of the competition, launched a continual stream of reviews and magazines onto the literary scene.

Practically all Bergamín's poet friends, at one time or another in their careers before 1936, came to edit their own journals. One of the key figures in this connection was the irrepressible itinerant poet-printer Manuel Altolaguirre. In Málaga in 1923 he published his first journal – *Ambos* – with the help of José María Hinojosa and José María Souvirón. This was followed in 1926 with *Litoral*, one of the major journals of the decade, which he co-edited with Emilio Prados and later, in 1929, with Hinojosa. In 1930 and 1931, in Málaga and Paris, he produced *Poesía*, and a year later, this time in Madrid, the six numbers of *Héroe*. His last and perhaps most ambitious enterprise before the war was *1616. English and Spanish Poetry*, published in London in 1934 and 1935.[2] Altolaguirre was joined by writers like Juan Larrea who, from his Paris refuge, launched his aggressive but short-lived *Favorables Paris Poema* with César Vallejo. While teaching in Murcia, Jorge Guillén shared editorial responsibilities with Juan Guerrero for the publication of *Verso y Prosa*, a worthy successor to the literary supplements of *La Verdad* that Guerrero had so painstakingly built up. In 1928, Lorca brought forth from his native city the journal *Gallo*, which soon foundered through lack of financial support. Alberti found an outlet for his left-wing militancy in the aptly entitled *Octubre*, while Salinas, from the relative calm of the Consejo Superior de Investigaciones Científicas, presided over the *Índice Literario*, seeking to construct (as the journal's subtitle indicates) a body of 'archivos de la literatura contemporánea.' These were accompanied by other publications like Giménez Caballero's *La Gaceta Literaria*, Araquistáin's *Leviatán*, the combative *Nueva España* edited jointly by Antonio Espina and José Díaz Fernández, and a host of others, both in Madrid and in the provinces.[3] Taken as a whole, they bear eloquent testimony to the range of interests and ambitions that gave the literary life of the period much of its vigour and variety.

It was inevitable that sooner or later Bergamín would match the initiatives of his friends and set up his own journal or else be entrusted with the direction of one. It would be a logical extension of his close association – as an assiduous contributor occasionally charged with editorial responsibilities – with many of the journals mentioned above. In 1923, following the demise of *Índice*, Bergamín's energies had for a while been channelled into editing the literary page of Los *'Lunes' del Imparcial*. At that time he must have seemed ideally suited to the task, being one of the leading lights of *la joven literatura*, extremely well connected and with a passionate interest in all things literary. It is not easy to reconstruct his activities, but in his letters to Unamuno of 1923 it is at least evident that he had marshalled an impressive array of talent to help him fulfil his obligations.[4] He was, however, not to hold the job for very long. Perhaps his youthful earnestness or intransigence did not endear him to his fellow-workers at the newspaper. Whatever the case, after only a few months as literary editor, he left *El Imparcial*, 'no sé si avisado o escarmentado,' as he wrote to Unamuno. The experience he gained during that short period may have been very valuable, but he was to wait ten years before he could put it to good use. When, however, in 1933 he eventually took charge of his own journal, it was to be with a range of responsibilities and a financial backing far greater than anything he had dreamed of a decade earlier.

The year 1933 was undoubtedly an opportune time to found a new journal. As Juan Chabás pointed out at the beginning of that year in a mournful 'Elegía de las revistas,' the productive initiatives that had given rise to the wealth of 'revistas juveniles de literatura' in the previous decade seemed to have petered out, leaving a depressing void in the literary world:

Inútil buscar las revistas que inquietan curiosidades o compendian esfuerzos de alguna desinteresada y espiritual empresa literaria; no existen ya. Se las llevó una ventolera de ansias y prisas, y en nuestra vida literaria, estrecha y sin aliento, ni parece advertirse su falta, mayor cada vez, porque la Prensa diaria, forzada por el interés de la contienda y el debate políticos, deja menos espacio al puro ejercicio y al goce lento de una literatura sin inmediata aplicación práctica.[5]

(It is pointless to go looking for journals that stimulate or arouse curiosity or bear witness to some disinterested spiritual enterprise. They no longer exist. They were swept away by a wind of anxieties and hurriedness, and in our narrow-minded, breathless literary world, their growing absence seems to pass unnoticed. The daily press, preoccupied with the latest political quarrel or debate, devotes less space to the pure exercise and leisurely enjoyment of a literature that lacks any immediate practical application.)

The appearance of *Cruz y Raya* a few months later would do much to remedy this uninspiring situation and to register some of the most significant 'ondas del temblor de nuestro espíritu' that Chabás felt were being neglected in the opening years of the Republic.

Bergamín himself has explained the circumstances in which *Cruz y Raya* came into being:

Por entonces existía el problema de la enseñanza religiosa. Un grupo de católicos pensó en montar un colegio, en el que se resolviera el problema de la enseñanza religiosa de forma opcional. Este grupo estaba formado por Miguel Maura, Gregorio Marañón, Ruiz Senén y, en fin, por la mayor parte de los que luego aparecerían como fundadores de la revista. Decidieron comprar el colegio de los marianistas, pero al fracasar este proyecto, se pensó en dedicar el dinero que ya habían reunido a otra actividad. Me llamaron y me encargaron del montaje de una revista.[6]

(At that time there was wide concern about the problem of religious education. A group of Catholics considered setting up a school in which the problem of religious instruction could be solved in an optional way. This group was made up of Miguel Maura, Gregorio Marañón, Ruiz Senén, and by the majority of those who would later figure as the founders of the journal. They decided to buy the school of the Marianist order, but when this plan fell through, they thought of using the money they had got together for some other purpose. They contacted me and gave me the job of setting up a journal.)

The journal emerged, therefore, from a specific set of political circumstances, though with the purpose of defending and promoting interests that went beyond the merely political. This is important to bear in mind, since it helps to explain *Cruz y Raya's* dual orientation: its sensitivity, on the one hand, to the social and political climate in Spain, and its concern, on the other hand, for values of a spiritual, 'unworldly' kind. This point will be looked at in greater detail later in this discussion.

Bergamín found himself, then, in the early months of 1933, in an enviable but somewhat alarming situation. He had what was to all intents and purposes unlimited financial backing: a budget of one million pesetas, an enormous sum for the time, was put at his disposal; but he had also been saddled with practically the entire responsibility of creating a journal from scratch. As he himself has written: 'Apenas se me confió su dirección y con ella su forma, pues la revista aún no existía, me encontré, por así decirlo, que tenía que concebirla, generarla, parirla o darla a luz y sustentarla o mantenerla' (I had hardly been given the task of directing and devising the format of the journal when I discovered myself in the situation of having to conceive it, give birth to it, provide it with nourishment and keep it alive).[7] This comment is important since it underlines the extent to which *Cruz y Raya* was very much Bergamín's own personal creation. Although the exact degree of responsibility that he was later prepared to accept for the journal as a whole has become something of a moot point, it is evident that from the outset, *Cruz y Raya* absorbed all his energies. Between 1933 and the summer of 1936, Bergamín was to be totally involved in the running of this enterprise. It was to give him the opportunity to become something more than an individual writer, and to assert himself in the Spanish intellectual world as a major cultural activist, concerned not only to promote literary excellence but also to use his authority and prestige to launch a whole range of initiatives that were to have considerable repercussions on life during the Second Republic.

In order to solve the initial problem of how to bring the journal into existence, Bergamín secured the advice of what he has called his 'mayores y maestros' (seniors and masters), namely Ortega, Falla, Unamuno, and Antonio Machado.[8] In different ways, these people gave him both practical support and general encouragement for the successful realization of the project. Bergamín was also able to count on the services of the best printer of the day, Silverio Aguirre. The latter's expertise, coupled with the meticulous professionalism of assistants like Cleto Patiño (who, with Bergamín at his side, would personally correct the proofs of each issue) was to guarantee both the artistic elegance and rigorous accuracy that characterized the presentation of *Cruz y Raya*. The responsibility for the design of the journal's front cover was entrusted by Bergamín to his friend Benjamín Palencia, the painter, who had already shown his talent in this area by designing, among other things, the logo for Lorca's theatre company La Barraca.

The distinctive character of the journal would be asserted above all in its title, which carried the suggestive imprint of Bergamín's own agile mind. His decision to baptize the new publication *Cruz y Raya* was a brilliantly inspired one and recalls the skill he had shown prior to 1933 – in his aphorisms, his prose, and the titles of his books – in imaginatively recreating a popular expression, placing it in a fresh context, and exploiting both its literal and figurative senses. It is of some historical interest to notice that the first time the phrase '*cruz y raya*' appears in Bergamín's writing is in the text of a lecture he gave in 1932 in the Palacio de Bibliotecas y Museos, bringing to a close an exhibition of drawings and paintings by Benjamín Palencia.[9] The lecture was entitled 'Cruz y raya de la pintura,' though when it was eventually published in 1936 in the second volume of *Disparadero español*, the title was changed to 'Un lenguaje de fuego de la pintura.'[10] Significantly, in the 1936 version of the text, all the passages making use of the expression '*hacer cruz y raya*' were deleted or rewritten. Bergamín evidently preferred to 'reserve' the phrase and all that he wished to make it imply for his journal alone.

Despite the subsequent changes to the text of 'Cruz y raya de la pintura,' it is instructive to see how, in 1932, Bergamín took hold of the popular expression and with his customary acuity incorporated it into his reflections on painting. The final paragraph of the lecture, as reproduced at the time in *El Sol*, reads as follows:

Si escuchamos con los oídos la luz, siguiendo el consejo evangélico; si abrimos los ojos a estos luminosos silencios, comprenderemos fácilmente cómo todos los lenguajes imaginativos se han originado y radicalmente se funden en un solo lenguaje común: el de la creación poética misma, que es voluntad sobrenatural de su propia naturaleza. Por eso cada uno de estos lenguajes es irreductible; por eso no puede decirse en palabras lo que ya se ha dicho en pintura o en música, pues cada uno de estos lenguajes es como actividad espiritual que es lo que llamó Hegel una especificación cada vez más determinada del pensamiento. Por eso la pintura como la música o la poesía empiezan por donde acaban: la puerta de sus laberintos es una sola: se entra y se sale por la misma; empiezan por donde acaban, que es por tomar una determinación, y por tomarla específicamente, o especificando espiritualmente el pensamiento: su pensamiento. Y esto no se hace más que por una voluntad, por la más pura y honda voluntad. Que así, por determinarse espiritualmente de ese modo, haciendo su santísima voluntad, haciéndose positivamente una voluntad, se hace la pintura cruz y raya de todo; haciendo cruz y raya con todo, porque finaliza y tiene por fin, por límite, por determinación de su voluntad, esa encrucijada espiritual – ese laberinto – de donde tiene que salir, como ha entrado, por su exclusiva voluntad: rectamente. Por eso la pintura, como ninguna otra determinación específicamente poética (creadora) del pensamiento o de nuestro pensamiento, es un misticismo; pero el que la hace, como el que la contempla, sí puede decirse que padece una especie de misticismo, una sumisión de su voluntad a otra voluntad más profunda. A esa santísima voluntad, a ese poder o potenciación de la voluntad, que significó Nietzsche en un 'más' y un 'menos,' en una cruz y en una raya, diciendo 'un sí, un no, una línea recta, un fin.' Que por eso hizo cruz y raya de todo y con todo; se hizo cruz y raya de todo, como hace toda verdadera creación imaginativa, toda verdadera poesía; como hace, y como hizo, siempre que hizo o creó imágenes, siempre las hizo como éstas: la pintura, cruz y raya sencillamente. Cruz y raya, ni más ni menos que pintura.

The spiritual emphasis that underlies Bergamín's interpretation of the process of artistic creation explains why he chose eventually to publish this essay together with 'El pensamiento hermético de las artes.'[11] The two essays have in common this idea of the divine element in creativity: the notion that inspiration and the act of composition convert the poet/composer/painter into a creator. It is in this initial sense that the usefulness of the expression '*hacer cruz y raya*' is first realized and exploited: 'toda verdadera creación imaginativa,' to return to Bergamín's phrase, creates or recreates anew, constituting a new beginning, submitting itself to the higher will of God at that 'encrucijada espiritual' from which it then departs, affirming and forging its own substantive present and future.

Although the style of the essay, like others of the period, is dense and elaborate (a fact that Bergamín appears to acknowledge with, perhaps, a hint of discomfort when he refers to 'el margen sombrío de mi palabra'), the ingenious way in which the writer makes use of the popular phrase is clear. By working out a variety of associations and incorporating them into his argument, Bergamín transforms the expression into a lyrical and rhetorical high point of the entire meditation on creativity.

Already in 1932, then, it was evident that Bergamín had hit upon an extraordinarily suggestive formula that could be put to a variety of purposes. All the possibilities that occurred to him when he was presented with the opportunity of setting up a journal, along with the hopes that as a writer and a restless unorthodox thinker he had entertained for a decade or more, seemed to be brilliantly condensed into the popular saying. On the one hand, for example, the *cruz* would stand as a constant reminder of the journal's (and Bergamín's) fundamental spiritual interests. On the other hand, the idiom would suggest what the journal hoped to achieve in general terms: a 'clean sweep' or 'fresh start.' In addition, the phrase could work as a conjunction of signs: a plus and a minus, a 'yes' and a 'no,' or, as the journal's subtitle asserted ('revista de afirmación y negación'), an affirmation and a negation. The journal's title eloquently summed up the stance that Bergamín planned for it to take up: a willingness to define, by acceptance or rejection, those values considered worthy of attention, and to move dialectically towards the promotion of new imperatives salvaged from the past or sifted critically from the present. Simultaneously, the title implied the weighing and balancing of ideas, the open scrutiny of positive and negative values, the rejection of a one-dimensional exclusivism, the encouragement of the meeting of opposites. And by means of the interaction between contrasting outlooks, it also meant the forging of a new direction, path or objective – hence the felicitous incorporation by Bergamín into the journal's opening declaration of the phrase from Nietzsche that he had quoted at the end of his lecture of 1932: 'un sí, un no, una línea recta, un fin.' Clearly, the title was a superb one, and it was largely Bergamín's responsibility to see that the journal lived up to the promises and expectations so cleverly condensed in its name.[12]

The first number of the journal appeared on 15 April 1933. Its price of three pesetas put it in the same category as the *Revista de Occidente* and *Leviatán* (which cost three and three and a half pesetas respectively), making it, like them, a publication with a fairly limited audience, drawn inevitably from the cultured middle and upper classes.[13] The quality of both its content and presentation, however, as well as the generous number of pages in each issue, made it a worthy rival of these other publications. Predictably, this first number opened with a 'Presentación,' written by Bergamín in collaboration with Falla.[14] Since this text makes explicit some of the main concerns that were to guide the journal, it is useful to draw attention to some of the points made in it. It begins:

No es el propósito de esta revista, al asumir todas aquellas manifestaciones del pensamiento determinadas por la pura actividad del espíritu, el de dirigirse en un solo sentido, exclusivo y excluyente, de una actividad religiosa positiva y negativa, sino en independencia de ella, pues esta actividad espiritual que es, para nosotros, la del catolicismo, está, como diría Unamuno, por encima y por debajo de todas esas manifestaciones del pensamiento: de todo ese conjunto, o conjuntos espirituales, que designan una cultura; y de la acepción misma, del propio concepto de la cultura ... Ninguna forma actual del pensamiento tiene que marcarse por adelantado con etiqueta confesional alguna para expresarnos a nosotros su significado espiritual más puro ...

The purpose of these lines was to underline the journal's plurality and independence. Even if its Catholic affiliation was specified, *Cruz y Raya* openly embraced all aspects of human creativity and reflection. Since these would not be judged by the narrow criteria of a traditional confessionalism, their 'spirituality' could and often would be implicit rather than explicit. This emphasis is important, since it explains why so little of the journal was overtly 'religious.' Only a small minority of contributors, for example, were clerics, and only a small proportion of the subjects treated in it were directly connected with religious matters. Bergamín's concept of spirituality was the wider one he had already advanced in essays like 'El pensamiento hermético de las artes' and 'Cruz y raya de la pintura.' It encompassed 'toda verdadera creación imaginativa,' and it would be the multiple forms of this that he would try to find room for in the journal.

The opening declaration goes on to say:

Esta revista de colaboración abierta, libre, independiente, se propone actuar sobre todos los valores del espíritu, sin mediatización que los desvirtúe. Precisamente, la razón más pura de ser de esta revista, la que la inspira y nos impulsa, quizás consista en eso: en nuestra viva voluntad de católicos para esclarecer bien las cosas; para darles, a cada una, el lugar que les corresponda en la vida como en el pensamiento.

This statement complements the passage quoted previously and stresses again the journal's openness and critical vigilance. Bergamín would continually insist – even in the face of condemnation and malicious misinterpretation – on the need to defend this principle of independence. Nobody connected with the journal, either as editor or contributor, was obliged to toe any particular line.[15] This enabled Bergamín as director to draw upon a wide variety of people: Catholics and Protestants, intellectuals of all shades of political opinion, poets, journalists, university lecturers, and so on. He spread his net outside Spain, too, enlisting in this general offensive the services of some of the most engaging minds of England, France, Germany, and Italy. All this would make of *Cruz y Raya* a genuine 'revista de encuentro' in which ideas and outlooks conventionally separated by unbridgeable gaps could be brought together in an implicit or explicit dialogue. Bergamín was able to encourage confrontations of this kind, guaranteeing with his own presence and supervision the constructive sense of the exchanges they produced. Some readers and critics would view this variety as a malignant eclecticism bordering on incoherence, but such criticisms overlooked the seriousness of the attitudes that lay behind it and which Bergamín championed so intensely: namely, that truth itself – or the truths that *Cruz y Raya* sought to affirm critically – were not unidimensional but rather contradictory, elusive, and multivalent. Out of the amalgam of elements that found expression in the journal, Bergamín hoped to assert the complex dualities of reality and reflection. This was, of course, very much a personal outlook and links up with some of the main features of his work discussed in previous chapters. *Cruz y Raya* was simply the most systematic, sustained and public affirmation of some of his most deeply held convictions.

Broadly speaking, the journal maintained the same format throughout its life. It was divided into two main parts, each characterized by its own intention and emphasis. This difference was underlined by the contrasting typesettings used in each part. Every number opened with a series of essays, followed by an anthology of some kind in which a selection of texts by a writer, past or present, Spanish or foreign, was presented by a critic with some competence in the field in question. This opening group of texts – essays and anthologies – constituted what might be termed the creative or aesthetic aspect of the journal. It was complemented by the contents of the second half, grouped under the headings 'Criba' and 'Cristal del Tiempo.'[16] The texts in these sections tended to be more critical. They were usually concerned with current events, both in Spain and abroad, which were judged to be of interest, either positively or negatively, to the journal's readers.

Bergamín actively contributed to both parts of the journal, though from a historical point of view, his most significant writing appeared in the 'Criba' and 'Cristal del Tiempo' sections. At any rate, in 1935, in a letter to Falla, he reflected on what he considered to be the different functions performed by the various sections of *Cruz y Raya*:

La revista, cumpliendo sus propósitos, fue pidiendo y publicando colaboraciones que fueran por sí mismas o por sus autores de tan indiscutible calidad poética o estética, literaria, científica, moral, etc. ... que la formaran como quiso, trató de ser, una revista 'de colaboración abierta, independiente.' Al mismo tiempo, yo quise que se transparentase siempre nuestra vida actual, en aquellas resonancias que, por su trascendencia propia o pública, manifestasen nuestra afirmación o negación, nuestra crítica, en suma, ante la compleja y difícil vida actual española y del mundo. Para esto, en su CRISTAL DEL TIEMPO, se fueron recogiendo diversos aspectos generales. No tantos, ni muchísimo menos tan ciertamente, como hubiera sido mi deseo. Pero yo mismo, con mi firma, en una serie de comentarios breves, cuya coherencia de conducta creo manifiesta, fui dando o haciendo una crítica, no sé si certera, pero puedo afirmar que sincerísima, en este sentido. A la vez que en la serie CRIBA se iniciaba un comentario permanente a los principales aspectos de libros o publicaciones o aun sucesos recogidos en la prensa diaria. Todo ello, tendiendo a fijar siempre claramente nuestro *sí* y nuestro *no*, nuestra *cruz* y nuestra *raya*.[17]

These statements clarify the sense of the internal imperatives that guided the journal as it developed, and of the role that Bergamín himself played in formulating them and putting them into practice. I shall refer in greater detail to some of the texts that appeared in these different sections when I come to assess the various aspects of *Cruz y Raya's* responses to life in the Second Republic.

Cruz y Raya enjoyed a mixed reception when it appeared. The fact that from the outset it had both supporters and detractors draws attention to the ambiguous reputation that, perhaps unnecessarily, has dogged the journal right up to the present time. A selection of the opinions voiced before 1936 helps to illustrate not only the contrasting judgments that the journal elicited at the time but also the central difficulty that critics have often had in grasping what Bergamín and *Cruz y Raya* were attempting to do.

Towards the end of April 1933, an unsigned statement appeared in *El Sol* commenting on the publication of the first issue. Although the writer expressed surprise at the nature of the initiative it represented and stressed the distance between *Cruz y Raya's* declared interests and those of *El Sol*, his response was generous and encouraging:

Acojamos con los honores que le son debidos a *Cruz y Raya*.

Más que en la Ciudad de Dios, se ha buscado divisa en la ciudad de los libros, que es corruptible, y a la vez que los métodos de salvación, dicta la 'libido sciendi' profana. Esta libertad en una revista católica sorprende, pero agrada.

Cuantos admiten que esta vida trasciende de sí hacia finalidades últimas para buscar su justificación más allá de la muerte, son para *Cruz y Raya* amigos.

Las posiciones de *El Sol*, las religiosas, las políticas o las de orden social se encuentran enfrente de las de *Cruz y Raya*. Esta disparidad ni nos veda ni nos cohibe el diálogo con la revista, y lo mantendremos aquí mediante escolios o glosas a sus ensayos, o bien mediante impugnaciones cordiales en las que el amor a la verdad nos guíe.[18]

(Let us welcome with the honours it deserves the appearance of *Cruz y Raya*.

This publication seeks an outlet not in the City of God so much as in the City of Books, which is corruptible, and along with the methods of salvation it preaches a secular 'libido sciendi.' This freedom in a Catholic journal is surprising but welcome.

All those who agree that this life has a transcendental sense and finds its true justification beyond death will be *Cruz y Raya's* friends.

The outlook of *El Sol* – on religious, political, and social issues – is opposed to that of *Cruz y Raya*. This difference, however, will not prove an obstacle in any dialogue with the journal, and we will gladly maintain that dialogue in this newspaper by publishing reports or extracts from its essays or by cordial dissent. We will only seek to be guided by the truth.)

Bergamín was undoubtedly pleased by this reaction, even though it judged prematurely some of the stances the journal would adopt. He did not expect everybody to share *Cruz y Raya's* basic outlook – least of all, perhaps, those republicans who professed anti-clerical opinions – but he did hope that it would be able to contribute in some way to a constructive dialogue in Spain. For this to happen he needed the tolerant, open-minded approach of the kind of people associated with *El Sol*: concerned intelligent liberals who were prepared to listen and debate, and perhaps eventually to absorb even some of the energies and expectations that impelled the new journal. Those responsible for the newspaper kept the promise given in this brief commentary of 1933, and right up until the outbreak of Civil War paid careful attention both to the ideas being advanced by Bergamín himself and to the stances being adopted by his journal.[19]

Other responses were not only less generous but were positively hostile. In *Hoja Literaria*, for example, no less a writer than Antonio Sánchez Barbudo – later to be so closely allied to Bergamín in the intellectual opposition to fascism – gave a vitriolic account of his impressions of the early issues of *Cruz y Raya* and of the current activities of its director:

Ha aparecido ya el segundo número de *Cruz y Raya*, revista, según ella misma dice, de afirmación y negación. Virguerías de más o menos a cargo de Sepepito Bergamín, trabajos espesos y algún nombre anodino escurrido, pero católico sin duda, en este último número, son las características de la revista catolizante recién aparecida. La dirección de *Hoja Literaria* declárase desde ahora por el refinamiento odioso, la hipocresía y catolicismo de *Cruz y Raya*, enemiga de este engendro. La declaración aparecida en el primer número de *Cruz y Raya* es un trasunto, una copia casi literal de la de Jacques Maritain, bien conocida, que ya comentamos últimamente al hablar de Les Isles. Lo que dijimos entonces podemos aplicarlo ahora, con el agravante en este caso de que tratamos con catolizantes españoles, vanguardistas, copistas y mediocres que se cuidan muy bien de ocultar el origen de sus 'ocurrencias.' Presenta pese a todo esta revista algún interés por varias de las firmas en ella aparecidas y por la calidad de ciertos trabajos (que ligan por cierto muy mal con el de Bergamín, hecho de rabillos deshilvanados) interesantes aunque sombríos como propios de una publicación fascista. Es triste, por lo demás, ver los nombres de grandes figuras, alternando en *Cruz y Raya* con los de figurillas para labor tan triste. El alto vuelo que pretende tener esta revista, no ya por vasalla, sino por la insolvencia de su animador José Bergamín, queda desde luego cortado. Es este Sepepito con cara de arrepentido el típico devoto católico de santos jesuitas. Manitas blancas, pañitos azules (en el pecho la medallita) va Sepepito, rebelde finito, sembrando una baba con voz de flauta, como un buen Luis a quien los padres quieren mucho. Los ataques que a J.R.J. y a las Misiones Pedagógicas dirige este J.B. en el primer número de *Cruz y Raya*, por injustos, por turbios, son algo verdaderamente despreciable que exigieron inmediatamente una respuesta que concretamos en una palabra: canalla.[20]

(*Cruz y Raya*, which describes itself as a journal of affirmation and negation, has brought out a second issue. This recent Catholic publication is characterized by the fancy frills of Bergamín, by its stodgy essays, and by the presence of the odd delicate, anodyne writer who undoubtedly professes the Catholic faith. *Hoja Literaria* declares itself the enemy of the odious refinement, the hypocrisy, and the Catholicism of *Cruz y Raya*. The declaration published in the first number is a crib, an almost literal copy of the well-known statement by Jacques Maritain, which we commented on recently when discussing Les Isles. What we said at that time can be repeated now, though in this case the situation is made worse by the fact that it involves Spanish Catholics, members of the avant-garde, a motley crew of mediocre cribbers who do their best to cover up the source of their ideas. Despite all this the journal does have some interest, thanks to some of the contributors and to the quality of particular articles (notably superior to Bergamín's own essay, which has neither head nor tail) that are interesting though gloomy – something to be expected in a fascist publication. It is depressing at any rate to see first class names in *Cruz y Raya* alongside insignificant ones, all working for such a sad cause. Because of the bankruptcy of its animator, José Bergamín, this journal has no hope of realizing its ambitions. Bergamín goes around with that look of repentance on his face like the typical worshipper of Jesuit saints. He has nice little white hands and is all dolled up in blue (and sports his nice little medal on his chest). He is an exquisite little rebel, and splutters about with that flute-like voice of his, behaving like mummy's little boy. The attacks that he published in the first number of *Cruz y Raya* against Juan Ramón Jiménez and the Misiones Pedagógicas are despicably unfair and demand a rejoinder, which we offer in a single word: swine.)

As Sánchez Barbudo would doubtless be the first to admit today, these remarks hardly constituted a fair assessment of the journal and its director. Their aggressive tone can be explained largely in terms of the references to the texts Bergamín had published in the first issue of *Cruz y Raya*, attacking both Jiménez and the Misiones Pedagógicas.[21] Since Sánchez Barbudo had been involved in the latter from the start and considered himself to be a loyal devotee of Jiménez at the time, he had every reason to feel indignant. Sánchez Barbudo essentially develops a counter-attack that Jiménez himself had launched from the pages of *El Sol* at the end of April 1933.[22] It was Jiménez who first sneeringly referred to Bergamín as 'Sepepito,' and Sánchez Barbudo, by using several other scornful diminutives, intensifies the contempt Jiménez had already voiced. He was obviously more concerned with attacking Bergamín personally than in formulating a balanced response to the contents of *Cruz y Raya*, which he confesses, grudgingly, do have a certain interest.

This text by Sánchez Barbudo is worth resurrecting, however, for other reasons. It draws attention to two aspects of the way in which *Cruz y Raya* was perceived by some readers during the Republican years and has sometimes been interpreted in more recent times. These concern, on the one hand, the debts that Bergamín and his journal owed to the examples set by leading French liberal Catholics such as Maritain, and on the other, the idea that because *Cruz y Raya* had openly declared its Catholic allegiances, it was to be dismissed, in Sánchez Barbudo's words, as a 'publicación fascista.' Both these views of the journal need to be examined with care and I shall do this when I look at the religious and political dimensions of Bergamín's initiatives in *Cruz y Raya*. For the moment, it is sufficient to notice that these interpretations were advanced in some quarters very soon after the journal began publication.

There is one other example of these early responses to the journal that is worth quoting. In the summer of 1935, José Herradón published a barbed and malicious review of *Cruz y Raya* in the communist journal *Nueva Cultura*. The writer's political affiliations largely explain why *Cruz y Raya* was denounced as part of a sinister conspiracy to win over the minds of middle-class Catholics by seducing them with the 'liberal,' 'European' side of what was essentially a corrupt and reactionary institution. Herradón is as aggressively hostile as Sánchez Barbudo – ironically describing Bergamín, for example, as a 'fino malagueño de playa' – but some of his remarks are reproduced, since they invite correction and clarification:

El 'agudo' José Bergamín, situado en el centro de la última generación literaria, ha recibido plenos poderes del genio dorado de los consejos de administración del trust jesuitista: del gran Don Valentín Ruiz Senén ... para que haga la competencia a la *Revista de Occidente* de Ortega, algo indiferente en materia religiosa. La colaboración se paga el doble, el papel es doblemente caro, no importa el déficit anual ... [23]

(José Bergamín, the writer of rapier-like wit who stands at the centre of our latest literary generation, has been given full authority by Don Valentín Ruiz Senén, the golden boy of the administrative councils of the Jesuit trust, to enter into competition with the *Revista de Occidente*, largely indifferent to religious affairs. Contributors are paid twice as much, the paper is twice as expensive, and no importance is attached to the annual deficit ...)

There are two points that can usefully be made in connection with these remarks. The first concerns the nature of Ruiz Senén's relationship with *Cruz y Raya*. The fact that he administered the journal's budget and was associated with the Jesuits has given rise to some speculation concerning the possible pressures that might have covertly been put on Bergamín as director. On this point Bergamín himself is adamant. He insists that he worked with total independence and consistently refused to allow the journal to be allied with any specific religious order or political party. When asked on one occasion, for example, if Ruiz Senén's administrative authority or his personal background affected in any way *Cruz y Raya's* orientation, he replied emphatically: 'Nunca. La revista perdió siempre dinero, y lo pagaba, en efecto, Ruiz Senén. Pero hasta tal punto no intervenía en la marcha de la revista que se negaba a leer los artículos antes de que aparecieran publicados. Cuando en alguna ocasión quisieron influir sobre él gentes a quienes les molestaba la orientación de *Cruz y Raya*, él respondía: "Yo soy el que menos manda en la revista, porque soy el que pongo el dinero"' ('Never. The journal always lost money, and that money did indeed come from Ruiz Senén. But he took no part in the direction of the journal, so much so that he even refused to read the articles that were submitted to it before they appeared in print. When on one occasion certain people who disliked the orientation of the journal tried to get him to do something about it, he replied, "I am the person who has the least influence since I am the one who supplies the money"').[24] More than anything, it seems to have been these more or less unlimited funds that Bergamín could draw on that have provoked suspicion of the kind that Sánchez Barbudo condensed into his reference to the journal's 'odioso refinamiento.' It was certainly true that no expense was spared with regard to the physical presentation of the journal, that contributors were generously paid, and that the journal continued to function irrespective of the considerable financial losses it incurred; but all this had no bearing whatsoever on the freedom with which Bergamín operated as director.[25]

The second point concerns the idea that *Cruz y Raya* was established in opposition to the *Revista de Occidente*. The simple fact that Ortega had generously given Bergamín both his advice and encouragement when the journal was being launched would tend to invalidate this interpretation. There is, moreover, evidence to suggest that rather than functioning as rivals, *Cruz y Raya* and the *Revista de Occidente* neatly complemented each other and coexisted harmoniously in the final years of the Republic. It is notable, for example, that out of a total of 113 contributors to *Cruz y Raya*, 34 also wrote at the same time for Ortega's journal. The two journals were not mutually exclusive but simply pursued different emphases. Marcel Brion noticed this as early as 1934 and mentioned it in a glowing review of *Cruz y Raya's* first year of activity:

La *Revista de Occidente* et *Cruz y Raya* se complètent utilement, en ce que l'une constitue principalement une vaste étude en surface des grandes activités intellectuelles mondiales, faisant une large place aux sciences naturelles et aux lettres étrangères, non sans une nuance de 'cosmopolitisme'; l'autre, au contraire, représente une volonté d'approfondissement de l'âme espagnole dans ce qu'elle a de plus singulier et de plus essentiel. Alors que la *Revista de Occidente* 's'étend,' *Cruz y Raya* 's'enracine': cela ne signifie pas qu'elle reste exclusivement espagnole; au contraire, les écrivains étrangers y trouvent une chaleureuse hospitalité, mais dès les premiers numéros de cette revue récente, nous avons remarqué avec beaucoup de sympathie d'ailleurs, son orientation spirituelle qui est absolument dans la tradition de l'esprit et de la littérature castillane ... [26]

There were certainly differences between *Cruz y Raya* and the *Revista de Occidente*, but it would be a mistake to view them (or their directors at the time of publication) as adversaries vying for the same readership. The one difference that critics have *not* mentioned up to now and which is important to bear in mind, since it explains *Cruz y Raya*'s appeal to many of the younger intellectuals of the period, is that by 1933, Ortega's journal had become rather dull and predictable, in a sense the organ of the senior establishment. Bergamín, however, always managed to introduce a provocative and sometimes polemical element into *Cruz y Raya*. The restless, combative, paradoxical, and often exasperatingly unorthodox nature of Bergamín's own outlook gave the journal much of its fascination. Domingo Pérez Minik's recollections of how he responded at the time to the journal's unashamed eclecticism are probably typical of the chord struck in the reading public then aged between twenty and thirty. Pérez Minik refers to 'la extraña conjunción de una España muy vieja, la del Barroco, ponemos como ejemplo bastante claro, y lo más moderno de nuestro pensamiento' (the strange conjunction of a very old Spain – the Spain of the Baroque period is the clearest example – and the most modern trends in our way of thinking) and comments:

Se intentaba conciliar a Lope con García Lorca, a Quevedo con Larra, y a Hernando del Pulgar con Américo Castro. Un acontecimiento insólito que a nosotros nos sacaba de quicio, aunque jamás dejáramos de admitir qué imaginación estupenda era necesaria para realizar tan extrañas maridajes, casamientos ilícitos, los peores contubernios.[27]

(There was an attempt to bring together Lope and García Lorca, Quevedo and Larra, Hernando del Pulgar and Américo Castro. It was done in such an unorthodox way that it used to enrage us, though we always recognized that it demanded a splendid imagination to arrange such strange marriages and illicit unions, such outrageous cohabitations.)

When he describes Bergamín as 'un español diferente, imposible de clasificar, de escudriñar, de definir' (a different kind of Spaniard, impossible to classify, to make sense of, to define), he puts into perspective the challenging aspects of *Cruz y Raya* and of the style with which it was directed.

The assortment of opinions and judgments quoted above may be limited, but it is enough to indicate that in many ways *Cruz y Raya*, like its director, was 'diferente, imposible de clasificar' (different, impossible to classify) and has consequently tended to provoke wildly differing responses, from direct condemnation to enthusiastic applause. Perhaps the most prudent way of evaluating its achievements – as well as its shortcomings – is to look at the role it played under Bergamín's leadership in the realms of literary, religious, and political activity.

* * *

The literary and general cultural dimension of *Cruz y Raya* constitutes the least controversial side of its activities and is therefore the most straightforward to describe and document. In brief, betwen 1933 and 1936 Bergamín brought together a wide variety of talents, both proven and potential, and focused interest on subjects ranging from literature, art, music, and history to science, philosophy, law, and architecture. In the first place, he enlisted the services of some of the most eminent figures of the intellectual establishment of the day: Menéndez Pidal, Falla, Marañón, Artigas, José María de Cossío, and Ortega. Names such as these gave *Cruz y Raya* a certain scholarly distinction, but they were never allowed to impose a pedantic, excessively academic tone on the journal. In the second place, Bergamín made full use of his extensive network of personal contacts and published work by the leading critics of his own generation, those reaching their maturity in the years of the Republic: Dámaso Alonso, José F. Montesinos, Joaquín Casalduero, Emilio García Gómez, Antonio Marichalar, José Camón Aznar, and Xavier Zubiri. Lastly, Bergamín's practically infallible instinct for spotting genuine intellectual promise combined with his generosity meant that *Cruz y Raya* was often used as an outlet for unknown or up-and-coming young writers and critics. Their careers were given a considerable boost when they were given access by Bergamín to the journal. Some of the cases in which *Cruz y Raya* functioned as a crucial launching pad for novice writers are well known: Miguel Hernández, for example, succeeded in making a name for himself in Madrid, thanks to the publication in Bergamín's journal of his *auto Quién te ha visto, quién te ve y sombra de lo que eras* (a title that was, in fact, suggested by Bergamín), and Luis Rosales gained invaluable momentum and prestige from publishing his first substantial essays in *Cruz y Raya*, as well as his first book of poetry – *Abril* – in the Ediciones del Arbol in 1935. There are several other examples, however, of the generous welcome that Bergamín gave to young people at the time: José Antonio Muñoz Rojas, Luis Felipe Vivanco, Leopoldo Panero, Ramón Sijé, José Antonio Maravall were all able to establish or consolidate their reputations by getting their work published in *Cruz y Raya*. It is a remarkable statistic that half the contributors to the journal were less than thirty years of age in 1933.

Bergamín also took pains to secure contributions from abroad, either from writers whose own outlook he judged to be compatible with the ideals that animated the journal, or from critics who simply had something illuminating to say about those 'manifestaciones del pensamiento' he had mentioned in the first issue and which he believed were indirectly but inextricably linked to man's spirituality. Thus, despite its pronounced interest in Spanish cultural affairs, *Cruz y Raya* also projected an international image of some distinction. Among the French writers, for example, whose work appeared in translation in the journal were Paul Claudel, Jacques Maritain, and Max Jacob. Essays by people as eminent as T.S. Eliot and Martin Heidegger were also published, the work of the latter reaching Spain for the first time in *Cruz y Raya*. Other notable foreign contributors were the refugee German philosopher Paul Ludwig Landsberg – who wrote for Bergamín's journal at the same time as he wrote for Emmanuel Mounier's *Esprit* in Paris – and the exiled Italian socialist Luigi Sturzo.[28]

There is one particular text that throws into relief the interest that Bergamín generously displayed in welcoming non-Spaniards into the *Cruz y Raya* enterprise. This is a letter that Bergamín wrote in 1933 to J.B. Trend, the distinguished Hispanist of the University of Cambridge. It gives a unique insight into the cordial relations Bergamín was establishing with intellectual circles outside Spain:

Recibí su carta, querido amigo, que me dio la gran alegría de ver cómo nuestra revista ha sido acogida por V. con tan afectuoso comprensión y elogio. Pero una cosa me faltó en ella: su respuesta a la petición que le hice – y le repito – de colaboración. V. puede darnos seguramente un trabajo de interés sobre cualquiera de los temas, de poesía o música, que le son familiares. En cuanto a la posible colaboración de Wilson, también le agradecería que V. mismo, si le parece, se lo indique. Yo le escribo, enviándole los seis números de la revista que hemos publicado.

¿Qué le parece este número seis, que habrá recibido últimamente? Pienso que un gran tema de ensayo para V. sería: *la Petenera*. Y que podría V. enviármelo, por ejemplo, para el número de diciembre.

Muchísimo me gustaría ir por esa Universidad en primavera: y más para hablar sobre Bécquer. Si esto se arreglase sería para mí una gran cosa, pues vivo deseando volver a ese Londres que conocí como al agua fría, según Nietzsche, de un modo rápido y profundo: a ese Londres que nunca olvido.

También quiero dar en la revista un Blake: y quisiera hacerlo con la reproducción de algunos dibujos. Dígame qué me aconseja para esto.

Espero sus noticias, rogándole que no se retrase mucho en enviármelas. Tiene V. que ser un colaborador mío en nuestra española *Cruz y Raya*. Tiene que darme colaboración y consejo; apuntarme las iniciativas que le sugiera. Tiene V. que ser, en una palabra, uno de los nuestros.

Le saluda con gran afecto su siempre amigo *y compañero*

José Bergamín[29]

It is clear from these lines that it was often Bergamín himself who personally took the initiative in securing contributions from abroad and in suggesting concrete topics for these contributions. The tone of the letter also underlines the way in which *Cruz y Raya* was genuinely a 'revista de colaboración abierta': the readiness to have the young Edward Wilson write for the journal; the interest in receiving Trend's advice on the Blake illustrations and any further suggestions he might have for the journal's growth and development. This combination of personal warmth and a belief in a common purpose indicates the kind of favourable impact *Cruz y Raya* began to have abroad during its brief existence.[30]

Bergamín's concern to widen the focus of *Cruz y Raya*'s interests by looking outside Spain is also evident in some of the anthology sections of the journal in which extracts from the work of foreign writers – 'classics' from the remote and recent past – were presented. Once again, the range of writers covered is impressive: from Milton and Pascal to Francis Thompson and Coventry Patmore, from Hölderlin and Novalis to Blake, Keats, and Gerard Manley Hopkins. Characteristically, it was a mixture of the specifically religious and the creatively superlative. In this particular initiative, Bergamín was lucky to have among his friends some of the best translators and most informed critics of the day: Marichalar, Souvirón, Cernuda, Muñoz Rojas, Altolaguirre, Pablo Neruda.

If the anthologies referred to above performed the useful function of introducing or reintroducing to the cultured reading public of Spain some of the past literary and spiritual high points of other European countries, the main virtue of others that Bergamín commissioned for *Cruz y Raya* was to focus attention on some of the excellences – often neglected ones – of Spain's own literature. It is in this area above all that the journal's contribution to a specifically national cultural awareness is most clearly seen. In these anthologies the emphasis, unsurprisingly, is placed on the Golden Age, though once again not exclusively on devotional writers. Alongside texts by Fray Luis de Granada, Pedro de Jesús, Fray Luis de León, and San Juan de la Cruz, room was also found for extracts from the work of Quevedo, Juan de Arquijo, Francisco de Medrana, Francisco de Rioja, and Villamediana. Each selection was prefaced by a critical and/or biographical introduction of some kind, written by some of the best critics, both young and old, with whom Bergamín was in contact: José María de Cossío, Francisco Maldonado, José María Semprún y Gurrea, Ramón Sijé, Cernuda. The scholarly excellence of some of these anthologies – Rodríguez-Moñino's of Gregorio Silvestre and Dámaso Alonso's of Gil Vicente's lyric poetry in Spanish, for example – explains why they have stood the test of time with such ease. This is to say that the successes of *Cruz y Raya* in this area of rehabilitating neglected classics were to leave a lasting impression on the way in which certain literary and cultural values of Spain's past have been critically perceived.

The permanence of the achievements of Bergamín's journal in the field of Spanish literature can also be seen in the way it responded to the best of the country's creative writers. In the issue of April 1934, Bergamín introduced a new supplementary section to *Cruz y Raya* that would continue to be a regular feature right up to the summer of 1936. This section carried different titles – 'Inventivas,' 'Historias,' 'Representaciones' – according to the nature of the texts it contained, but basically it was devoted to creative writing previously unpublished. It was in this section, for example, that Miguel Hernández's *auto* was published in three successive issues in 1934. Other young writers like Vivanco and Antonio Morón also had the good fortune to have their work accepted in these supplements. On several occasions Bergamín was able to give financial help to his destitute friend Gómez de la Serna by publishing his texts in this section.

These supplements were distinguished from the main body of the journal by the coloured paper on which they were printed. This was a device that would be used later in journals like *Hora de España* and is a sign of the impact that the presentation of *Cruz y Raya* had subsequently on other literary and cultural publications. The different coloured paper emphasized the fact that the texts in question were creative rather than critical, meditative, or scholarly.[31] They met with immediate success and were made available to the public in offprint form. It was this circumstance that led Bergamín to consider the possibility of setting up a publishing company in order to complete and complement the journal's activities. In this way, the Ediciones del Arbol of *Cruz y Raya* were founded and Bergamín embarked on his career as a publisher. This development constitutes a separate aspect of the journal and of Bergamín's role as a cultural activist in the Second Republic and deserves a brief commentary.

At an early stage in the journal's life, Bergamín decided to use a woodcut of the *hortus philosophae* as a kind of emblem for *Cruz y Raya*. It was another boldly suggestive move on his part. The tree depicted in the woodcut symbolically expressed the scope of the journal's interests and ambitions: the harvesting, as it were, of the fruits of man's labours in areas as far apart as medicine and metaphysics. The logic here, as I have suggested before, was that these disparate disciplines shared a common origin and ultimate purpose, namely the affirmation of human spirituality through creative and critical meditation. The symbol of the tree, however, went much further than that, and Bergamín obviously realized that it had as much exploitable potential as the very title of the journal. The tree also represented nature – the classical source of art – and the process of creation: roots burrowing into the traditions of the past, branches reaching upwards to the sky, which expressed the final goal. The fruits the tree bore and would continue to bear were a sign of cyclical renewal, of man's fertile imagination, and of the promise of his future – a promise reflected in a sense in the first steps taken by the Spanish Republic and the new age it theoretically heralded. In view of these interpretations, it was entirely apt that the publishing offshoot of *Cruz y Raya* should be baptized the Ediciones del Arbol.

In the two years or so during which it operated, this publishing branch of *Cruz y Raya* produced a series of books that were remarkable for a number of reasons. In the first place, they consolidated the reputation the journal had established for being tastefully and impeccably presented. Silverio Aguirre made good use of the funds placed at his disposal, and on several occasions was joined by Manuel Altolaguirre, the latter being personally invited by Bergamín to take charge of the printing of particular texts.[32] Second, the books published in the Ediciones del Arbol did not constitute a uniform collection. As director of the company, Bergamín adopted unusually generous procedures: he worked in close collaboration with the writers whose work he published, allowing them considerable personal freedom in deciding the layout and presentation of their own books.[33] Third, these writers were not only Bergamín's personal friends, but also the major figures of the literary world of the thirties. As a result, Ediciones del Arbol was able to produce editions of the most important poetic works of the Republican period: *Razón de amor* by Salinas; the second edition of Guillén's *Cántico*; Alberti's collected poetry to date, along with his *Verte y no verte*; Lorca's *Llanto por Ignacio Sánchez Mejías* and *Bodas de sangre*; Rosales's first book *Abril*; the first version of Cernuda's complete works, *La realidad y el deseo*; and the first Spanish edition of Neruda's *Residencia en la tierra*.

Although the Ediciones del Arbol showed a marked preference for creative writing – works by writers like Max Aub and Gómez de la Serna appeared alongside those of the poets mentioned above – they were in principle run along the same flexible lines as *Cruz y Raya* and accordingly display a considerable range of interests. Some notable texts on literary criticism, for example, came out in the collection: Azorín's *Lope en silueta*, Karl Vossler's *Introducción a la literatura española del Siglo de Oro*, and Menéndez Pelayo's previously unpublished *Introducción y programa de la literatura española*. Bergamín also began a special series – 'La Rosa Blanca' – devoted to *fábulas* of the Golden Age, though because of the pressure of circumstances, only three titles had appeared by the summer of 1936: Cristóbal de Castillejo's *Fábula de Polifemo*, Gaspar de Aguilar's *Fábula de Endimión y la luna*, and Pedro Espinosa's *Fábula de Genil*. In addition, attention was paid to research of a purely scientific kind – evidenced in the publication of José Sánchez Rodríguez's *Anemias y alimentación* – and also to works from abroad that in some way touched upon the spirit of *Cruz y Raya* – hence the translation of Etienne Gilson's *Pour un ordre catholique* in 1936.

It is regrettable that Bergamín had neither the time nor the opportunity to develop further this aspect of the journal's activities. It is possible, however, to reconstruct the future plans that he had for the Ediciones del Arbol in the summer of 1936. In an interview he gave shortly before the outbreak of the Civil War, he outlined the direction in which he planned to move as publisher:

José Bergamín me habla con voz suasoria, permanente y suave; pero voz interior al cabo. Dice de próximas publicaciones: *Arquitectura española del Renacimiento*, por Camón Aznar, viene a llenar un tremendo vacío en la arquitectura nacional esta obra realmente importante; *Yerma*, del gran poeta Federico García Lorca; *La música en el siglo* xx, de Adolfo Salazar, fino espíritu crítico; *Lope de Vega*, por José F. Montesinos, y los volúmenes tercero y cuarto del *Disparadero español* de Bergamín.

En término más lejano, tres libros de poetas jóvenes: *Pérdida fija, Ardiente jinete* y *Cantar de la luna,* por Luis F. Vivanco, José A. Muñoz Rojas y Cayetano Aparicio. Este último compuso su obra a los quince años.

Luego comenzará la colección de libros olvidados de nuestros siglos xv y xvi, con *Jardín de las nobles doncellas* y *La visión deleitable,* por Alonso de la Torre.

Edita *Cruz y Raya* una colección que, bajo el título de *La Rosa Blanca,* agrupa numerosas y magníficas fábulas, y paralelamente empezará en breve a salir otra colección de églogas.

Pero no se olvida lo que por actual tiene un sentido nuevo y agudo de ventanas entreabiertas, y así están en prensa dos libros de Juan Larrea, uno en verso y otro en prosa. El libro de estética de Malraux, aguardando turno, y seguidamente textos de Cassou, Gide ...

En lo que a teatro se refiere, prepara una pequeña serie de comedias, encabezada por M. Altolaguirre, Moreno Villa, Claudio de la Torre, José Antonio Muñoz Rojas y Bergamín.

La voz de Bergamín se ha ido haciendo más fina, es un hilo pálidamente sinfónico que parpadea sombras y espacios silenciosos ... [34]

Clearly, the Ediciones del Arbol would have continued to cultivate those fields of interest that are discernible – albeit in embryonic form – in the early published titles. The emphasis on Spanish literature, both creative and critical, from the past and the present, would have been kept; but Bergamín would also have remained alert to what was happening outside Spain, ready to translate and publish what he considered to be stimulating or illuminating. We can only speculate on the kind of impact that such a program of publications, had it come about and been able to continue to evolve naturally, might have had on Spanish literary and intellectual life.

*   *   *

The spirituality of *Cruz y Raya,* as I have already outlined, was expressed in large part indirectly, through the general literary, cultural, and creative achievements alluded to above. It did, however, assume other forms. Although the journal avoided the limitations that an exclusive commitment to a particular order or institution would have imposed, it did respond directly and systematically to a whole range of matters related to religious life in Spain. Thanks largely to Bergamín, *Cruz y Raya* adopted an alert and combative attitude to such pressing issues as the status of the Church within the State, and the relationship between the individual believer and his social and historical circumstances. An examination of this aspect of the journal (the implications of which will lead on to a discussion of its political dimension) helps to clarify the radical nature of the type of Catholicism that Bergamín promoted in it. One of the main reasons why *Cruz y Raya* came into being was a feeling of dissatisfaction within a minority of enlightened intellectuals at the condition of the Church in Spain. What the journal sought to do, therefore, was to combat the decline or corruption of religious sentiment and to reaffirm the elemental doctrines of Christianity. Its stance on this matter is most clearly communicated in a text by Bergamín of 1935:

Decía un ingenioso escritor francés que el catolicismo era, en Francia, *la forma más elegante de la indiferencia religiosa*. La famosa frase tendría que modificar su calificativo para aplicarse a la sediciente religión de la mayoría de los que se manifiestan pública y políticamente como católicos en España. Habría que decir que para esa enorme mayoría de españoles *el catolicismo es la forma más inelegante de la indiferencia religiosa*: la más chabacana y mentirosa o hipócrita: cuando no supersticiosamente estúpida; el antifaz picaresco de intereses bastardos, por políticos o comerciales, con los cuales la propia política o mercadería se mixtifica, desnaturalizándose; se corrompe y corrompe todo lo que le rodea.
Tiene sobrada razón Unamuno al venir denunciando entre nosotros estos hechos, contra los que repetidas veces hemos levantado en estas mismas páginas nuestra voz. Pues precisamente contra todo eso: contra todos ésos, y aquéllos, se hizo, desde un principio, y se viene haciendo, cada vez más firme en su empeño, nuestra *Cruz y Raya*. Nuestra crítica afirmación y negación.[35]

The militant tone here is entirely characteristic of the many commentaries Bergamín devoted to this subject in the journal. He tried in *Cruz y Raya* to launch a sustained protest at the distance that had come to separate the Church from its fundamental mission. Any aspect of the activity of the Church or clergy that deviated from this mission or that highlighted the way essential responsibilities had been cynically abdicated was vehemently attacked by Bergamín. In an aggressive text entitled 'Dar que decir al demonio,' for example, he denounced the 'corrupción secular de la actividad religiosa en España,' lamenting 'la inmensa desmoralización producida en el ambiente religioso español por la confusión o mixtificación de tantos intereses prácticos con los espirituales, que debieran serles tan ajenos y tan contrarios.'[36] The emphasis in this text on the need to purify the Church, its outlook and interests, was to be a constant in his treatment of this point: 'Nada tan distante de la pobreza espiritual evangélica (Saber supremo) como estos truquistas de la seudociencia, estos pragmatistas rebajados al empirismo circundante y totalizador de una pan-ignorancia crónica.'

In *Cruz y Raya*, Bergamín in effect assumed the task of salvaging the credibility of the Church, attempting to decontaminate it at a time when its integrity had been seriously called into question. This idea comes across in the conclusion he appended to 'Dar que decir al demonio':

¿No habrá que buscar en palabras como las del gran cardenal [Mercier], antes citadas, las causas que han podido destruir la sensibilidad católica de los españoles hasta estos extremos, de tan honda corrupción y degeneración, que llega a poderles ofrecer a los enemigos de la fe motivos más que justificados en que hacer su presa segura para el ataque moral, la burla y el escarnio?

Va siendo ya hora de que se alcen algunas voces de católicos, menos *prácticos*, que lo denuncien: en protesta indignada, por lastimada, contra todo eso.

Nosotros, católicos, lo hacemos queriendo traspasar el rumor de esos éxitos escandalosos de los más, para llegar hasta el silencio escandalizado y temeroso de otros muchos, aunque los menos, a quienes especialmente nos dirigimos con estas palabras doloridas; intentando también cercar con ellas aquel otro silencio inerte de una complicidad farisea, blanqueada por fuera como los sepulcros: silencio sepulcral, en efecto, que esconde y cobija tan profunda corrupción mortal en su seno.

The stress Bergamín lays here on the *unpractical* side of his own religious outlook, and of the outlook he wishes to disseminate in *Cruz y Raya*, requires some clarification. It will already be evident that he considered the root cause of the Church's degeneration to be the way in which spiritual affairs had become sullied by political or commercial interests. His conviction that they needed to be kept strictly apart from each other was stated time and time again in the journal, and is forcefully put, for example, in the early text, 'Un gran vuelo de cuervos mancha el azul celeste': 'Que no es en la política donde vamos a encontrar los exponentes supremos de la vida del pensamiento ... No es el catolicismo bandería ni cepo de ningún partido.'[37]

Faced with the spectacle of a Church tarnished by its interventions in business and politics, Bergamín adopted the strategy of reiterating the importance of basic, *unpractical* Christian virtues. Commenting, for example, on the violent confrontations in Austria between workers and the officially Catholic government, Bergamín drew attention to the higher responsibilities, beyond the political, that the Catholic should seek to respect: 'la única sangre que puede derramar un creyente en cuanto lo es, es la suya propia por el martirio: dándose en testimonio vivo de su fe. El único deber que tiene que cumplir, religiosamente, en tal caso, es el del sacrificio.'[38] He repeated this idea on many occasions, stressing that 'la responsabilidad del cristiano, en todo *momento presente*, es decir, en todo momento, en cualquier momento, es una responsabilidad ante Dios.'[39]

It would be tempting to draw the conclusion that both Bergamín and *Cruz y Raya* as a whole simply turned their backs on political realities, preferring to take refuge in these responsibilities before God. Bergamín certainly gave the impression at times that the values and policies he was promoting in the journal were powerless to affect the social and political situation in Spain. His definition, for example, of the 'active' role that the Catholic could play when caught up in the kind of dramatic events that had engulfed Austria seemed to constitute a retreat from the possibilities of direct intervention: 'La acción cristiana, católica, no existe, no puede existir, fuera del exiguo, y enorme, recinto de la caridad.'[40] It would be mistaken, however, to view such declarations as these as an advocation of passive resignation and nothing more. Despite their concern to reaffirm the essential teachings of Christ and the Bible, Bergamín and his companions recognized the paradoxical situation of the Christian. They were fully aware that the believer, while focusing his aspirations on another world and another life, was also firmly rooted in this world, with a life to live in the here and now. In the 1930s this 'here and now' happened to be especially turbulent. *Cruz y Raya* responded to the challenge of the times and devoted considerable attention to the civic responsibilities of the concerned Catholic.

The initial problem posed by *Cruz y Raya*'s interest in these issues concerns a point alluded to earlier, namely the degree to which, in this connection, the journal followed the lead given by other groups elsewhere in Europe. The implication of Sánchez Barbudo's comment on this matter was that Bergamín and the enterprise he headed functioned merely as echoes or appropriators of initiatives that had already been taken in France.[41] This is an unfair simplification. Bergamín's remark that 'CRUZ Y RAYA respondía, dentro como fuera de España, a una situación religiosa y política de desesperación esperanzadora' comes closer to the truth.[42] Bergamín did not set out to model himself on Jacques Maritain, nor did *Cruz y Raya* come into being as a carbon copy of the journal *Esprit* that Mounier set up in Paris in 1932. It was a matter not of servile imitation but of a natural recognition that in both France and Spain there were radical minorities in the Catholic world that shared the same basic concerns. The situations at the time in the two countries were similar from several points of view; therefore, what happened in one could illuminate – and warn against – what might happen in the other. It was, in other words, a question of parallel preoccupations and of an ongoing dialogue between two communities on subjects of common interest.

The sense of this dialogue is clear in the commentaries that Bergamín himself wrote on the various texts imported, so to speak, from France and reproduced in *Cruz y Raya*. In March 1934, for example, he published a short commentary on a manifesto signed by people like Maritain, Mounier, and Roland Manuel that had been sent to the president of the Austrian Republic. The signatories expressed their concern at the conflictive political situation in Austria and hoped that the consequences for Austrian Catholics would not be too grave or compromising. Having quoted from the manifesto, which had already appeared in both *Esprit* and *La Vie Intellectuelle*, Bergamín wrote:

Hay en estas palabras algo que merece ser subrayado. Y no para discrepar del sentido en que se dirigen, sino para esclarecerlo mejor, si cabe, en relación con aquellos presupuestos que a nosotros más nos inquietan, por posibles, y ya apuntadas analogías o equivalencias entre esa gran *desdicha histórica* de Austria y las que hace más de un siglo vienen produciéndose en España.[43]

In other words, Bergamín refers to the French text not only to inform but also to instruct: to make use of the analogy suggested by the situation for the purpose of bringing home to his readers the kinds of pressures at work in Spain.

His procedure was identical in the case of the declaration made by the same group of Catholics entitled *Pour le bien commun. Les responsabilités du chrétien et le moment présent*, which Bergamín commented on a few months later in 1934. He again stresses both the intrinsic significance of the text and the lessons it contained for concerned Catholics in Spain:

La recta voluntad de quienes escriben: *político, temporal y espiritual; humano y divino; complicidades y combinaciones; violencias de guerra civil* ... , nos advierte de aquellos peligros que aquí, en España, nosotros también bordeamos ...
    ... Toda esta especie de profecía nos llega a nosotros en tan clara correspondencia que apenas si exige otro comentario que su lectura.[44]

This is characteristic, then, of *Cruz y Raya*'s alertness to what was happening in France and its wish to bring to the notice of readers in Spain the sense of these outside actions. It would be wrong to view this as simple imitation; it reflects, rather, a coincidence of concern, a readiness to learn from each other, and a shared desire to reassess the Catholic's role in societies subject to the same religious and political pressures.[45]

This coincidence of outlook is especially evident in the way these minorities in Paris and Madrid attempted to resolve the dilemma of the Christian who 'está en el mundo sin ser del mundo.'[46] Both groups believed that religion should not be used as an instrument or ally of temporal, political power, but this did not mean that religion could play only a marginal role in modern society. They proposed, essentially, that spiritual values should be affirmed with greater vigour and purity of motive than had been done before. They hoped that by doing this, they could dignify political life, injecting into it those basic human concerns that lay at the heart of Christian teaching. This attitude is expressed in an extract from *Pour le bien commun* quoted in *Cruz y Raya*:

Tienen, lo político y lo temporal, muchos más recursos que aquellos tan sólo debidos a las energías exclusivamente materiales, que son las que no escapan nunca al juego de las combinaciones y de las complicidades si no es para pasar a las violencias de la guerra civil. Será reintegrar al orden político en toda su fuerza y su dignidad, acrecentándolas, el destacar aquellos otros recursos espirituales, de más alto rango, recordándole que son los que deben penetrarle y envolverle con una vida superior ...

... En todo momento debe repetir el cristiano su NON POSSUMUS ante las más brutales apariencias de necesidad, cuando éstas tratan de querer inclinarle a lo que su conciencia le prohibe. Lejos de ser una deserción o una retirada, este NO requiere una actitud activa, impulsando nuestras energías hacia trabajos positivos. Y, antes que nada, testimonia aquella pureza necesaria, expresándola al rechazar ambigüedades que son claudicaciones.[47]

This became Bergamín's own approach to the problem, what he called 'la calle de en medio.' What it represented was the independent but active critical vigilance of *Cruz y Raya*: the refusal to support any political party and the vigorous championing of those ideals (justice, peace, freedom, and so on) upon which the Christian outlook was based. It was in this sense that the spiritual concerns of Bergamín and his journal came to perform a political function. While this view constitutes a major aspect of the journal's originality and radicalism in Spain, it also poses the most difficult problems of interpretation.

*   *   *

Bergamín has adamantly maintained that *Cruz y Raya* can only be understood in political terms:

El enfoque que debe hacerse para entender cabalmente hoy la revista debe serlo desde un punto de vista político, dándole a esta palabra su más claro y hondo y verídico valor y sentido. De aquí a deducir que fue ante todo una revista política no hay más que un paso.[48]

(The approach that needs to be taken today in order to understand the journal correctly is a political one, if we give this word 'political' its clearest, deepest, and truest value and sense. It follows on immediately from this that *Cruz y Raya* was above all a political journal.)

This opinion conflicts with that of Jean Bécarud, the only critic who has written at length on the journal, and who has argued, equally emphatically, that 'Cruz y Raya nunca fue una publicación política' (*Cruz y Raya* was never a political publication).[49] These points of view appear to be irreconcilable because they approach the notion of 'politics' from different angles, with contrasting expectations. Bécarud's argument is based on the conviction that a journal that was not devoted exclusively to politics and that did not formulate systematically a clear political doctrine cannot be termed a 'political' publication. In a sense he is quite right, but his mistake is to take Bergamín and his journal to task, albeit implicitly, for failing to do something that he, Bergamín, expressly declined to do, namely to draw up a political program that could in some way have served as a viable practical alternative to the parties existing in Spain at the time. As will be clear by now, Bergamín had no wish to institutionalize in some secular movement the ideals that animated *Cruz y Raya*. It was precisely the journal's independence that enabled it to function as a kind of impartial watch-dog of the political scene. When Bergamín speaks of the 'más claro y hondo y verídico valor y sentido' of the term 'political,' he is referring, I believe, to this critical alertness to current affairs that went beyond partisan allegiances and that constituted one of the main functions – *political* functions – performed by the journal. This is why Bergamín insists that *Cruz y Raya* 'estuvo al nivel de su tiempo: "a la altura de las circunstancias" – diría Antonio Machado – y no por encima ni por debajo de ellas; ni muchísimo menos "al margen," con una especie de neutralidad – como se ha dicho equivocadamente.'[50] This clarifies the sense of the journal's commitment – and that of its director – to what Bergamín described to Falla as 'la compleja y difícil vida actual española y del mundo.'[51]

The presence on the Spanish cultural scene of a *Catholic* journal prepared to express *political* opinions would give rise to persistent misunderstandings of the kind that characterize Sánchez Barbudo's dismissal of *Cruz y Raya* as a 'publicación fascista.' In some ways the tendency in 1933–34 to interpret Bergamín's journal in this manner is understandable, since right-wing ideologues like Giménez Caballero were busy at that time developing their ideas on the 'Catholic essence' of the imperial Spain they wished to resurrect.[52] The attention that *Cruz y Raya* paid to Spanish Catholic culture of the sixteenth and seventeenth centuries could easily be misread as a sign of sympathy with that outlook. In addition, as later critics like Bécarud have been quick to point out,[53] a number of writers associated with the Falange from the moment of its foundation – García Valdecasas, Sánchez Mazas, and Luis Santa Marina most notably – were active contributors to Bergamín's journal. Because of the gravity of the charges that these remarks implicitly – if not explicitly – lay against *Cruz y Raya*, this point requires clarification.

Bécarud's suspicions can be dealt with fairly easily. What he fails to take into account is precisely the journal's declared intention of adopting an open, independent policy to all shades of opinion. If *Cruz y Raya* was to live up to its promise of being a 'revista de encuentro,' then Bergamín was practically under the obligation to give people like Sánchez Mazas access to it. This is not to suggest (and in this Bécarud overstates his case) that there was anything overtly 'fascist' about Sánchez Mazas's contributions to the journal or that his presence in it somehow compromised Bergamín. Bergamín's procedure suggests, rather, that even though people like Sánchez Mazas were developing political ideas with which he was in absolute disagreement, he still felt that their voices should be heard in *Cruz y Raya*. Even in a negative sense, as an invitation to a categoric '*no*' from Bergamín, they had a useful contribution to make to certain matters under review.

Bergamín was, in recent years, surprisingly candid about the approaches that were made to him by Primo de Rivera and his cohorts to become involved in the Falange and indeed to make *Cruz y Raya* the official organ of the movement. It is not difficult to grasp the logic behind these overtures even if it is riddled with flaws. Primo de Rivera, for example, just like Sánchez Mazas and García Valdecasas, had been a personal friend of Bergamín's for some time. The two had even worked together for a while in Bergamín's father's law practice. In addition, the Falange was originally planned as a radical movement, though steeped in national traditions and with a commitment to solid Catholic values. It was conceivable, therefore, in the summer of 1933 at least, that some would view *Cruz y Raya* and the embryonic Falange as essentially moving in the same direction. Bergamín's own commentary on this situation is the best explanation of the misunderstanding involved:

Rafael Sánchez Mazas trataba entonces de convencer a José Antonio de hacer el fascismo español. Ya estaba en pie *Cruz y Raya* – su primer número había salido el 15 de abril de 1933 – y José Antonio piensa en la revista para su movimiento españolista. Y entonces, antes de que la Falange Española exista, nos convoca Sánchez Mazas a José Antonio, a Alfonsito García Valdecasas y a mí para que, reunidos los cuatro, decidamos fundar un partido español, tradicionalista y fascista. Nos reunimos en la Plaza de Santa Bárbara, tomando horchata en verano, José Antonio, Sánchez Mazas y yo, y Alfonsito García Valdecasas no viene. Yo creí siempre que no había venido porque no quiso, pero fue porque no le avisó a tiempo Sánchez Mazas. José Antonio me habló entonces de su intención de fundar un partido fascista español y me ofreció un puesto en él. Yo, claro, me negué, diciendo que para mí el catolicismo y el fascismo eran incompatibles.[54]

(Rafael Sánchez Mazas was at that time trying to persuade José Antonio to create a Spanish fascist party. *Cruz y Raya* was already in existence – its first number had appeared on April 15th, 1933 – and it ocurred to José Antonio that he could use the journal to support such a movement. So even before the Spanish Falange came into being, Sánchez Mazas arranged a meeting between José Antonio, Alfonso García Valdecasas, and myself with the idea that, between the four of us, we could set up a traditionalist, fascist, Spanish political party. We met for a drink in the Plaza de Santa Bárbara that summer: José Antonio, Sánchez Mazas, and myself, but Alfonso García Valdecasas didn't show up. I always thought that he didn't come because he didn't want to, but in fact it was because he hadn't heard about the meeting in time to attend. José Antonio then outlined to me his plan to found a Spanish fascist party and offered me a position in it. Naturally I refused the offer, saying that as far as I was concerned, Catholicism and fascism were incompatible.)

In part this statement simply confirms Bergamín's reluctance to allow *Cruz y Raya* to become identified with any political party, but it obviously goes much further than that, too. The last sentence sums up the main problem. For many people – as the Civil War would make graphically clear – Catholicism was indeed compatible with fascism. One of Bergamín's most crucial and laudable contributions to the drama of the mid-thirties – as André Gide rightly pointed out in 1938[55] – was to maintain the dignity of the Catholic Church in Spain, or at least a part of it, by denouncing the cynicism with which Catholics had lent their faith to a questionable political cause. The difficulty that Bergamín experienced between 1933 and 1936 was to convince the public that he and *Cruz y Raya* represented something different and were to be considered a voice that, far from endorsing the complacency and opportunism of the Church, spoke out militantly against its conservatism and corruption. Although this would have been evident to anybody who knew Bergamín's writings (even before 1933) and who read *Cruz y Raya* with any care, the weight of the Church's reputation as a bastion of self-interest was such that the distinctions Bergamín tried to draw in his journal were not always clearly grasped. I shall return to this point at the end of the chapter.

*   *   *

Bergamín not only emphasized the political character of *Cruz y Raya*, but stated that it was identified specifically with the Republic:

CRUZ Y RAYA nacía en aquella República, diríamos que de aquella República y hasta que para aquella República, identificándonos con ella, con su íntima lucha o agonía. Por eso, el primer SÍ de la revista fue para la República misma: fue decir SÍ a aquella vida republicana naciente. Y al mismo tiempo, en consecuente decisión afirmativa, NO a quienes la negaban para destruirla. Por definición CRUZ Y RAYA se afirmó a sí misma como católica y republicana.[56]

To a critic like Bécarud this declaration must have seemed to be an exaggeration. There may indeed be some grounds for saying that Bergamín was indulging in melancholic, tendentious retrospection when he wrote these lines in 1973. Some would say that he simply seized the opportunity offered by the republication of *Cruz y Raya* (while Franco was still in power) to make a defiant public statement reiterating the political beliefs for which he had suffered nearly thirty years in exile. Yet if the emphasis Bergamín gives his description may be rooted in sentimental factors, there is nothing fanciful about its substance. Both Bergamín and *Cruz y Raya* openly endorsed what the Republic stood for and what it promised Spain. As Bergamín himself has explained: 'De Azaña fue la frase o definición que resumía lo que primeramente aquella República significaba y quiso; como lo que quiso y significó *Cruz y Raya*: "Independencia de juicio y libertad de espíritu"; que es, en definitiva, lo que adelantaba la revista en su primer número de presentación.'[57]

It is legitimate to identify the spirit that guided *Cruz y Raya* with the essential foundation of republicanism. The problem, historically speaking, lies in the Republic's failure to live up to its initial promise and the disillusionment this produced in supporters like Bergamín, who saw that promise slowly frittered away and ultimately stifled. This disillusionment explains who so many of Bergamín's political commentaries in *Cruz y Raya* are attacks on the Republican government or warnings against the dangers its policies represented. They were not inspired by anti-Republican feeling; quite the contrary. They reveal a conviction that genuine Republicans had to speak out against the errors and ineptitude of people who were wasting a unique historical opportunity. Some of these commentaries are worth reviewing because they draw attention to the unequivocally Republican sympathies that motivated Bergamín and to his characteristic vigilance in the journal.

These writings on the contemporary political situation in Spain are basically informed by the disappointment and anger Bergamín felt at the way the Republic was veering away from the course it had been set. In 'Las manos vacías,' for example, he lamented the bankruptcy and small-mindedness of Republican politicians that had created a void in national political life, adding, 'Sólo puede colmarlo un estilo, una inteligencia: una política de verdad; sin maneras y maniobras, ni manipulaciones escamoteadoras.'[58] Bergamín continually reminded his readers of what the Republic had so far failed to achieve, and in a text entitled 'El tris de todo y ¿qué es España?' he stressed the fact that the original mandate of the Republic was to do what the monarchy had been unable to do, namely to create a popular state based on elementary principles of justice and freedom for all: 'Tuvo razón de ser una república española que vino para eso: para hacer un Estado, para causarlo. Para ser cosa o causa pública o popular de razón y no de pasión: de paz civil y no de guerra.'[59] Bergamín believed that the Republic had become hamstrung by constant party squabbles that had swamped this fundamental responsibility. Such behaviour had led to confusion and disorder – 'la ausencia terrible de Estado' – for which the people rather than the politicians were paying the price. In 'El Estado Fantasma y ¿en qué país vivimos?' he develops this idea and bitterly denounces the government for the repressive internal measures it had adopted and for giving every sign of returning to the kind of régime from which Spaniards believed they had escaped in 1931.[60]

There is an obvious parallel in the approach that Bergamín took to religion and politics. In both areas he defended the pure motives and ideals that had inspired, on the one hand, the original mission of the Church, and on the other, the original trajectory of the Republic. As a result, he was led to speak out strongly against those who, in either case, deviated from that original path, vitiating those fundamental ideals through their own cynicism, opportunism, or incompetence. That Bergamín was prepared to accept the consequences of this approach, working it out to its final conclusions, is a tribute to his intellectual integrity and to his stubborn loyalty to his own convictions. The full effect of this on his religious outlook would only become clear during the Civil War, and therefore falls outside the limits of this study. It is possible to gauge its sense, however, by examining the immediate political consequences that are discernible before the summer of 1936. These show how, through *Cruz y Raya*, Bergamín came to adopt an extremely radical political stance while remaining faithful to those elemental Christian values he never ceased to advocate.

The first incident that puts these developments into perspective is the Asturian revolution of October 1934 and the way in which it was handled in *Cruz y Raya*. Bergamín's commentary on the event is a sensitive, searching piece of writing, which tried to establish the reasons for the apparent degeneration of national affairs into confrontation and anarchy. He succeeds in drawing a positive lesson from this episode by quoting from the report that his friend and co-founder of the journal Alfredo Mendizábal had given of his personal experience of the uprising during which he had been held prisoner by communist miners. Despite the personal trauma that he had suffered, Mendizábal had only praise for the way he had been treated: 'El mero hecho de tratarles nosotros con afabilidad y con simpatía despertó en ellos sentimientos tan cordialmente humanos y tan fraternalmente cristianos (cristianos sin saberlo y aun creyéndose enfrente), que hicieron del grupo de *burgueses* y del de *comunistas* una sola *comunidad*, mejor una *hermandad*.' What Mendizábal had experienced touched the very centre of *Cruz y Raya*'s ambitions: the overcoming of the barriers dividing the country (at a political or social level) through the joint affirmation of certain elemental values, which for the Catholic were Christian and for the communist were revolutionary and fraternal. Above and beyond hatred, exploitation, and injustice, a common ground had been found on which the two ostensibly opposing 'sides' could come together. Mendizábal saw in this an invitation to revise an entire social and political outlook and to combine forces in a common offensive for change:

Camaradas mineros que la convivencia cambió tan pronto de nuestros adversarios en nuestros amigos. Vosotros decíais buscar una sociedad justa para oponerla a la injusticia del capitalismo. Y por esa sociedad que creíais más justa os habéis sacrificado en vuestro presente y en vuestro porvenir, y habéis estado dispuestos a dar vuestra vida. Sabed que desde campo distinto, y distante, otros hombres repudian también el capitalismo, por su injusticia y por su materialismo. Y repudian al mismo tiempo la violencia de la revolución externa y el materialismo radical del marxismo, porque postulan una revolución interna, una revolución de cada uno en sí mismo que transforme la sociedad de todos en sus cimientos. Tras el engaño de la lucha de clases, tras el fracaso de la violencia, aun contra un Estado desprevenido y tardígrado, ha llegado el momento de la confluencia en una superación de egoísmos, en un desinterés que sólo el cristianismo puede vivificar.[61]

The point was that the Christian ideals of justice, peace, equality, and charity could and should find an outlet in a social and political reality. They did not exist in a vacuum but echoed ideals that came from an incongruously remote political doctrine. The kind of world to which the idealist Catholics of *Cruz y Raya* aspired was basically akin to that which the most purely motivated insurrectionists of Asturias struggled for. They shared a common conception of Utopia, though each approached it from a different angle. Mendizábal had simply realized that the transformation of society could best be achieved by the transformation of man.

Bergamín immediately saw the significance of the events in Asturias and of Mendizábal's response to them. He described his co-contributors' words as

el mejor testimonio de que aún hay voces que atender en este angustioso vocerío de odios, de injurias, que ha desatado locamente la triste fase de sucesos recién pasados. Al menos una voz católica, entre tantos sospechosos silencios, y, lo que es peor, entre tanto ruido acusador y vengativo, viene a recordar, sencillamente, como digo, los *porqués* del creyente. La verdadera palabra de paz: por encima de todo y de todos.

Pero estos *porqués* son exclusiva, universalmente personales. Dicen de una revolución más honda, de un Estado más vivo.

('El estado fantasma y ¿en qué país vivimos?')

Both Mendizábal and Bergamín stood at the point at which Christian commitment and political idealism intersect. They accepted the need to set aside prejudice, class differences, and animosity to concentrate their energies on this *personal* revolution through which society itself, ultimately, could be changed. It was an outlook that naturally went beyond the limitations of party politics and violent subversion, but which was prepared to come out and embrace all those elements opposed to the worship of materialism, the injustices of capitalism, the violent inequalities of a corrupt state. For Bergamín the incident provided the first graphic insight into the potential alliance between Catholic and communist.

*   *   *

His stand on this matter of the political implications of a radical religious outlook was further developed in 1935, in one of the most significant polemics of the years of the Republic. This took the form of a public exchange of letters between Bergamín and the young Marxist writer Arturo Serrano Plaja. It was prompted by the publication in *Cruz y Raya* of a commentary by Bergamín on a speech that André Gide had given at the International Congress of Writers held in Paris in June 1935. Although the substance of these letters has been looked at before by a number of critics in the context of intellectual life in the thirties, they have not been examined specifically for what they reveal concerning the evolution of Bergamín's attitudes at the time. For this reason it is worth reviewing the circumstances in which the letters were written.[62]

Gide's speech centred on the problem of the writer's role in society and the contribution that he could make to the improvement of that society. In 1935, Gide was in sympathy with communist opposition to social injustice, and while emphasizing the writer's need to retain his independence, placed the full weight of his authority behind the commitment to liberating the individual through social change. In brief, Gide argued that literature should not limit itself to mirroring the situation of the proletariat, but should also 'ayudar a este hombre nuevo que amamos y que deseamos, a que se desprenda de las trabas, de las luchas, de las falsas apariencias; se trata de ayudarle a formarse y a perfilarse él mismo' (24).[63] Given the injustices of capitalism, the writer has to struggle against society so that this 'hombre nuevo' can be brought into being. The role of culture as a whole should be to work towards 'la emancipación del espíritu' (30). The contribution of communism would be to produce 'un estado social que permita el mayor desenvolvimiento de cada hombre, la aparición y desarrollo de todas sus posibilidades' (30).

The fact that Bergamín entitled his review of Gide's speech 'Hablar en cristiano' is indicative of the highly personalized and loaded way he interpreted it.[64] By exploiting, predictably, both the figurative and literal meanings of the idiom 'hablar en cristiano' Bergamín drew attention simultaneously to the admirable frankness with which Gide had broached the subject of the relationship between culture and society, and the specifically Christian implications he felt his remarks contained. Just as Mendizábal had seen Christian values in action in the conduct of communists who were declared enemies of the Church, so Bergamín saw in Gide's words an affirmation, albeit unconscious, of the kind of Christian ideals that inspired Cruz y Raya. Gide's speech was, therefore, according to Bergamín 'un hablar en cristiano sin saberlo.' What brought Catholic and communist together was their common concern for this 'hombre nuevo.' What for Gide implied a *social* revolution, for Bergamín signalled a *personal* revolution, hence full of religious significance: 'Se trata, entonces, de la obtención de ese hombre nuevo. Fuesen cuales fueran las precisiones técnicas de laboratorio revolucionario que se necesitasen para esto, esta obtención sería un hecho que, en definitiva, pudiera llamarse religioso' (43).

What Gide expects from communism is precisely what Bergamín expects from Christianity: the affirmation and renovation of the individual. Gide is praised for accepting the consequences of his outlook and expectations and for making 'una profesión moral de fe' (46). His stance is defined as 'una actitud religiosa ... que no se puede diferenciar en nada, esencial-mente, de una fe religiosa en cuanto a la actitud vital' (46). This is the sense of the link that is perceived and stated: that Catholics of Bergamín's ilk share the same kind of 'radicalismo humano' that 'ignorándolo tal vez sus mismos poseedores, contiene una afirmación espiritual tan cristiana del hombre' (47). Bergamín leaves no doubt about the sense of this parallel when he writes 'que el hombre sea siempre nuevo es una de las primeras verdades del cristianismo. Del cristianismo no histórico, ni evolutivo o progresivo: del cristianismo revolucionario permanente. El cristianismo nos dice del hombre que se puede novar o renovar siempre, *haciéndose de nuevas*. Pues esto, y acaso no otra cosa, quiere decir evangelizarse' (48). This bold mixing of religious and political terminology is indicative of Bergamín's growing public commitment to radical humanism and of his own wish to 'hablar en cristiano' to the readers of Cruz y Raya who were prepared to listen.

Bergamín's commentary prompted Serrano Plaja to write a long letter which, though spelling out the points on which he disagreed with Bergamín, sought to establish an open dialogue on a subject of such central importance at the time. Serrano Plaja argued that the attitude of the Christian – exemplified in Bergamín – was to resign himself passively in the face of suffering, to accept despair but to relegate it to the sidelines of society. He believed that in this sense Christianity was inferior to Marxism, since the latter could play a much more active and effective social role, working systematically against the injustices of a capitalist society in order to accelerate the birth of the 'hombre nuevo.' He accused Bergamín of being opportunistic in his use of the term 'Christian' to describe what were essentially classic Marxist doctrines. He emphasized the differences between a Marxist approach – which allowed for the structured organization of this radical humanism so as to achieve specific political ends – and a Christian attitude, like Bergamín's, which was limited to a faith in the individual irrespective of his social circumstances.

Bergamín's reply to Serrano Plaja is extremely revealing. As is usual in his case, when called upon to justify or defend a particular stance in this way, he writes in a much more direct and explicit fashion. His letter, therefore, is crucial to an understanding of the kind of outlook he was developing in the years of the Republic and which, as I have said before, would reach its fullest and most militant expression during the Civil War.

It is apt that Bergamín should begin by thanking Serrano Plaja for the way in which he had communicated his disagreement with his interpretation of Gide's speech. Nothing could have been more in tune with Bergamín's hopes in *Cruz y Raya* than the concern Serrano Plaja had shown to establish an intelligent, civilized debate on a subject that, though approachable from contrasting viewpoints, affected in one way or another all enlightened writers. Bergamín wrote in an introductory note: '¡Ya hubiera deseado yo que estas consonancias y discrepancias con la revista se nos hubiesen manifestado con la misma franqueza y claridad, tan verdaderamente ejemplares, como éstas de Arturo Serrano Plaja en su "carta abierta"!'[65] Bergamín's reply is highly charged emotionally. He begins by denouncing the use of violence that has produced such lamentable results in Spain, directing his scorn not only at the 'cazadores con pistola' but also at the 'sedicientes católicos, anarquistas, que practican en nombre de un Estado suicida ... este enmascarado terrorismo' (76). He rejects Serrano Plaja's view of his 'misticismo desesperado' and 'pasividad resignada' and reflects:

Usted sabe, probablemente, con quiénes verdaderamente simpatizo. Es decir, con quiénes me siento coincidir en el aliento animador de sus rebeldías. Cuando yo estuve en Rusia, en 1928, traje de aquel rápido contacto vivo, una lección moral inolvidable: algo que, como dije entonces, me había enseñado para siempre, aún más que el sabor de la sangre, el gusto y regusto del pan, entero y compartido. (77)

Communion and communism become subsumed into a single experience: the fraternal breaking of bread. Bergamín here openly took up the challenge that Mendizábal had thrown down in the previous year. Like Gide, he accepted that this kind of conviction entailed social and political consequences and demanded of him a responsibility towards the plight of the common man. His definition, in this context, of what he understands the term 'pueblo' to mean is especially interesting: 'Pues esto, entre otras cosas, significa para mí el pueblo: la personificación viva y verdadera del cristianismo al historiarse el *hombre nuevo* en un revolucionario, y no evolutivo ni progresivo, afán de salvación humana, eterna, permanente' (81).

It is a carefully worded combination of the socially radical and the devoutly Christian. As he develops his idea of the Christian's active responsibility towards the *pueblo*, he comes to acknowledge the common ground he shares with his Marxist interlocutor. His indignation, for example, at the brutalizing effects of the injustices of a capitalist system is entirely in harmony with Serrano Plaja's: '¡Esa sí que es miseria total, definitiva! ¿Qué cristiano va a tolerar siquiera, a soportar sin repugnancia, esta situación *capitalista*?' (82). The crucial step that Bergamín takes, however, is to recognize that if Marxism is a more effective means of opposing these injustices than Christianity, then he, as a Christian, is under a moral obligation to lend his support to it:

En lo que éste [el marxismo] se pueda hacer cauce de expresión – acaso brutal, pero auténtica – de la angustia popular española y de su ímpetu revolucionario, contenido y enervado por la persecución terrorista de un Estado-fantasma, ese mal llamado marxismo me parecería a pesar de todo, la mejor, la más noble esperanza viva, hoy por hoy, y sobre todo, por mañana, de nuestro pueblo, de nuestra España. (83)

Such a declaration may sound rather bland in the 1980s when the dialogue between Marxists and Christians enjoys a sound base in many parts of the world; but in 1935, in a country still dominated by an arch-conservative Catholic hierarchy, it must have taken considerable courage to make it publicly in this way. For right-wing politicians and clerics in Spain, Marxism was at that time a terrifying threat and – as the Civil War would show – they were prepared to go to any lengths to eradicate the danger it was seen to pose. Bergamín, to say the least, was sticking his neck out by giving his public blessing to this element of social protest contained in Marxism.

Bergamín went on equally boldly to suggest that the Catholic Church itself in Spain might even end up by admitting that in certain respects the Marxist approach to the critical situation through which the country was passing was a sound one:

Y en lo que es, en realidad, como método o sistema, cuya eficacia y logro nos dirá la historia de nuestra revolución presente, permanente, creo, por lo menos, que de sus raíces se han nutrido muchas verdades de ésas, en cierto modo *galileas*, por lo que el desenvolvimiento social alcanza; verdades como aquéllas (*e pur si muove*) que la misma Iglesia católica, a que pertenezco – aunque no le afecten esencialmente – acaba, cuando no empieza, por reconocer en su día. Día que tal vez no tarde mucho. (83–4)

If Bergamín admitted the relief that he felt at finally being able to make these statements publicly and to resolve once and for all the apparent inner contradictions of the faith he professed and the social ideals he cherished, he did not miss the opportunity of reiterating the fact that he still maintained his absolute independence. He rejected the notion that he could be called a Socialist or a Marxist – 'mi sueño no es de este mundo' (84) – even though he was prepared to take a stand and to commit himself in the same way Gide had done. Predictably, then, he underlines the element in Gide's speech with which Serrano Plaja had concurred, namely the affirmation of 'su independencia de escritor, de su libertad de pensamiento y de expresión, de arte' (85). This principle was still of central importance to him, and as a Christian he would always refuse to become formally allied to a political faction. He had at least joined his voice with that of Serrano Plaja to specify what needed to be salvaged from the bickering and confusion of Republican political life. Together they had given a memorable example of how complex and controversial issues could be debated in a dignified and honest way. Despite the distance that ostensibly separated their respective viewpoints, both writers had shown a readiness to find the common ground on which the fundamental ideals of each one could be respected.

This admirably frank but unorthodox assessment of the Christian's responsibility within Spain's dramatic domestic situation would win for Bergamín a unique place in the history of contemporary intellectual life. From a personal point of view, his letter to Serrano Plaja was a symbolic high point of the outlook he had tried to promulgate in *Cruz y Raya*: the rejection of violent solutions, the call to unify all idealisms behind a single cause, the addition and subtraction of possibilities and imperatives, the signalling of a path at the end of which all hopes for freedom, justice, and peaceful coexistence could become a living spiritual and social reality. But it required great integrity, exemplary flexibility, and boldness to hold all these disparate attitudes and expectations together in a single coherent outlook. The task was made especially difficult by the pressures at work in the situation: the unavoidable way in which in 1935 and 1936 political outlooks became polarized and mutually antagonistic. The skill with which Bergamín performed this balancing act could not easily be emulated. He had set a fine example but could expect to win few followers at once. It was unfortunate that, like the Second Republic itself, Bergamín was deprived of the time and opportunity to develop the lead that he had given in *Cruz y Raya*. The constraints imposed by history determine the conclusion that needs now to be drawn on the journal's limitations.

*   *   *

Cruz y Raya operated in a set of historical circumstances that prevented the journal from realizing its true potential. Since publication was necessarily suspended when the Civil War broke out, Bergamín had in effect been given only just over three years in which to make something substantial out of the enterprise he headed. To return to a point made earlier, if the journal was 'a la altura de las circunstancias,' it was also doomed to suffer the consequences when those circumstances degenerated into armed conflict. Thus, Bergamín is justified in tying *Cruz y Raya*'s fate to the historical destiny of the Republic: 'La revista ... venía navegando por un mar tempestuoso que terminó por destrozarla contra las rocas: como a la República: o sea a España' (The journal ... was navigating on a tempestuous sea, finally crashing against the cliffs: like the Republic: just like Spain).[66] The historian Javier Tussell has also taken the view that *Cruz y Raya* was a victim of the times. Emphasizing that the promise it represented in the Republican period was simply cut short by the outbreak of war, he includes Bergamín's journal among

aquellos movimientos políticos de raíz democrática y de inspiración cristiana que surgieron a la vida pública en la década de los años treinta y que, en el caso de que la República hubiera logrado estabilizarse, hubieran venido a significar algo muy semejante a lo que en el resto de Europa occidental (y luego también en América Latina) supusieron los grupos políticos demócrata-cristianos.[67]

(those political movements of a democratic nature and Christian inspiration that emerged in the thirties and which, had the Republic enjoyed some degree of stability, might have come to represent in Spain something similar to what the Christian democratic political groups meant in the rest of Western Europe and later in Latin America.)

Tussell makes a supplementary comment on the journal's limitations that leads on to another point that can fruitfully be made, though not without qualification. He links *Cruz y Raya* to other movements at the time in Spain that he describes as 'los solitarios' (the solitary kind), justifying the label in the following terms:

En primer lugar, porque su acción o su pensamiento, aunque influyera sobre la vida política del país ... no alcanzó la relevancia suficiente, debido al mentado hecho de no haber llegado a ser inspiradores de ningún grupo político; en segundo lugar, porque no viviendo estos personajes en la España periférica (la del nacionalismo vasco o catalán), evidentemente se encontraban más aislados desde el punto de vista espiritual, pues la CEDA ... no llegó nunca a tener un carácter demócrata-cristiano. (207)

(In the first place, because their impact or outlook, despite having an influence on the country's political life, were not sufficiently wide ranging, for the simple reason that they never inspired any political group; second, because since these people did not reside at the edges of national life (i.e. associated with Basque or Catalan nationalism), they were obviously more isolated from the spiritual point of view, since the CEDA never acquired a Christian Democrat character.)

The first point can easily be dealt with since it coincides with a view of the journal that has already been discussed. That is, it is misguided to reproach Bergamín and his journal for failing to inspire a specific political party or program when their intention was to influence the conduct of political life as a whole, promoting attitudes and ideals that went far beyond a narrow *partidismo*. The second part of Tussell's comment is more suggestive, however, even though it takes no account of the changes that were due to be introduced in the summer of 1936. Bergamín was in fact perfectly aware of the dangers that the journal's isolation posed and realized the need to widen its scope so that it could assimilate those regional groups that were basically in sympathy with its outlook. In an interesting text of 1953, reviewing a recently published volume of correspondence between Unamuno and Maragall, Bergamín recalls his plans of 1936, which were frustrated by the Civil War:

Recuerdo que cuando el año 1936 ... quedó suspendida la publicación de mi revista *Cruz y Raya* (aquí sí digo mía porque asumo toda su responsabilidad ahora como entonces), suspensa por motivos de fuerza mayor, motivos de guerra, estaba preparando exactamente aquello mismo que idealmente proyectaban en sus cartas – en las finales de su vida, Maragall – una revista ibérica, donde nuestros tres lenguajes aparecieran juntos: el gallego-portugués, el catalán y el castellano. Una revista íntegramente española, como la proyectada, soñada más bien, desde los primeros años de siglo, por Unamuno y Maragall. ¡Cómo no ha de conmoverme ahora leer esas cartas![68]

(I remember that when in 1936 the publication of my journal *Cruz y Raya* (and here I certainly do say 'my' since now as then I assume all responsibility for it) was suspended for reasons beyond my control, for reasons of war, I was working on exactly the same project that these men – Maragall at the end of his life – were outlining in their correspondence: an Iberian journal in which our three languages, Galician-Portuguese, Catalan, and Castilian, would appear side by side. An integrally Spanish journal, just like the one planned, or dreamed of, rather, by Unamuno and Maragall at the beginning of this century. It is unsurprising that I am so moved by reading those letters now!)

Bergamín clearly saw the need to raise *Cruz y Raya* and the values it stood for out of the rarified isolation of Madrid and to make of it a journal that could attract and harness those parallel energies at work in other parts of the country. Again, this is a sign of what Bergamín's journal *might* have come to mean in Spain – both spiritually and politically – had there existed the possibility of natural development and expansion.[69]

The isolation of *Cruz y Raya* can also partly be explained by the strength of the established Church it sought to defy. Bergamín's spiritual radicalism inspired a vanguard minority that neither had the power to undermine the entrenched conservatism of the Catholic Church in Spain nor the time to effect any substantial change in the way Catholics in general were perceived, especially by left-wing parties. It should be remembered that ever since the proclamation of the Republic, the Church had been seeing satanic adversaries everywhere and so felt justified in closing its ranks and strengthening its own reactionary outlook. Bergamín's voice, therefore, was bound to be a solitary one in an extremely inhospitable Catholic wilderness. Given the fixed image projected by the Church in Spain and the monumental difficulties involved in modifying it in any way, Bergamín was condemned to remain associated in the minds of some people with a type of conduct that he himself rejected and abhorred. This problem is most clearly seen in an incident dating from July 1936 to which I have already obliquely referred. In that month Bergamín was appointed to a tribunal that was to assess candidates for a university lectureship in Spanish literature. His appointment was sharply criticized in the left-wing daily newspaper *El Socialista*, which described Bergamín as 'reactionary.' The point was, as Bergamín himself made clear in a strongly worded reply, that *El Socialista* had made the mistake of automatically equating 'Catholic' with 'reactionary':

Si la calificación de reaccionario puede ser injuria a un republicano de izquierda o a un socialista, no sé por qué no ha de serlo, por la misma razón, aplicada de este modo a un católico. Esto es, según ustedes, porque los católicos españoles 'prácticamente' lo son. No olviden ustedes que esto no es una consecuencia moral ineludible de su catolicismo. Yo creo todo lo contrario. Y lo practico, al actuar políticamente desde su fundación en un partido republicano de izquierda.[70]

(If a left-wing republican or a socialist is offended by being called a reactionary, I see no reason why a Catholic should not feel the same way, and for the same reason, when the word is used to describe him. Your reasoning is that in practical terms Spanish Catholics are, indeed, reactionary. But you should not forget that this is not an unavoidable moral consequence of their Catholicism. My own beliefs are entirely opposed to this. And I have put these beliefs into practice by being politically active in a left-wing republican party ever since it was founded.)

The fact that Bergamín felt compelled to defend himself against the accusation indicates, ultimately, his lack of success between 1933 and 1936 in communicating (to some circles at least) the radical spirit that guided his particular brand of Catholicism. Even after the unequivocal statements he had made in his much-publicized letter to Serrano Plaja, and despite the constant militant and outspoken tone of his writings in *Cruz y Raya*, he still needed to explain publicly that all Catholics should not be herded together and dumped on the far political right:

La religión política en España, corrompida hasta sus raíces espirituales por un costumbrismo supersticioso y politiquero, pudo hacerse prácticamente por algunos, muchísimos, católicos, compatible, como todos sabemos, con la reacción y hasta llegar a la colaboración inmoral, y a veces encubrimiento criminal, de la política más sanguinaria y deshonesta; los católicos que lo denunciamos y combatimos, en reacción contra la reacción, ¿debemos ser llamados honradamente reaccionarios? ...

... ¿Por qué ha de llamarse reaccionario hoy en España al católico que dedica su actividad intelectual desde una revista independiente, como yo lo hago, a difundir y propagar la cultura española entre nosotros y fuera de España, sin eludir en momentos determinados, de grave responsabilidad, su comprensión y hasta simpatía a los movimientos revolucionarios del proletariado, en su ímpetu justo y justiciero: por ejemplo, Asturias, como hizo, 'entonces,' *Cruz y Raya*. Y sin eludir sobre todo, ahora y siempre, en cuanto las circunstancias lo han exigido, la declaración expresa y firme de combatir cualquier intento de fascismo español por considerarlo, eso sí, incompatible con la libertad, con la democracia, con la cultura, y sobre todo, con la religión católica de Cristo.

(Even the deepest spiritual roots of religion in Spain have become corrupted by superficiality, superstition and politicking, and as a result religion, as we all know, has indeed become, for many, a great many Catholics, allied to reaction. It has even stooped to being immorally involved with the most callous and dishonest politics, and has at times sought to cover up that involvement. Is it fair to call Catholics like me reactionary, when we denounce and combat this corruption, as a reaction against that reaction? ...

... Why should the word reactionary be used today in Spain to describe the Catholic who, like me, devotes his intellectual activities from the pages of an independent journal to propagating Spanish culture both within the country and outside it and who, at specific times of grave responsibility, expresses his understanding of and even his sympathy with the revolutionary movements of the working class, inspired by a just and righteous cause: as in the case of Asturias, for example, which is what *Cruz y Raya* did at the time. When the circumstances have demanded, I have never refrained and will never refrain from voicing an unwavering opposition to any attempt to promote a Spanish fascism since I consider it – and I underline this – incompatible with freedom, democracy and culture, and above all with the Catholic religion of Christ.)

Despite all he had done since 1933 to activate his radical views publicly through *Cruz y Raya*, Bergamín was still, on the eve of the Civil War, something of a rare and misunderstood species on the intellectual scene, a victim not only of the dramatic times in which he launched his offensive but also, perhaps, of the very originality and boldness with which he applied himself to that difficult task.

7

'De veras y de burlas':
A Provisional Conclusion

Yo prefiero decir mis veras entre burlas. Es cuestión de estilo.

J.B.

Dudo que en otro pueblo alguno moleste tanto el que se mezclen las burlas con las
veras.   M. DE UNAMUNO

A number of aspects of Bergamín's role in *Cruz y Raya* omitted from the
previous chapter can fruitfully be examined here, both as a postscript to
what has already been said about the journal and as a means of
formulating a provisional conclusion to this study as a whole. The central
issue concerns the degree to which Bergamín and *Cruz y Raya* can
legitimately be seen as one and the same thing. This matter is a
fundamental one because the journal's distinctive appeal as well as its
shortcomings can be viewed as dependent upon the style and personality
of its director. An examination of this point illuminates not only the
energies that simultaneously pushed the journal forward and held it back,
but also the conflicting strengths of Bergamín's work as a whole in the
pre-war period.

Bergamín himself has made what appears to be contradictory statements on the nature of his relationship with *Cruz y Raya*. On the one
hand, he has sometimes insisted that what he calls the journal's
physiognomy was a product of its contributors as a whole.[1] Echoing this
sentiment elsewhere, he has listed the most distinguished of these
contributors and stated boldly: 'inician y consolidan con sus colaboraciones la personalidad de la revista misma' (they initiated and consolidated
with their own contributions the personality of the journal itself).[2] In
other words, he has at times preferred to stress the collective nature of an
enterprise in which his own voice was only one among many. On the
other hand, as I have indicated in the previous chapter, he has on
different occasions referred to '*mi* revista *Cruz y Raya*' (*my* journal *Cruz y
Raya*), acknowledging the extent of his personal responsibility for the
journal 'ahora como entonces' (now as then).[3]

The distance between these two viewpoints is probably less great than might seem to be the case at first sight. *Cruz y Raya* was clearly not a unipersonal publication in the same way that his quarterly *El Pasajero* would later be in Mexico.[4] Javier Tussell is quite right in this respect to emphasize the journal's plurality and the diversity of its opinions when he writes that 'Bergamín no era toda la revista: otros de sus colaboradores no hubieran suscrito, de modo total, sus palabras' (Bergamín was not the entire journal: other contributors would not have subscribed without reservations to his words).[5] Yet, as I have argued, *Cruz y Raya* was from the start largely Bergamín's personal creation: its format, style, and orientation were determined by his personal tastes and by his conception of what the publication could be and should try to be. Throughout its life, the journal depended for its substance and presentation on the initiative he was able to exercise with total freedom: the invitations to contributors, the suggestions on topics they could cover, the choice of foreign texts to be translated, the pointed titles that commentaries carried, and so on. In addition, as Falla and the other founding editors distanced themselves from the journal in 1934 and 1935, Bergamín's own personality and individual ideas tended naturally to come to the fore.[6] This is to say nothing of the assiduousness with which he himself contributed to the journal, both as commentator in the 'Cristal del Tiempo' section and as an essayist and anthologizer.

We might conclude appropriately that while Bergamín was happy to call upon a wide variety of people and opinions to demonstrate that *Cruz y Raya*'s openness was a genuinely held principle, he also took every opportunity to assert his own views on topics that he found personally engaging, as well as of potential interest to his readers. It was not that he used the journal as a personal mouthpiece, but rather that the strength of his convictions coupled with the forcefulness and originality with which he expressed them meant that it became natural to associate *Cruz y Raya* with him and to identify its particular spirit and outlook with his own.

The process whereby *Cruz y Raya* became inseparable from its director proved to be both a boon and a hindrance. On the positive side, Bergamín's combative, paradoxical nature stimulated and provoked people, drawing them – almost against their will, it must have sometimes seemed – towards the curious mixture of culture and politics, serene contemplation and militant protest that he somehow managed to incorporate into each issue. His appeal as an individual became *Cruz y Raya*'s appeal as a whole, and both were felt particularly, as I have already pointed out, by the young generation of writers and intellectuals emerging in the years of the Republic. They responded to Bergamín's stimuli and to his generosity, rising to the challenge that his vigilant unorthodoxy posed. They did not read Bergamín and his journal for easy answers, but rather for insights into how to approach the problems created by the critical times in which they all lived.

Bergamín's style and personality, however, could alienate as well as enchant. On the negative side, his outspoken views and the elegant, involved subtlety of his writing could unnerve and distract readers who in principle might have been prepared to support him. Falla's alarm at the radical edge Bergamín gave *Cruz y Raya* is one obvious example of the counterproductive effect that his boldness and originality could sometimes have. It is revealing, too, that Angel Ossorio, who sympathized wholeheartedly with the ideas that inspired the journal, expressed disappointment at its 'tono conceptista' – presumably a reference to Bergamín's commentaries and essays. Ossorio confided to a friend that *Cruz y Raya* needed 'no sólo quienes escribieran bien, sino los que lo hicieran con claridad' ('not only people who could write well but also people who could write clearly').[7] Evidently there were people like him who felt that the clarity with which the journal's mission had originally been conceived was somehow clouded by the acrobatics and baroque intricacies of Bergamín's style. This, in turn, explains the sense of the charges that critics like Bécarud have laid against Bergamín and the journal, namely that they were excessively intellectual, too bound up with literary refinement and stylistic niceties.

The kind of double-edged response that Bergamín and his journal could elicit is most clearly seen in the literary almanac published in the Ediciones del Arbol in 1935: *El aviso de escarmentados del año que acaba y escarmiento de avisados para el que empieza*. This is worth dwelling on for a number of reasons. First, *El aviso* was in many ways Bergamín's own personal achievement: he instigated and supervised its composition, was responsible for securing contributions and devising its format, and generally channelled a vast amount of creative energy into choosing its texts and illustrations.[8] Understandably, therefore, it bears all the hallmarks of his literary style and temperament. Second, it was the publication of *El aviso* that brought the uneasy relationship between Falla and Bergamín to a critical impasse, underlining the ultimately irreconcilable differences existing between them. Third, it was in *El aviso* – and in the earlier almanac of 1934, *El acabóse* – that Bergamín condensed with great creative flair the fundamental sense of *Cruz y Raya* and of a whole range of personal concerns. The different ways in which these almanacs can be (and were) viewed consequently throws into relief the potential strengths and weaknesses of the journal, its director, and, by extension, the latter's creative style in general.

It is important to make it absolutely clear initially the degree to which the almanacs did indeed represent the highest expression of the spirit that animated *Cruz y Raya*. As Bergamín himself has put it:

El *sí* y *no* de *Cruz y Raya* fueron a su tiempo respuesta y pregunta. Su significado completo: 'hacer cruz y raya,' que es poner fin a algo para volver a empezar de nuevo ('acabóse' y 'aviso' a su vez), era, en una palabra, el de una ruptura.[9]

(The *yes* and the *no* of *Cruz y Raya* were both an answer and a question. Its complete sense is in the phrase *hacer cruz y raya*, which means to put an end to something in order to begin again: an 'ending' and a 'warning' at the same time. In a word, it signified a break.)

Bergamín's concern in *Cruz y Raya* to make a 'fresh start,' to draw his reader's attention to the new awareness he was trying to foster, was succinctly summed up in the titles he gave both almanacs. These titles embodied the sense of the break with the past, the rejection of complacency, and amplified the caution that he hoped to offer his readership: the need to be alert, to combat insensitivity and indifference, and to work towards a renewed commitment to fundamental ethical and Christian ideals.

This notion of renewal, of cyclical renovation, is a central aspect of Bergamín's initiative in producing the almanacs. In a separate and equally revealing commentary he alludes to what he considers to be *Cruz y Raya*'s finest achievement: 'su tomarle el gusto al tiempo pasajero tratando de percibir en él un sabor que es un saber de siglos' (the way it captured the flavour of fleeting time striving to perceive within it a taste laden with the knowledge of centuries).[10] His subsequent remarks clarify the way in which this achievement was complemented in *El acabóse* and *El aviso*:

La expresión poética de ese 'tomarle el gusto' a lo tradicional español nos la dan claramente sus almanaques ... El tiempo ha confirmado sus títulos en su expresa y expresiva significación. El primero se tituló EL ACABOSE. El segundo EL AVISO. Muy diversos de forma y estilo, aparentemente caprichosos, ambos significan igual: lo que se sintetiza en el 'CRUZ Y RAYA para todos' que los subtitula. Para todos y para nadie hubiera dicho Nietzsche. Aviso y escarmiento, acabóse y principio, fueron la razón de ser, que fue pasión de ser, de la revista misma. La continuidad de una vida y una cultura en su renovación permanente. (XI)

(The poetic expression of that 'capturing the flavour' of what is traditionally Spanish can be most clearly seen in the journal's almanacs. The passing of time has confirmed the express and expressive meaning of their titles. The first was called EL ACABOSE. The second, EL AVISO. Although they are very different in their apparently whimsical style and form, their meaning is identical and is compressed in the subtitle that they both carry: 'CRUZ Y RAYA for all.' For all and for none, as Nietzsche would have said. A warning and a lesson, an ending and a beginning: these were the justifications and the causes of the journal itself. The continuity of a life and a culture continually renewed.)

The concepts specified here of continuity and renovation recall the symbol of the tree chosen with such acuity by Bergamín to represent both *Cruz y Raya* and its publishing offshoot. If the tree itself is subject to decay as the time passes and the seasons change, its roots – deep in the past – provide the nourishment that annually restores and the vitality of the entire organism. In the short prologue he wrote to *El acabóse*, Bergamín underlined the obvious parallel between this cyclical rejuvenation and the full trajectory of the life of the Christian: 'Acabóse no cabe mayor que el de la muerte y con ella empieza el cristiano la nueva vida verdadera' (There is no greater ending than death and with it the Christian begins a truly new life) (5). The Christian sense of this *acabóse*, with its implicit moral *aviso*, encouraging the 'fresh start' that the title of *Cruz y Raya* adumbrated, is clarified still further in an additional comment:

Empezamos un año con el *acabóse* del otro, por este principio de todos nuestros *acabóses* juntos: lo que es como un *cortar por lo sano* el tiempo y hacernos *cruz y raya* de nuestra vida. (6)

(We begin a year with the ending of another, through this principle of all our assembled endings: which is like going straight to the root of the trouble of time itself and making a fresh start in our own lives.)

In comparison with *El aviso*, *El acabóse* was a fairly modest compendium of texts. Those that Bergamín and his co-editors chose came chiefly from the Golden Age – Valdivielso, Quevedo, Lope, Fray Luis de Granada, and so on – and were accompanied by others from medieval sources, such as the work of Saint Augustine. They had in common the articulation – albeit in an implicit literary fashion at times – of the moral concerns that informed the entire *Cruz y Raya* enterprise and much of Bergamín's own writing in the twenties and thirties: the belief in the vanity and impermanence of this world, the potential security offered by faith, and the promise of salvation. In *El acabóse*, Bergamín in essence reactivated the spirit of the Baroque period that had produced so many remarkable literary and artistic expressions of this particular view of the world. By following the practice he had established in *Cruz y Raya*, he allowed the most eloquent and creative voices from the past to affirm naturally the spiritual and moral values he was concerned to revitalize in the present.

The procedure adopted in *El aviso* was basically the same, though the project was a much more ambitious one in terms of its size and scope. Again, Bergamín chose not to wag his finger directly at his readers: the almanac was not designed to be a pulpit from which to deliver a solemn, confrontational sermon. Instead, as was the case in general terms in *Cruz y Raya* and in some other areas of Bergamín's own work, the substance of the Christian imperatives that preoccupied him would be communicated implicitly, through artistic creativity and literary excellence. This comes across clearly in the explanation he gave Falla:

En este AVISO mío ... puse, con más empeño que nunca, mi propósito de siempre, de ir penetrando en el ánimo, tan distraído, del lector español, con las palabras más hondas y verdaderas de nuestra fe, sin que, por las *apariencias* y *tramoyas*, como diría Calderón, en que este espectáculo de la vida humana se le ofrece, se aperciba casi de la intención piadosa, compasiva, cristiana que le penetra. Y para ello tomé por el camino más corto: el de la belleza, el de la poesía.[11]

(In this AVISO of mine I followed with greater determination than ever before the purpose I have always had: that of penetrating the mind of the distracted Spanish reader with the deepest and truest words of our faith. And I sought to do this in such a way that, through the tricks and illusions with which the spectacle of life is viewed by that reader, he would almost fail to notice the devout, compassionate, Christian intention that permeates it. And in order to do this, I chose the shortest path: the path of beauty and poetry.)

And by choosing this particular option, Bergamín was able to produce an extraordinary book: impeccably and imaginatively presented, a memorable combination of ethical reflection and aesthetic elegance.

In a review he wrote at the time, Guillermo de Torre described *El aviso* as 'el libro más caprichoso del año' (the most capricious book of the year).[12] His reaction was an understandable once since Bergamín had housed under a single roof such contrasting writers as Heraclitus and Juan Larrea, Lope de Vega and Apollinaire, matching the devotional texts from Spain's Golden Age with surrealist photo-montages by Benjamín Palencia, photographs of Greta Garbo, babies, and smiling Cheshire cats. With typical expertise he was able to harness disparate energies for the sake of a common cause: Unamuno alongside Gómez de la Serna, Neruda alongside *falangistas* like Sánchez Mazas and Santa Marina, recruits from the younger writers of the time like Vivanco, Rosales, and Muñoz Rojas. This was *Cruz y Raya in nuce*: a variety of outlooks and interests held together by Bergamín's subtle supervision. By leading all these talents along the same 'camino de la belleza, de la poesía' (path of beauty and of poetry), he was able to create not an incoherent pot pourri, but an exquisite literary design.

The problem was how to see and appreciate the underlying pattern of this design. In many ways this was the problem that Bergamín posed in much of his own writing of the period: how to perceive the true concerns that were so playfully and elegantly packaged. For a pious reader like Falla, *El aviso* could never be more than an irreverent collage: 'en conjunto, el Almanaque me parece *monstruoso* en el exacto sentido de la palabra' (as a whole, the Almanac strikes me as monstruous, in the exact sense of the word).[13] His interpretation of Bergamín's flamboyance was perhaps typical of the strictly orthodox sensibility that expected Christian truths to be conveyed with the seriousness they conventionally received. But Bergamín was no meek defender of such conventions. By temperament he was incorrigibly playful, impelled by a need to clothe his most deeply felt concerns in a provocative, almost mischievous guise. He knew full well that the confrontation with Falla ultimately revealed a difference in style, and he admitted this candidly when replying to Falla's scandalized criticisms: 'Yo prefiero decir mis veras entre burlas. Es cuestión de estilo' (I prefer to state my truths in jest. It's a question of style).[14] Some of Bergamín's readers would be too distracted by the *burlas* to see the *veras*; others would see that his delightful originality did not undermine or neutralize the seriousness of his beliefs, but made them more challenging, palatable, and accessible. His style may not have been one for every common reader, but it was a style that gave his own writing – as well as *Cruz y Raya* and its almanacs – their distinction and their singular, if perhaps restricted, appeal.

Guillermo de Torre goes on in the review mentioned above to describe *El aviso* as 'un espejo de las diversidades que tironean a su compilador' (a mirror of the different interests that tug at its compiler) and writes:

Sólo viéndolo así podremos explicar rectamente la disparidad, la lejanía polar – y la secreta unidad, muy al fondo – de los textos que llenan sus páginas.

(Only by looking at it in this way can we understand correctly the disparity, the wide-ranging differences – and the hidden unity deep within – of the texts which fill its pages.)

This *secreta unidad*, sensed by Guillermo de Torre and seemingly over-looked by Falla, was a moral and spiritual one, focusing the kinds of preoccupation that Bergamín had grappled with in his own work up to that time. Its overall sense is defined in the epigraph that the almanac carries, chosen by Bergamín from Calderón:

¡Oh monstruo de la fortuna!
¿Dónde vas sin luz ni aviso?
Si el fin es morir, ¿por qué
andas rondando el camino?

Bergamín took it upon himself in *El aviso* – as elsewhere – to provide the enlightenment and the ethical sign-posting that his readers might be in need of. He reformulated the lessons that seventeenth-century Spain had taught concerning the tireless industry of time, the inevitability of death, the call to reflection and reform. Taking the traditional structure of an almanac, he used the seasons, the divisions of the year, to plot man's trajectory through life. Each stage was marked by a quotation taken from some of his favourite writers: 'La vida nueva que en niñez ardía' (Quevedo); 'Loca ambición al aire vago asida' (Lope); 'La juventud robusta y engañada' (Quevedo); '¡Oh flor al hielo! ¡Oh rama al viento leve!' (Lope). The movement described by these lines summarized for Bergamín that shift in man and in nature from exuberance to decay. It was a decline that was continually emphasized beneath the almanac's playful exterior. But it was an emphasis that was pitched in a low key, designed not to harass readers, but to allow them to absorb it naturally as they savoured the literary curiosities and visual delights that the book contained.

When Bergamín answered Falla's charges of frivolity and irresponsibil-ity – of having taken God's name in vain – he gave a frank explanation of how he had sought to convey the serious message contained in *El aviso*:

Yo he quitado del almanaque mi andamiaje después de haberlo armado. Pero a Ud. no puede escapársele su coherencia, su sentido: su honda, *jonda*, razón de ser auténtica. Monstruo, sí lo hay en él: pero 'monstruo en su laberinto.' Es un sueño de la vida y del mundo en que Ud. puede encontrar el *espejo* y el *enigma* con que los cristianos, desde la palabra de San Pablo, nos lo explicamos todo. Pero con el afán constante, que hay en mí siempre, no sé si exagerado, de eludir toda pedantería.[15]

(Having erected the almanac I dismantled my scaffolding. But surely you cannot fail to see its coherence, its meaning: its deep and genuine purpose. There is indeed a monstrous presence within it, but it is of a 'monster in its labyrinth.' It is a dream of the life and the world that you can find in the *mirror* and the *enigma* with which we Christians, ever since St Paul, have understood everything. But with the constant concern that I have always had, perhaps to an excessive degree, to avoid all trace of pedantry.)

This can be interpreted not simply as an account of his intentions and procedures in *El aviso*, but also as a comment on his own literary outlook as a whole, framing the '*cuestión de estilo*' on which the reader's response to the almanac of 1935, to *Cruz y Raya*, and to the writer's work itself largely depends. From Falla's point of view, the comment suggests Bergamín's shortcomings: the ability to mislead, confuse, or alarm his readers unintentionally, the tendency to place too much emphasis on playful ingenuity and to become too enthralled with the originality of his own finely wrought literary artefacts. Viewed in a different perspective, these features become transformed into his distinctive strengths: his lack of pedantry, his blending of tradition and originality, his capacity to rejuvenate even the most well-worn ideas, his stylish and challenging subtlety, his concealed depth.

*   *   *

Bergamín's natural dominance in *Cruz y Raya* and the effects produced by the publication of *El aviso* demonstrate the overall energies that operated in his work during this period. The discussion above draws attention to those twin impulses – critical vigilance and restless non-conformity – that are discernible in his literary career from its beginnings. Playing complementary roles throughout the pre-war years, they came to determine a basic style and outlook giving an underlying unity to a corpus of writing that must have appeared fragmented and disjointed. The alertness Bergamín showed as a young man gave him an insatiable appetite for knowledge, an absorbing interest in everything he came into contact with: language, literature, ideas, people, institutions. His curiosity was a discerning one, however, and led him to question critically all the data he amassed. This can be seen in his general reluctance to accept passively anything that was already given or to conform to any established norm, whatever the nature or scale of that norm might be.

The effect of this was to encourage what can be termed the 'recreative' side of his work. His theatre, for example, shows how this overall principle worked. He was fascinated by the situations and characters devised by other writers, but his procedure was to locate and realize a potential that they had left untapped. His originality, therefore, lay in his 're-writing' or 'reinvention' of those characters and situations, constructing highly personal schemes out of material that had already been quarried. His approach to language in general traced a similar pattern, revealing what amounted to an allergy to established meanings, a compulsive need to go beyond dictionary definitions, and to look at any fixed formula from a fresh critical and creative standpoint. In handling words and phrases, then, Bergamín was constantly experimenting with the possibilities they offered for the generation of new meaning. This strategy enabled him to forge a completely personal idiolect through which he patented the versions and subversions of language that he devised. His rejection of univalent meanings sustained what I have described as his *conceptista* mentality: an inquisitive attitude that determined the shape and form that his ideas assumed.

From this creative non-conformity, Bergamín derived his independence. He preferred always to steer his own course, refusing to become constrained by any narrow allegiance, even though his own sympathies often coincided with particular political parties or literary and religious factions. While he lent his support to these groups when a constructive purpose could be served, he usually went his own way, concerned only, in the final analysis, with his sense of loyalty to his own convictions. This intransigent individuality made him, even before the Civil War, an unclassifiable element on the intellectual scene – a unique kind of stylist and thinker. Whatever the nature of the comparisons that his work invites, it is unable to do justice to this radical singularity.

Bergamín's temperament set him apart even from those groups and trends with which he appeared to be closely associated in the twenties and thirties. His writing could be productively suggestive but it could also often be volatile and uncooperative. It betrayed an outlook that was partly defined in the heavily loaded epigraph from Rimbaud that *Tres escenas en ángulo recto* carried: 'Je m'évade? Je m'explique.' The phrase was a warning, albeit an oblique one, that the frequent elusiveness of Bergamín's texts was part of a consciously conceived plan. It was precisely in that elusiveness that his 'explanations' were given and need now to be sought. His approach was founded on a passionate aversion to confessionalism, a feeling he summed up in *La cabeza a pájaros* when he wrote: 'Si no declaro mi fe ante las gentes – ante ciertas gentes – no es por respeto humano, sino por respeto divino' (If I do not declare my faith before people – before certain people – it is not out of human respect but out of divine respect) (108). This same idea reappeared in the explanation he gave to Falla of the playfully elusive appearance he had given *El aviso*: 'Yo no soy de los que gustan de espectáculos de confesionalismo repugnante, en ningún sentido' (I am in no way the kind of person who enjoys spectacles of repulsive confessionalism).[16]

As a consequence of this feeling, Bergamín's creative strategy was to opt for the enigma, the veiled truth, the subtle insinuation. It ties in exactly with what he said to Falla concerning 'el *espejo* y el *enigma* con que los cristianos ... nos lo explicamos todo.' Bergamín has often quoted a declaration he once heard made by a character in a film: 'Prefiero pegarme un tiro que dar una explicación' ('I prefer to blow my brains out rather than give an explanation'). This would certainly make an appropriate epigraph for much of his work in this period where the explicit spelling-out of what he was intent on conveying was often avoided. In one sense, this reluctance to say too much too openly reflects the *pudor* that Dámaso Alonso saw as characteristic of the writing of the twenties: the tendency to conceal personal feeling and commitment beneath the objective perfection of the purely intellectual creation. But in another sense, it simply explains a temperamental need in Bergamín: his irony was protective, his subtlety made him less vulnerable. 'Al que media palabra basta,' he once wrote, 'una palabra sobra' (If half a word is enough, a whole word is too much).[17]

Bergamín tended, therefore, to take refuge behind this *media palabra*, not simply in the quantitative sense of condensation or fragmentation, but in the qualitative sense of enigmatic evasiveness. In the twenties and thirties he can be viewed as adopting a series of poses or donning a variety of masks. Although the effect of these was usually to eliminate explicitness from his writing and to project an image of a frivolous *dilettante*, they were still able to guarantee – as Unamuno, Salinas and others realized – a high degree of sincerity and serious personal commitment in his work. When Oscar Wilde wrote 'Man is least himself when he talks in his own person. Give him a mask and he will tell the truth,'[18] he formulated a typically witty contradiction that gives an insight into Bergamín's outlook. In his case, the act of self-concealment, of evasion, becomes – paradoxically – the most authentic means of self-revelation. In the terms posited by a famous phrase from Nietzsche that Bergamín himself has often alluded to – 'la mejor máscara es el rostro' – it is as if the mask becomes transparent, thereby revealing the exact features of the face it purports to hide. It is pertinent to recall that the generic title suggested by Manuel Abril for Bergamín's early theatre was 'Máscara de cristal.'[19] Those early plays gave a clear illustration of how Bergamín put those beliefs into practice. The *Arlequín*, for example, who appears in *Tres escenas en ángulo recto*, is described as *camouflage* (14). It is the *antifaz* he wears – rather than the conventional mask – that *camouflages* the truths conveyed in the play, obliging the reader to be constantly on the alert in order not to miss the issues being examined in such an oblique way. In this connection, it is worth recalling a suggestive aphorism from *El cohete y la estrella*: 'La careta tapa la verdad con una mentira; el antifaz la disimula, incitándonos a descubrirla. La careta es una mala sustitución; el antifaz, un estimulante' (60).

The *'verdad'* that Bergamín was loath to express in too direct or confessional a way was linked to the great imponderables of life and death to which his restlessness as a thinker inevitably led him. At the root of much of his writing lay a struggle with faith, a search for illumination from both within and without. His dissatisfaction with the answers conventionally preferred in this area stemmed from his non-conformity and produced the characteristic *agonismo* of his religious outlook. It also accounted for his condemnation of a Church that in its corrupt institutionalized form seemed little concerned with these fundamental mysteries. As an antidote to that indifference, Bergamín's own work would constantly explore these concerns, though the seriousness of the quest would often be refracted through his temperament: broken down into a mocking playfulness, rendered in poetry rather than in dogma. Or as Luis Felipe Vivanco aptly put it: 'Una cosa es decir cosas importantes y otra darle importancia a lo que se dice' (It is one thing to say something important and quite another to give importance to what one says).[20] All this leads back to the double-edged response that *El aviso* had provoked. While its underlying seriousness would be clear to the reader who could appreciate the 'imaginación estupenda' – to return to Pérez Minik's phrase – with which it had been compiled, for certain others, like Falla, only its exterior pose would be perceived. And for them the almanac would always be an arbitrary and irreverent collection of texts, a creative dead end.

If the critic had to choose a single item or character from Bergamín's work that seemed to sum up his outlook as a writer in this period, he might well take the *mirlo* from *Los filólogos*. It appears in the play as closely associated with the author himself, or at least with a particular modality of his voice. In the opening scene, it makes the following statement to the audience:

El que esto escribió me quiere mucho, porque cuando era niño, en los parques, yo fui su mejor amigo, y hasta su negro preceptorcillo juguetón. (12)

(The person who wrote this is very fond of me because when he was a child, in the parks, I was his best friend, even his playful little black teacher.)

This suggests that the *mirlo* and the attitudes it represents in the play inspired that part of Bergamín that always posed the uncomfortable, impertinent, searching question. It can be seen as embodying that aspect of his personality that ridiculed – with exquisite but sometimes vicious irony – the pretentiousness and complacency of the ideas, people, and institutions with which it came into contact. The *mirlo*'s voice is like the solitary voice of that rebellious, outspoken, indomitable, playful, and deadly serious part of Bergamín that, indifferent to the hostility it often aroused, appeared constantly in his writings. Although this voice is especially noticeable in the twenties, it has in a sense accompanied the writer throughout his career. Its most recent reincarnation was the *duendecito burlón* whose indiscretions Bergamín faithfully transcribed in his polemical articles of the mid-seventies in *Sábado Gráfico*.

Bergamín's use of this voice has had an ambivalent effect. For those readers in the pre-war period who intuitively shared his misgivings, his readiness to confront even the most sacrosanct ideas and institutions and to taunt them with his wit and intellectual agility was a sign of his courage and integrity, of a healthy and productive non-conformity. For those opposed or indifferent to his concerns, his temperament must at times have seemed to be an aberration. In their case, the elegance and humour with which he often expressed his beliefs – even those to which he was most deeply committed – must have muffled their potential resonance. The following exchange in *Los filólogos* between the *Maestro Inefable* and the *Coro de Monos* suggests that Bergamín himself was not unaware of the risks he was running by courting this playfully iconoclastic image:

MAESTRO
Yo temo más al mirlo, porque es un cínico capaz de cualquier cosa con tal de ponernos en ridículo.

CORO
No lo creas. El mirlo, como se burla de todo, ha perdido mucha autoridad. (65)

(MASTER
I fear the blackbird most because he's a cynic capable of anything as long as we're made to look ridiculous.
CHORUS
Don't be too sure. Since the blackbird makes fun of everything, he's lost a good deal of authority.)

The analogy need not be taken too far, since it cannot stand as an absolute definition of Bergamín and his many facets; but it does at least draw attention to the dangers inherent in this creative dependence on the *burla* as a means of conveying the truths that concerned him. The suggestion in *Los filólogos* is simply that this tendency to give opinions a light-hearted veneer can have the effect of corroding – in the minds of his unconvinced readers – the authority they might otherwise have claimed. On the reader's ability to relate to or to distinguish between a flippant arabesque and a serious reflection depended in many ways the reputation that Bergamín acquired in the years under review.

*   *   *

This study has covered only a part of a long, eventful, and productive literary career. Within the limits that it has set, I hope it has been able to suggest that no assessment of the pre-war period can afford to overlook Bergamín's contributions to it as writer, critic, and activist. The point at which I have called a halt to these investigations into his work – the outbreak of Civil War – does not mark a break or decline in his prestige and inventiveness; quite the contrary. The year 1936 is simply a convenient resting place at which to consider the kind of overall momentum that he had acquired in peacetime and in Spain, and to assess his achievements in the first fifteen years or so during which he practised his chosen profession. In the turbulent years immediately prior to the Civil War, Bergamín reached maturity, adapting simultaneously to the external pressures of the times and to the evolving internal imperatives of his own attitudes and expectations. By 1936, he had begun to shed the less useful aspects of his style, become more direct and authoritative, making fuller use of the weight that his voice had come to carry as a commentator on the literary and cultural scene, as an observer of political events, as an agent of reform and renovation, and as a creative force in his own right. He was perfectly prepared by that time for the leading role he was to play in the Civil War as a spokesman for the kinds of cultural and political values that the Republic had tried to promote. This would be a climax to the conspicuous promise he had shown in the twenties and early thirties, a promise that continued to sustain his activities in Mexico in the forties before it was tempered by the realities of exile and isolation. The nature of his experiences as a *peregrino español en América* – to take the subtitle of his journal *El Pasajero* – and as a *peregrino en su patria*, as he later preferred to define himself, remain to be examined in other studies. In identifying the mark they left on his work, future critics will doubtless discover new emphases in his outlook and draw different conclusions.

Notes

INTRODUCTION

1 See Landsberg's prologue to Bergamín's *Ewige Spanien. (Don Tancredo und Don Quijote)* (Lausanne 1940), 3. The Spanish text of this prologue was published in *El Nacional* (Caracas), 28 September 1947, 9, on the occasion of Bergamín's departure from Caracas to Montevideo.

2 Francisco J. Laporta, 'Los intelectuales y la República,' *Historia 16* (Madrid) 6, 60 (April 1981): 86–93, at 92

3 A typical example would be Jorge A. Marfil, 'José Bergamín, una inteligencia inclasificable,' *El Viejo Topo* (Madrid), March 1978, 23–7.

4 See my 'José Bergamín: ilustración y defensa de la frivolidad,' *Cuadernos Hispanoamericanos* 342 (December 1978): 603–13.

5 Examples of this tendency would be Elías Díaz, *Pensamiento español 1939–1973* (Madrid 1974), 45, and José Carlos Mainer, *La edad de plata*, 1st ed. (Barcelona 1975), 319–20.

CHAPTER 1

1 See Claude Aveline's 'Présentation de José Bergamín,' which serves as an introduction to Bergamín's *Aphorismes* (Avignon 1959), 9.

2 He was a prominent member of the Real Academia de Jurisprudencia and often spoke at the Madrid Ateneo. As Minister of Education in 1914, he was responsible for having Unamuno removed from the rectorship of the University of Salmanca, though a reconciliation was later effected between the two, thanks to the intervention of the minister's son.

3 Aveline, 'Présentation ... ,' 9

4 A surprising number of critics and publishers have wrongly given Bergamín's

date of birth as 1894 or 1897. José was the only child not to be born in Málaga, though this did not stop him sharing their Andalusian allegiances. In many ways, Bergamín's work embodies the same kind of local strength as that of his more eminent companions of the twenties.

5 Among his neighbours in the square were the novelist Palacio Valdés and, of his own age, Antonio Marichalar, who would become his constant companion. Bergamín evokes some of his childhood experiences in this apartment in his introduction to *Caballito del diablo* (Buenos Aires 1942), 7–15.

6 This document, originally written for the benefit of one of his grandchildren, was made available to me by Bergamín himself.

7 'Ahora que me acuerdo. (Fragmentos del capítulo I del libro *Recuerdos de esqueleto*),' *Entregas de la Licorne* (Montevideo) 1 and 2 (November 1953): 51–69, at 63–4. Elsewhere Bergamín has underlined the literary sense of the debt he owed to those maids of his childhood: 'Aprendí a escribir oyendo hablar a los analfabetos, rodeado de una muchedumbre numerosa procedente de todas las regiones de España, porque los niños andaluces comían en la cocina. Aquellas muchachas contaban chismes, infundios, leyendas de sus aldeas en un lenguaje poético, que constituía mi dialecto literario, que decía Unamuno, siempre dificilísimo de entender de los doctos profesores,' in an interview with Carlos Gurméndez, 'La irreductible personalidad de José Bergamín,' *El País* (Madrid), *suplemento* 14 November 1982, 12–14, at 13.

8 I quote from the autobiographical sketch referred to in note 6.

9 In *El caballo griego*, Altolaguirre's largely unpublished autobiography, quoted by M. Smerdou Altolaguirre in the introduction to her critical edition of Altolaguirre's *Las islas invitadas* (Madrid 1972), 10.

10 Autobiographical sketch (see notes 6 and 8)

11 From an interview dating from 1977, the text of which is unpublished. I am grateful to Bergamín for having lent me a copy of this document and for giving me his authorization to quote from it.

12 Bergamín alludes to his early interest in anarchist writings in 'Por nada del mundo. (Anarquismo y Catolicismo),' written during the Civil War and collected in *Detrás de la cruz. Terrorismo y persecución religiosa en España* (Mexico 1941), 59–90. There he argues that during the Civil War anarchists and Christians shared fundamental beliefs and were in effect fighting for the same cause.

13 Bergamín appears alongside the other 'amigos de primera hora' in José Gutiérrez Solana's famous portrait, now in the Museo de Arte Contemporáneo in Madrid.

14 The *Hombres Jueves*, so named because of the day on which they met, are mentioned by Juan Chabás in his *Literatura española contemporánea (1898–1950)* (Havana 1952), 582.

15 The expertise of Martínez Sierra was enlisted to attempt the staging of some of Bergamín's dramatic works dating from the early twenties. The plays were so outlandish, however, and presented such complex technical problems that Martínez Sierra gave up in despair and the enterprise was abandoned.
16 Alberti, *La arboleda perdida* (Barcelona 1975), 256. Full details of Bergamín's long and stormy association with Jiménez are given in my forthcoming book *Perfume and Poison: A Study of the Relationship between José Bergamín and Juan Ramón Jiménez* (Cassel 1985).
17 Bergamín himself has admitted that he owed his initiation into Góngora's work to Alfonso Reyes. See his 'Alfonso Reyes, maestro en letras humanas y divinas,' *Cultura* (San Salvador) 9 (May–June 1956): 95–8, especially 95.
18 According to the chronology of Jiménez's *caricaturas* established by Ricardo Gullón in his edition of *Españoles de tres mundos* (Madrid 1969), the portrait of Bergamín was one of the earliest to be published. It appeared in *España* (Madrid), 5 January 1924.
19 By Antonio Marichalar in the journal *Intentions* (Paris) (April–May 1924): 23–4. The other writers represented were Dámaso Alonso, Rogelio Buendía, Juan Chabás, Gerardo Diego, Antonio Espina, Guillén, García Lorca, Marichalar, Quesada, Salazar, Salinas, and Fernando Vela. A variety of translators participated: Marcelle Auclair, Jean Cassou, Valéry Larbaud, and others. Extracts from *El cohete y la estrella* were reproduced in translation by Mathilde Pomès (pp. 14–18).
20 Since Bergamín never actually lived or stayed at the Residencia, his connections with it have rarely been alluded to. He in fact attended all the cultural events that took place there, and with his friend Marichalar was responsible for suggesting to Jiménez Fraud the names of contemporary French writers who could be invited to give talks there.
21 Consider, for example, the early date of Bergamín's commentary on surrealism: 'Nominalismo supra-realista,' *Alfar* (La Coruña), 50 (May 1925): 3. The article was inspired, significantly, by the talk that Louis Aragon gave on the subject at the Residencia de Estudiantes. Bergamín's essay on Gil Vicente – 'El arte católico dramático de Gil Vicente,' *Criterio* (Buenos Aires) 60 (April 1929): 531–3 – is, to my knowledge, the earliest critical attempt to reassess the qualities of this forgotten poet and dramatist. Later, as editor of *Cruz y Raya*, Bergamín invited Dámaso Alonso to edit a complete collection of Gil Vicente's lyric poetry written in Spanish.
22 Alberti writes in his memoirs: 'Nadie como Pepe comenzaba a escribir con más fervoroso entusiasmo de la poesía española, convirtiéndose a la larga en el mejor comentarista de la nuestra, ya casi perfilada por aquellos años,' *La arboleda perdida*, 203.
23 Full details of Bergamín's role in the Góngora celebrations can be found in

Gerardo Diego's 'Crónica del centenario gongorino,' *Lola (amiga y suplemento de 'Carmen')* (Gijon/Santander) 1 and 2 (December 1927 and January 1928), n.p.

24 The meeting was arranged by J.B. Trend, the distinguished British Hispanist who, through his friendship with people like Jiménez Fraud, Falla, and J.R. Jiménez, had met nearly all the major writers of the twenties, including Bergamín. In the library of the University of Cambridge, where Trend taught Spanish for many years, there is preserved a curious testimony of this meeting in 1927: a copy of Bergamín's *Enemigo que huye*, published in that year, dedicated to Eliot. Presumably Eliot, who could not read Spanish, gave the book to Trend who, in turn, deposited it for safekeeping in the university library.

25 Bergamín recorded his impressions of the Soviet Union in an interesting article 'Rusia, capital,' *La Gaceta Literaria* (Madrid) 46 (15 November 1928). I have described the literary significance of one particular encounter he had in Norway in my 'Rafael Alberti, José Bergamín y la Eva Gúndersen de *Sobre los ángeles*,' *Nueva Estafeta* (Madrid) 15 (February 1980): 60–70.

26 In the interview with Carlos Gurméndez, p. 13

27 Ibid., 14

28 For full details concerning Bergamín and *Cruz y Raya*, see chapter 6.

29 The articles published in *Cruz y Raya* are discussed in chapter 6, but see also '¡Adelante con los faroles! o los aficionados al fascismo,' *Luz* (Madrid), 31 October 1933, and 'Los enemigos de la República y ¡otro gallo nos cantará!' *Luz*, 25 November 1933.

30 The embassy did in fact already have an official attaché at that time in the person of Max Aub. Bergamín's role was that of an 'agregado cultural libre,' which meant that he exercised his responsibilities according to his own initiative.

31 Bergamín's emotional depiction of the plight of the Spanish people during the Civil War had a notable effect on many French intellectuals, a good number of whom came to support the Republican cause as a result. In a letter of 9 November 1936 to his friend J.A. Lesourd, Roman Rolland, for example, wrote: 'J'ai reçu – entre autres – la visite d'un des plus grands écrivains catholiques espagnols: José Bergamín – qui venait de Madrid et qui y est retourné. Il s'est donné tout entier, ainsi que la plupart des meilleurs intellectuels, à la cause du Frente Popular. Il me parlait, avec une emotion enflammée, de la révélation qui lui avait été la découverte du peuple d'Espagne, et son admiration et de son amour pour lui, de sa honte et de ses remords de l'avoir si longtemps méconnu, de sa volonté de le servir jusqu'à la mort.'

32 See, for example, Bergamín's denunciatory essays 'La cruzada y el desquite' and 'Carta entreabierta,' both collected in *Detrás de la cruz*, 11–58 and 141–58.

Bergamín is also mentioned in K. Deschner, *Med Gud og Fascisterne* (Oslo 1971), especially in chapter 2, 'Vatikanet og den Spanske Bogerkrig,' 51–88.

33 Bergamín describes his trip to North America in 'De mi viaje a los Estados Unidos,' *La Voz de Madrid* (Paris) 1 (18 July 1938): 8.

34 The congress, along with Bergamín's role in it, is examined and documented in detail in the three-volume work that carries the general title *II Congreso Internacional de Escritores Antifascistas (1937)* (Barcelona 1978–79): vol. I, *Inteligencia y guerra civil española* by Luis Mario Schneider (1978); vol. II, *Pensamiento literario y compromiso antifascista de la inteligencia española republicana* by Manuel Aznar Soler (1978); vol. III, *Ponencias, documentos y testimonios*, edited jointly by Aznar Soler and Schneider (1979).

35 The Junta de Cultura Española was actually founded in Paris in March 1939. Bergamín later shared the presidency with José Carner and Juan Larrea. It seems that soon after they began to function in Mexico, both the Junta and the journal *España Peregrina* ran into problems that were not only financial, but also stemmed from personal differences between Bergamín and Juan Larrea. See P.W. Fagen, *Exiles and Citizens. Spanish Republicans in Mexico* (Austin 1973), 89–90, and Larrea's epilogue to the facsimile reprint of *España Peregrina* (Mexico 1977), 75–86. Among the titles Bergamín published in the Editorial Séneca in 1940 were Antonio Machado's *Obras completas*, Lorca's *Poeta en Nueva York*, and Vallejo's *España, aparta de mí este cáliz*.

36 Bergamín was denounced as a Trotskyite agent, for example, by Diego Rivera at an official enquiry.

37 Bergamín refers explicitly to his disappointment in 1945 and sums up what must have been the feelings of many Spanish exiles at the time in the important article 'Prólogo – epílogo – apostillas a *La niña guerrillera*,' *Retablillo Español* (Montevideo) 1 (January 1954): 1–4.

38 One of Bergamín's unusual procedures as a teacher was to award all students full marks in examinations (which he only agreed to hold under pressure from the university authorities), regardless of their ability to answer the questions. The circumstances of his departure from Caracas are described in a famous article '¡Goodbye Míster Ciruela!' *El Nacional* (Caracas), 23 September 1947, 4.

39 In the interview with Carlos Gurméndez, 14

40 In an interview with Guy Suarès, Bergamín recalls his feelings in exile in the early fifties: 'j'ai recontré mon ami Rafael Alberti, comme moi en exil. Je me rappelle notre promenade aux alentours de la Huchette et ma soudaine question, "Que faisons-nous içi, Rafael? Regardons-nous. Nous vieillissons. Je me refuse à devenir un fantôme vivant et à crever loin de la terre natale. Telle qu'elle est, l'Espagne a besoin de nous. Nous devons lui façonner un nouveau visage et nous n'avons pas le droit d'attendre que 'cela change' pour

commencer.'" ('Un entretien avec José Bergamín. Espoirs et désillusion d'un intellectuel espagnol,' *Le Monde* [Paris], 30 November 1963).

41 In the interview with Carlos Gurméndez, 14

42 The text of the lecture was published in *Indice de Artes y Letras* (Madrid) 15, 147 (March 1961): 5-7.

43 Many details surrounding this episode remain to be clarified. The text of the manifesto, of the letters that passed between Bergamín and Fraga, and of the individual protest on Bergamín's behalf written by Dionisio Ridruejo were all published in a *Boletín Informativo del Centro de Documentación y de Estudios* (Paris) 19 (November 1963), entitled 'Los intelectuales y la represión de las huelgas de Asturias.'

44 The interviewer on these programs was André Champ. During these years, Bergamín deliberately cultivated the image of 'phantom,' and was amused when the French official reviewing his identity card – ostensibly the only document attesting to his existence at that time – defined his nationality as 'à déterminer.' See also, in similar vein, the text of the interview with B. Porcel, 'José Bergamín, fantasmagórico,' *Destino* (Barcelona), 3 January 1970.

45 This was the result of a 'convocatoria' organized in 1977 by *Litoral* to celebrate both the tenth anniversay of the journal's reappearance and the fiftieth anniversary of the Generation of 1927. A total of 44 critics were consulted of whom 30 voted for Bergamín. The full texts of their remarks on his literary career were collected in a pamphlet entitled *Resultado de una convocatoria*, which was published together with Bergamín's *Por debajo del sueño. Antología poética* (Málaga 1979).

46 The homage was organized by José Monleón as part of the cycle *Análisis del teatro español*. The two works by Bergamín that were covered were *Medea la encantadora* and *Melusina y el espejo*.

47 See, in relation to this event, Bel Carrasco, 'Presentación de *Al fin y al cabo* y *Poesías casi completas* de José Bergamín,' *El País*, 22 February 1981.

48 His anti-monarchical feelings are condensed in his polemical pamphlet entitled *La confusión reinante* (Madrid 1978).

49 The circumstances in which the Cervantes Prize was awarded in 1982 – ironically to Bergamín's protegé from the days of *Cruz y Raya*, Luis Rosales – provoked a number of outraged responses in the Madrid press. A typical example of the political interpretation of the incident is Manuel Arroyo-Stephens, 'El Cervantes como premio a la conducta,' *Diario 16* (Madrid), 2 November 1982.

50 Published in *Punto y Hora* (San Sebastian) 281 (15–22 October 1982): 12

CHAPTER 2

1 *Revista de Occidente*, First Series III, 7 (January 1924): 127

2 In an unpublished letter to Unamuno dated 15 February 1924, for example, Bergamín wrote: 'He tenido durante esos primeros días de la publicación de mi librito una penosa impresión de aislamiento, de insensibilidad alrededor mío, cuando no de hostilidad o interpretaciones torcidas.'

3 *Nuevo Mundo*, 7 March 1924. The text of the review has been included in successive editions of Unamuno's *Libros y autores contemporáneos*.

4 The copy of *El cohete y la estrella* that Bergamín gave to Unamuno is conserved in the Casa Rectoral at the University of Salamanca. In it, the aphorisms that Unamuno discusses in his review are marked with a pencil. In the letter mentioned in note 2, Bergamín, referring to Unamuno's declared intention of reviewing his book, wrote: 'Me ha dado una gran alegría leer su carta. Si Vd. supiera cómo *la necesitaba*, me perdonaría mi impaciencia ... Entretanto mi humildísimo librito – vivido en el secreto íntimo y universal del pobre pensamiento mío – ha encontrado un eco en Vd., dándome la mejor alegría ... ' The italics are Bergamín's.

5 Jiménez, 'Historias de España y México. Carta obligada a mí mismo,' *Letras de México* 4, 20 (1 August 1944): 7. The reader should bear in mind that Jiménez's phrase contains a good dose of malice.

6 See Salinas's review of *La cabeza a pájaros*, 'Los aforismos de José Bergamín,' *Indice Literario* 3, 5 (May 1934): 93–8, at 95. Salinas returns to this idea of the 'desintegración' of discursive prose in an essay entitled 'El signo de la literatura española del siglo xx,' originally published in 1940 and included in his *Literatura española siglo xx* (Madrid 1972), 34–45.

7 With regard to Bergamín's elders, the examples are too well known to require illustration here. In connection with his contemporaries, see B. Jarnés, *Ejercicios* (Madrid 1927); E. Giménez Caballero, *Julepe de menta* (Madrid 1927); A. Salazar, 'Bocetos: Jeroglífico y arabesco,' *Indice* 3 (1921), xi–xii; G. Diego, 'Mínimas estéticas,' *Meseta* (Valladolid) 1 (January 1928): 5. The subject of the fragmentation in Spanish prose in the twenties is examined by Anthony Leo Geist, 'Estética de lo pequeño' in *La poética de la generación del 27 y las revistas literarias: de la vanguardia al compromiso (1918–1936)* (Barcelona 1980), 142–5.

8 *El cohete y la estrella*, 21. This particular aphorism is an echo of Pascal's famous definition of man as a 'thinking reed.' All subsequent references to this work and to *La cabeza a pájaros* are taken from *Caballito del diablo* (Buenos Aires 1942), which is a republication of both, together with *Caracteres* (1927). Page numbers are indicated parenthetically. In the case of certain aphorisms omitted from this second edition, I have used the parenthetical reference CE I to indicate that I am quoting from the first edition of 1923.

9 In the past critics have referred to most of the names mentioned as possible 'sources' of Bergamín's aphorisms, though the comparisons and parallels have never been examined in any detail. Angel Valbuena Prat, for example, alludes

to the presence of Pascal in *El cohete y la estrella* in his *Historia de la literatura española*, 3 vols (Barcelona 1963), III, 705. Gonzalo Sobejano suggests an affinity with Nietzsche in his *Nietzsche en España* (Madrid 1967), 497. Luis Felipe Vivanco finds traces of both Cocteau and Nietzsche in Bergamín's aphorisms, 'El aforismo y la creación poético-intelectual de José Bergamín,' in G. Díaz-Plaja, ed., *Historia general de las literaturas hispánicas*, 6 vols (Barcelona 1968), VI, 599–609. In the introduction to his otherwise unilluminating critical edition of *El cohete y la estrella* and *La cabeza a pájaros* (Madrid 1981), José Esteban makes the point that 'es a Ramón Gómez de la Serna al que en alguna ocasión [Bergamín] llamó su maestro aforístico,' 26. Critical allusions to the similarity between the styles of Bergamín and Gracián will be dealt with later.

10 For the impact of Pascal on the young Bergamín, see the latter's confession in an unpublished and undated letter (probably of 1923) to Unamuno: '¡Pascal y Renan! Al primero – le diré en confesión – lo llevo sobre mi alma desde la adolescencia, y lo llevaré toda mi vida – y hasta, creo, que pensaré en él cuando vaya a morirme.' It may also be of interest to know that according to Antonio Marichalar, there was a striking resemblance between the young Bergamín and Domat's portrait of Pascal. See his 'Introduction,' *Intentions* 23–24 (April–May 1924): 8–10, at 9.

11 Pascal, *Pensées*, 133. All quotations are taken from the Garnier edition (Paris 1964). Page numbers of subsequent references will be indicated in parentheses.

12 Bergamín's ideas on the Devil are developed at length in his essay 'La importancia del demonio,' first published in *Cruz y Raya* 5 (August 1933): 7–51.

13 In the review referred to in note 1

14 Full details of Bergamín's separation from Jiménez are given in my *Perfume and Poison* ...

15 See note 1

16 José Esteban's edition of *El cohete y la estrella*, referred to in note 9, is inexplicably based on the edition of 1942 rather than the first of 1923. He consequently makes no attempt to account for the disappearance of this section of aphorisms.

17 Since this information is not provided by Esteban in his edition of the book, it is useful to point out here that the following series of aphorisms are included, though sometimes with modifications and omissions: 'Aforística inactual,' *Alfar* 40 (May 1924): 3; 'Transparencia y reflejo,' *Mediodía* (Seville) 5 (October 1926): 1–3; 'Molino de razón,' *Verso y Prosa* (Murcia) 1 (January 1927): n.p.; 'Veleta de locura,' *Verso y Prosa* 2 (February 1927): n.p.; 'Martirio de San Sebastián,' *Verso y Prosa* 9 (September 1927): n.p.; 'Carmen: enigma y soledad,' *Carmen* 2 (January 1928); 'El grito en el cielo,' *Gallo* (Granada) 1 (February 1928):

7–8; 'Hermes, encadenado,' *Mediodía* 9 (January 1928): 4–6; 'Por debajo de la música,' *Mediodía* 11 (March 1928): 9–10.

18 Pérez Ferrero's untitled review was published in *El Heraldo de Madrid*, 14 June 1934, 6. G. de Torre's review entitled 'Del aforismo al ensayo' appeared in *Luz*, 6 July 1934, 8. For the details of Salinas's review, see note 6.

19 Maravall's review, entitled 'Pasión y vida de José Bergamín,' was published in *Literatura* (Madrid) 4 (July–August 1934): 127–8. Sijé's review, under the title 'Péndulo y carbonería,' appeared in the first number of *El Gallo Crisis* (Orihuela), Corpus de 1934, 31–2.

20 First published in *Cruz y Raya* 3 (June 1933): 61–94.

21 In the review referred to in note 6

22 In the review referred to in note 18

23 A typical example would be G. Torrente Ballester: 'Heredó (Bergamín) de Unamuno el gusto por desentrañar las palabras, añadiendo de su cosecha el amor a las expresiones populares, igualmente desentrañadas, interpretadas … Su elección de Unamuno como más cercano guía obedece tanto al gusto por la contradicción, por la paradoja, por el pensamiento en lucha consigo mismo, como a la pasión española,' *Literatura española contemporánea* (Madrid 1964): 303–4.

24 'The Picture of Dorian Gray,' in *Plays, Prose Writings and Poems*, edited by Isobel Murray (London 1975), 126. Other references to Wilde's writings are taken from this edition with page numbers indicated in parentheses.

25 It is uncertain whether or not Bergamín knew enough English at the time to appreciate fully the subtleties of Wilde's style, though there were certainly competent translations of his work available in Spain in the twenties. It is at least clear that Bergamín knew Wilde's work: he refers to Wilde's theatre in *El cohete y la estrella* (49), and to *De Profundis*, in *La cabeza a pájaros* (123). The interest in Wilde's work in general in Spain between 1908 and 1923 and the translations available at that time are studied by Luis Fernández Cifuentes in his excellent book, *Teoría y mercado de la novela en España del 98 a la República* (Madrid 1982), 96–104 and 134–41.

26 In the review mentioned in note 6

27 G. Torrente Ballester, *Panorama de la literatura española contemporánea* (Madrid 1956), 439; A. Amorós, *Introducción a la literatura* (Madrid 1979), 191. The techniques displayed in Gracián's 'Crítica reforma de los comunes refranes' demonstrate most clearly the similarities with Bergamín's style in his aphorisms. See the section entitled 'El saber reinando' of *El criticón*, ed. G. Correa Calderón, 3 vols (Madrid 1971), iii, 143–69.

28 See, for example, the following *discursos* in Gracián's *Agudeza y arte de ingenio*: xxxi, 'De la agudeza nominal'; xxxii, 'De la agudeza por antonomasia, retruécano y jugar del vocablo'; xxxiii, 'De los ingeniosos equívocos.'

29 Quoted by T.E. May, 'An Interpretation of Gracián's *Agudeza y arte de ingenio*,' *Hispanic Review* 16 (October 1948), 275–300, at 279.
30 Vivanco, 'El aforismo y la creación poético-intelectual de José Bergamín,' 601
31 See F. Ynduráin's examination of this feature of Gracián's style in 'Gracián, un estilo,' *Homenaje a Gracián* (Zaragoza 1958), 163–88
32 A similar pattern is discernible in the following aphorisms: 'La duda no es una comodidad para el espíritu, es un esfuerzo' (58); 'La poesía no tiene historia: tiene estilo' (99); 'El poema no es criatura, sino cosa enigmática' (136). This tendency to define ideas positively by means of an initial negation heralds the dialectical method employed in *Cruz y Raya*.
33 See the following *discursos*: XXIII, 'De la agudeza paradoja'; XXIV, 'De los conceptos por una propuesta extravagante, y la razón que se da de la paradoja'; XLII, 'De la agudeza por contradicción y repugnancia en los efectos y sentimientos del ánimo.'
34 Jiménez, *Libros de prosa*:I (Madrid 1969), 946
35 *Expeditions of an Untimely Man*, quoted by R.J. Hollingwood in *A Nietzsche Reader* (Harmondsworth 1977), 20
36 Jiménez, *Selección de cartas (1899 – 1958)*, ed. F. Garfias (Barcelona 1973), 80–1
37 Jarnés, *Ejercicios*, 29

CHAPTER 3

1 Readers sceptical of the nature of the friendships Bergamín had at the time with writers of his own age – from Alberti and Lorca to Altolaguirre and Guillén – should consult my 'Epílogo prologal' to Bergamín's *Prólogos epilogales* (Valencia 1985). As I suggest in this text, if any critical label accurately describes this disparate group of writers – Bergamín included, naturally – it is José Luis Cano's 'La generación de la amistad.'
2 Bergamín recalls that in about 1920 he completed a book of poems entitled *Lamentaciones en primavera*. He read them to Jiménez who is supposed to have commented: 'No me interesan los poemas, pero sí el poeta.'
3 The phrase appears in Ramón Gaya's 'Epílogo para un libro de José Bergamín,' in Bergamín's *La claridad desierta* (Málaga 1973), 209–14, at 209. The full implications of this remark, together with the formal characteristics of Bergamín's discursive prose style, are examined in the next chapter.
4 Gerardo Diego, 'La nueva arte poética española,' *Síntesis* (Buenos Aires) 20 (January 1929): 183–99, at 192.
5 The collection of articles by Bergamín, dating roughly from the period 1926–46, that I have grouped under the heading *Prólogos epilogales* is partly designed to enable the interested reader to reassess Bergamín's role as a critic during this period, making all the relevant texts easily available.

6 Guillermo de Torre, 'Alquimia y mayéutica de la imagen creacionista,' *Cosmópolis* (Madrid) 21 (1920), reproduced in Juan Manuel Rozas, *La generación del 27 desde dentro* (Madrid 1974), 137–40, at 138.

7 Diego, 'La nueva arte poética ... ,' 185

8 Cansinos-Assens, 'Un gran poeta chileno: Vicente Huidobro y el creacionismo,' *Cosmópolis* 1 (1919), reproduced in René de Costa, ed., *Vicente Huidobro y el creacionismo* (Madrid 1975), 119–24, at 122. It should be borne in mind that Cansinos-Assens was referring specifically to the effect of Huidobro's arrival in Madrid upon the conventional approaches to poetry that until 1918 had been largely unchallenged in Spain.

9 G. de Torre, 'Alquimia y mayéutica ... ,' 140

10 It was doubtless fortunate that the better poets of the twenties largely refused to allow themselves to be rigidly tied to these dogmatic theories and unequivocal declarations. Guillén's advocation of a 'poesía pura, *ma non troppo* ... ' opened up more fruitful possibilities and was symptomatic of the way in which absolute ideals were wisely qualified by common sense.

11 Diego, 'La nueva arte poética ... ,' 188

12 Manuel Abril, 'Itinerario del nuevo arte plástico,' *Revista de Occidente* 14 (1926): 343–67, at 358. The fact that Abril was writing about painting draws attention to the close parallel that existed, in the early twenties at least, between poetry and painting. Guillermo de Torre commented on this point as early as 1920, describing 'la escuela creacionista,' for example, as 'emergida teóricamente de los postulados esenciales del cubismo.' See his essay 'La poesía creacionista y la pugna entre sus progenitores,' reproduced in René de Costa, *Vicente Huidobro y el creacionismo*, 129–43, at 134.

13 G. de Torre, 'Alquimia y mayéutica ... ,' 138

14 Vicente Aleixandre, 'Mundo poético,' *Verso y Prosa* 12 (October 1928), n.p. Ortega had already used the same idea when he wrote in *La deshumanización del arte* that 'el placer estético tiene que ser un placer inteligente.'

15 The phrase is Jorge Guillén's and appears in his 'Carta a Fernando Vela,' *Verso y Prosa* 2 (February 1927): n.p.

16 Diego, 'La nueva arte poética ... ,' 190

17 See Antonio Machado's '¿Cómo veo la nueva juventud española?' originally published in *La Gaceta Literaria* (1 March 1929) and later collected in *Los complementarios* (Buenos Aires 1957), 152–6.

18 Fernando Vela, *El arte al cubo y otros ensayos* (Madrid 1927), 16

19 G. de Torre, *La aventura estética de nuestro tiempo* (Barcelona 1962), 78

20 Juan Cano Ballesta, *La poesía española entre pureza y revolución (1930–1936)* (Madrid 1972), 24

21 Diego, 'La nueva arte poética ... ,' 191–2

22 The first was originally published in *Cruz y Raya* 1 (April 1933), and collected in

the second volume of Bergamín's *Disparadero español* (Madrid 1936), 169–223. All references are to the 1936 text with page numbers indicated parenthetically. The second appeared in *Verso y Prosa* 8 (August 1927): n.p. The title of the 'Notas ... ' is modelled on Kant's *Prolegomena zu einer jeden kunftigen Metaphysik die als Wissenschaft wird auftreten können.*

23 The notable exceptions of critics who have realized the importance of Bergamín's critical writings of this period are Gerardo Diego, at the time, in his 'La nueva arte poética ... ,' and in more recent years, apart from Cano Ballesta: G.W. Connell in the introduction to his anthology, *Spanish Poetry of the 'Grupo poético de 1927'* (Oxford 1977); Francisco Javier Díez de Revenga, *Revistas murcianas relacionadas con la generación del 27*, 2nd ed. (Murcia 1979); and Anthony Leo Geist, *La poética de la generación del 27 y las revistas literarias: de la vanguardia al compromiso (1918–1936)* (Barcelona 1980).

24 There may well be a connection between Bergamín's idea of the work of art as a substantive artefact and Huidobro's well-known contention that the *creacionista* poem affirmed itself as 'un objeto nuevo,' 'un hecho nuevo inventado,' 'un fait nouveau ... indépendant de tout autre phénomène externe' that actually competed with the objects created by nature.

25 As a confirmation of this point see, for example, G. de Torre: 'El poeta creacionista aspira a construir un orbe distinto en cada poema. Quiere dotar a éste de una vida independiente y propia, fundiendo diversos elementos, que aisladamente tienen existencia real, para producir un conjunto totalmente nuevo e insólito, como una maquinaria' ('Alquimia y mayéutica ... ,' 140); G. Diego, ' ... una poesía absoluta o de tendencia a lo absoluto; esto es, apoyada en sí misma, autónoma frente al mundo real del que sólo en segundo grado procede' (in his prologue to *Primera antología de sus versos* [Buenos Aires 1941], 19); D. Alonso, ' ... en los años inmediatamente anteriores a 1927, nada de estridentismo: se trataba de trabajar perfectamente, en pureza y fervor; de eliminar del poema los elementos reales y dejar todos los metafóricos, pero de tal modo que éstos satisfacieran a la inteligencia con el sello de lo logrado' ('Góngora entre sus dos centenarios,' in *Cuatro poetas españoles* [Madrid 1962], 49–77, at 64).

26 Details of Bergamín's response to the publication of *La deshumanización del arte* are given in my 'Combates y confluencias: Bergamín y Ortega,' forthcoming in the *Revista de Occidente.*

27 The image of the faulty *cerradura* recalls Bécquer's description of the conflict between inspiration and expression in poem no. 11 of the *Libro de los gorriones:* ' ... no hay cifra / capaz de encerrarle ... ' Bécquer also alludes to the same idea in poem no. 42 ('Sacudimiento extraño'), using verbs like *ordenar, enfrenar, atar, reunir, agrupar*, as well as *encerrar*, in order to convey how reason subjugates inspiration.

28 The debts here to the principles of *creacionismo* as expounded by Huidobro are obvious. Compare, for instance, Bergamín's argument with the following declaration by Huidobro: 'Il ne s'agit pas d'imiter la nature, mais de faire comme elle, de ne pas imiter ses extériorisations, mais son pouvoir extériorisateur,' quoted by G. de Torre, 'La polémica del creacionismo: Huidobro y Reverdy,' reproduced in Costa, ed., *Vincente Huidobro y el creacionismo*, 151–65, at 159.

29 Cano Ballesta, *La poesía española entre pureza y revolución*, 25.

30 I am referring specifically to the aphorims collected under the title 'Arte de temblar' in *La cabeza a pájaros* mentioned in the previous chapter. Since 'Arte de temblar' does not include all the aphorisms on poetry that Bergamín published between 1925 and 1930, and since certain aphorisms were modified when incorporated into the book, I have preferred in all cases to go back to the original texts as they appeared in literary journals.

31 I have examined this point at greater length in my '"Dueño en su laberinto." El ensayista José Bergamín (de la Irreal Anti-Academia),' *Camp de l'Arpa* 23–24 (August–September 1975): 13–19.

32 The texts of the aphorisms I have referred to are 'Carmen: enigma y soledad,' *Carmen* 2 (January 1928); 'Hermes, encadenada,' *Mediodía* 9 (January 1928); 'Martirio de San Sebastián,' *Verso y Prosa* 9 (September 1927); 'Aforústica y epigrométrica,' *Ley* 1 (1927); 'Trasparencia y reflejo,' *Mediodía* 5 (October 1926); 'Aforística permanente,' *Alfar* 47 (February 1925). In incorporating references to these texts into my discussion, the abbreviations I have used are self-explanatory.

33 *Verso y Prosa* 6 (June 1927), n.p.

34 Alberti, *La arboleda perdida* (Barcelona 1975), 235

35 Obvious examples would be *El arte de birlibirloque* (1930), *La cabeza a pájaros* (1934), and *Detrás de la cruz* (1941). Bergamín's most successful exploitation of a popular expression was undoubtedly the title of his journal *Cruz y Raya*.

36 *La Gaceta Literaria* 54 (15 March 1929)

37 Bergamín, 'El idealismo andaluz,' *La Gaceta Literaria* 11 (1 June 1927)

38 Idem, 'La poética de Jorge Guillén,' *La Gaceta Literaria* 49 (1 January 1929). Full details of Jiménez's reaction to this review and of the general tensions it gave rise to are given in my *Perfume and Poison* ...

39 Idem, 'Figura de cera: el arte romántico de Antonio Espina,' *Verso y Prosa* 3 (March 1927): n.p.

40 Idem, 'Literatura y brújula,' *La Gaceta Literaria* 51 (1 February 1929)

41 It would be possible to extend, as Bergamín himself did, the scope of aesthetics to include other creative activities. See, for example, his 'El arte poético de bailar: La Argentinita,' *El Heraldo de Madrid*, 20 April 1933. His book *El arte de*

birlibirloque is in many ways an 'estética del toreo' as its dedication implies: 'Al toreo andaluz, escuela de elegancia intelectual.' In the introduction to this book Bergamín writes: '... en el toreo se afirman, físicamente, todos los valores estéticos del cuerpo humano (figura, agilidad, destreza, gracia, etc.); y metafísicamente, todas las cualidades que pudiéramos llamar deportivas de la inteligencia (rápida concepción o abstracción sensible para relacionar).'

42 Alberti, *La arboleda perdida*, 203

43 Anon., 'Poesía sin historia,' *Extremos a que ha llegado la poesía española* 1 (March 1931): 3–5, at 3. The fact that these comments were made a year after the publication of Valbuena Prat's book – *La poesía española contemporánea* (Madrid 1930) – suggests that it had a relatively limited impact.

44 'Literatura y brújula' is in fact specifically referred to in the text in *Extremos a que ha llegado la poesía española*, mentioned in note 43.

45 Published in *Luz*, 30 January 1934

46 C. Vallejo, *Trilce* (Madrid 1930), 9–17, at 9–10. Bergamín is referring specifically to the idea of the 'translatability' of poetry championed by *creacionistas* like Larrea and Huidobro who preferred to write in French rather than in Spanish.

47 Cernuda, 'Gómez de la Serna y la generación poética de 1925,' in *Estudios sobre poesía española contemporánea* (Madrid 1957), 165–76. While apparently being unaware of Bergamín's writings on this subject, Cernuda echoes exactly his feelings on the importance of Gómez de la Serna for the poets of the twenties: 'Se ha hablado mucho, acaso demasiado, acerca de la influencia de tal o cual poeta de la generación de 1925, pero que yo sepa nada se dijo acerca de la influencia sobre ellos de Gómez de la Serna. Sé que la importancia de la obra de este escritor, que por sí sola equivale a la de toda una generación literaria, a toda una época de nuestra literatura, requería un comentario general y no uno parcial acerca de este aspecto de la misma ... ' (177).

48 An interesting attempt to revise the influence of Gómez de la Serna on the poetic techniques of the twenties is Susana Cavallo's article, 'Un antecedente del 27: Gómez de la Serna y la greguería,' *Insula*, 368–369 (July–August 1977): 26.

49 There are two essays by Bergamín on Gómez de la Serna dating from this period: 'Solo de Ramón. Trompeta con sordina,' *Papel de Aleluyas* (Huelva) 6 (April 1928): n.p. and 'Ramón y el eco,' *La Gaceta Literaria* 72 (15 December 1929).

50 The main aspects of this breakdown are documented in my book *Perfume and Poison* ...

51 Bergamín, 'Aforística inactual,' *Alfar* 40 (May 1924): 3

52 See the following comments: 'En mis recuerdos personales, Manuel Altolaguir-

re y Emilio Prados son siempre inseparables. Cuando los encontré primero juntos y luego separados en su vida, siempre me parecía sentir, como una sombra, con presencia invisible, al otro en cada uno de ellos. En su poesía también me parece sentirlos de ese modo, casi complementario. Pero no quisiera que este recuerdo mío personalísimo desviase el juicio valorativo de su obra poética por separado: como hay que hacerlo ahora al leer o releer sus libros de poesía' ('Homenaje y recuerdo,' Indice de Artes y Letras [Madrid] 13, 128 [August 1959]: 5). Also ' ... no es [Antonio Espina] figura de cera en museo romántico: entre su cuerpo y la mirada no se interpone un cristal de vitrina (ni Solana ni Ramón Gómez de la Serna ni Larra; aunque los evoque) ... ' ('Figura de cera'). Bergamín also takes the trouble to draw a distinction, in his prologue to Trilce, between Gerardo Diego and Vallejo, even though the comparison, to my knowledge, has not often been made: 'De la poesía de Gerardo Diego se aproxima Trilce por la aparente incoherencia de los enlaces imaginativos, acusadores de una honda coherencia poética más exacta; se aparta totalmente del poeta de Manual de espumas por el estremecimiento humano que la determina, por la rapidez, por la vibración, por el acento ... '

53 In addition to the articles already mentioned, see Bergamín's 'De veras y de burlas' (on Alberti), La Gaceta Literaria 71 (1 December 1929); 'Verdad de poesía' (on Salinas), Luz, 6 February 1934. On Lorca, see his prologue entitled 'La muerte vencida' to Lorca's Poeta en Nueva York (Mexico 1940), 17–27.

CHAPTER 4

1 These examples from Jiménez's work are not meant to represent exact equivalences but rather the chronological limits within which Jiménez refined his own style as a prose poet. The most suggestive parallels between the poetry of Guillén, Alberti et al., and Jiménez's prose are to be found in the kind of work the latter published in the late twenties and early thirties in his cuadernos: Obra en marcha (1928), Sucesión (1932), Presente (1933), and so on. Many of his 'caricaturas líricas' appeared first in these publications.

2 Cernuda, 'Gómez de la Serna y la generación poética de 1925,' in Estudios sobre poesía española contemporánea (Madrid 1957), 165–76, at 174. Page numbers of references to this essay will be indicated parenthetically.

3 El cohete y la estrella, 21. Additional quotations from Bergamín's aphoristic works will be taken from the 1942 edition, as in chapter 2, with page numbers given in parentheses.

4 Bergamín, Duendecitos y coplas (Madrid/Santiago de Chile 1963), col. 'Renuevos de Cruz y Raya.' Page numbers to references will be given in parentheses.

5 Bergamín has adoped this saying of Unamuno's as his own and offers a

commentary on it in his *La música callada del toreo* (Madrid 1982), 7. I would not like to leave the reader with the impression that *Duendecitos y coplas* is nothing more than a poet's re-encounter with the ideas he formulated in a remote past. Though many of the ideas in this book are familiar within the context of Bergamín's thought as a whole, much new ground is broken. The short verse forms become genuine lyrical poetry as they acquire a more personal, introspective tone and cease to be simply vehicles for philosophical reflection.

6 Exactly the same can be said of the essay 'La importancia del demonio,' the essence of which is summed up in the aphorism, 'Donde no está la voluntad de Dios está siempre la del Diablo' (*La cabeza a pájaros*, 118).

7 The texts contained in this book were all written in 1926 though the book itself did not appear until February 1927.

8 Evidently, the criteria used by Altolaguirre and Prados, the writers responsible for the series, were the same as Cernuda's when he included his essay on Gómez de la Serna in a collection of studies on poets and poetry. Bergamín contributed regularly to *Litoral* from the moment of its foundation in 1926, and the texts he published in it are among his most 'poetic' (i.e. in the style of *Caracteres*) of the decade. It was planned to publish Bergamín's *El arte de birlibirloque* in a second series of supplements that never materialized. According to details given by the publishers (in a publicity leaflet distributed with *Caracteres*), this second series would have included Moreno Villa's *Jacinta la pelirroja*, and other works by Hinojosa, G. Diego, Aleixandre, Alberti, Cernuda, Altolaguirre, and Larrea.

9 In connection with this sometimes only thinly disguised biographical element in *Caracteres*, the reader may be interested to know that the final text, fittingly entitled 'El admirable' (40), is a portrait of Juan Ramón Jiménez. 'El espinado' (19) turns out to be a self-portrait of Bergamín who recently identified some of his other models in his introduction to the facsimile reprint of the book (Madrid 1978). Further details of the historical interest of this book are given in my 'Caracterología bergaminiana. (Verso y prosa en la joven literatura),' *Nueva Estafeta* 3 (February 1979): 75–7.

10 Lorca's comment on the problem of gaining access to Góngora's poetry clarifies the sense of what is expected of the reader: 'Es un problema de comprensión. A Góngora no hay que leerlo, sino estudiarlo. Góngora no viene a buscarnos como otros poetas para ponernos melancólicos, sino hay que perseguirlo razonablemente,' in 'La imagen poética de Don Luis de Góngora,' *Obras completas*, 18th ed. (Madrid 1974), i, 1001–25, at 1006.

11 Angel del Río, *Historia de la literatura española* (New York 1963), ii, 347

12 Pedro Salinas, 'España en su laberinto,' *Indice Literario* iii, 5 (May 1934): 93–8, at 95

13 Luis Felipe Vivanco, 'El aforismo y la creación poético-intelectual de José Bergamín,' 602
14 Max Aub, *Manual de historia de la literatura española* (Madrid 1974), 524
15 More recent instances of the way in which this approach has been developed would be Luis Cañizal de la Fuente's untitled review of Bergamín's *Beltenebros y otros ensayos sobre literatura española* in *Insula* 329 (April 1974): 4, and my own 'El neobarroquismo en la prosa española de pre-guerra: el caso de José Bergamín,' *Revista de Occidente* 14 (June–July 1982): 85–96.
16 The major scenes from this nightmare are played out in my PH D dissertation (Cambridge 1976). I have restricted my discussion of the subject here to the necessary minimum in order not to get bogged down in an interminable discussion.
17 See James Mark, 'The Uses of the Term "Baroque,"' *Modern Language Review* 33 (1938): 547–63.
18 René Wellek, 'The Concept of Baroque in Literary Scholarship,' *Journal of Aesthetics and Art Criticism* 5, 2 (December 1946): 77–109
19 See H. Hatzfeld, 'A Clarification [sic] of the Baroque Problem in the Romance Literatures,' *Comparative Literature* 1, 2 (Spring 1949): 113–39 and his *Estudios sobre el barroco* (Madrid 1964). See also Mme de Mourgues's *Metaphysical, Baroque and Précieux Poetry* (Oxford 1963), especially the first chapter entitled 'The Welter of Terminology.'
20 The idea of baroque politics is put forward by José Antonio Maravall, *La cultura del barroco* (Barcelona 1965). Despite its occasional oddities, this book is to my mind the best study of the phenomenon of the Baroque as a whole.
21 Emilio Orozco Díaz, *Lección permanente del barroco* (Madrid 1952), 8
22 José Ortega y Gasset, 'Góngora. 1627–1927,' *Obras completas*, 6 vols (Madrid 1957–8), III, 580–6, at 584
23 Jiménez, *Libros de prosa*: I, 981
24 Dámaso Alonso, 'Claridad y belleza de las *Soledades*,' in Góngora, *Soledades* (Madrid 1927), 7–36, at 31
25 The book is based on a series of lectures Bergamín gave in 1930 at the Residencia de Señoritas in Madrid. Some extracts were published under the title 'Las raíces poéticas del "Teatro independiente español y revolucionario del XVII"' in the *Boletín de la Biblioteca Menéndez Pelayo* (Santander) 13 (1931): 223–60. The first edition of the book was published by the Editorial Plutarco in Madrid. All my references are taken from the 1974 reprint (Madrid: Ediciones del Centro), with page numbers indicated in parentheses. The reader should bear in mind that the substance of what I say about *Mangas y capirotes* can be applied to any of the long essays Bergamín wrote from 'El pensamiento hermético de las artes' up to 'Laberinto de la novela

y monstruo de la novelería' (1935) and 'El disparate en la literatura española' (1936).

26 Although five volumes of the *Disparadero español* were originally planned, only two appeared in Spain before the outbreak of the Civil War. A third was published in Mexico in 1940.

27 Alonso, *Ensayos sobre literatura española* (Madrid 1964), 64

28 The history of the debate on *conceptismo* and the various difficulties that interpreters have encountered are covered in Andrée Collard, *Nueva poesía. Conceptismo, culteranismo en la crítica española* (Madrid 1967).

29 Samuel Coleridge, *Biographia Literaria*, quoted by K.K. Ruthven, *The Conceit* (London 1969), 7

30 Gracián, *Agudeza y arte de ingenio*, ed. E. Correa Calderón, 2 vols (Madrid 1969), I, 55

31 Quoted by T.E. May, 'An interpretation of Gracián's *Agudeza y arte de ingenio*,' *Hispanic Review* 16 (October 1948): 275–300, at 279

32 The reader interested in these self-contained examples may examine the use Bergamín makes of expressions such as *andarse por las ramas* (53), *andarse con contemplaciones* (67), *hacer constancia* (84), *hacer mangas y capirotes* (94).

33 Quoted by Hugh H. Grady, 'Rhetoric, wit and art in Gracián's *Agudeza*,' *Modern Language Quarterly* (Seattle) 41, 1 (March 1980): 21–37, at 32

34 There is one other notable example in the book of an entire section being constructed on these lines. It concerns the use made of the expression *tener ley* on pp. 73–82.

35 See again the attention Gracián devotes to different aspects of the paradox in his *Agudeza y arte de ingenio*: Discurso XXIII, 'De la agudeza paradoja'; Discurso XXIV, 'De los conceptos por una propuesta extravagante, y la razón que se da de la paradoja'; and Discurso XLII, 'De la agudeza por contradicción y repugnancia en los efectos, y sentimientos del ánimo.'

CHAPTER 5

1 This work dates from 1924 and there is some evidence that Jiménez planned to publish it in the 'Biblioteca de Indice' in that year. Bergamín ended up, however, by having it privately published in 1925.

2 It may be of some interest to give these titles in full here, with an asterisk to indicate the plays: *Santoral de un escéptico*, **Farsa de los filólogos*, **El clave mal temperado*, **El hombre, la sombra y el fantasma*, **Don Lindo de Almería*, *Molino de razón*, **Coloquio espiritual del pelotari con sus demonios*, *El arte de birlibirloque*, *Balada en forma de fuga*, **Comedia de las musarañas*, **El príncipe inconstante*, **La zarza ardiendo*, *Burla y pasión del hombre invisible*. The contents of this list pose

typical problems in the compilation of a complete bibliography of Bergamín's work. For example, *El clave mal temperado* was the early provisional title of a collection of playlets that were published under the new title of *Enemigo que huye* in 1927. This book contained the 'Coloquio espiritual ... ' mentioned above, and two other plays entitled 'Variación y fuga de una sombra' and 'Variación y fuga de un fantasma,' which may well correspond to *El hombre, la sombra y el fantasma*. Additional difficulties are posed because the list given in *Caracteres* is evidently incomplete. Bergamín himself refers to a work entitled *El auto de la Mari-Chiva* in a letter published in *Verso y Prosa*: 'He dado a Esplá un proyecto de "Auto" que llamo "de la Mari-Chiva" y que llevará ilustraciones suyas y alguna cancionilla de Alberti,' 'Epistolario,' no. 4 (April 1927). Some time later he worked on another play with Alberti and Esplá, which has similarly never come to light; it was to have been entitled *Electra electrocutada*. See Alberti's 'Autobiografía,' *La Gaceta Literaria* 49 (1 January 1929). Bergamín also recalls having written another dramatic work in the late twenties that he called *Ramón Ramírez*. The complications created by unfinished projects, changed titles, and lost texts need to be examined in detail one day.

3 There are no references to Bergamín's plays, for example, in Francisco Ruiz Ramón's *Historia del teatro español. Siglo* xx (Madrid 1975), and no mention is made of his use of the Don Juan theme even in specialised studies such as L. Weinstein, *The Metamorphoses of Don Juan* (Palo Alto 1959).

4 A marginal interest in staging some of Bergamín's plays from this period was shown in Spain in the sixties. Scenes from 'Variación y fuga de un fantasma,' for example, were performed under the title *Hamlet,solista* at the Teatro Guimerá in Madrid in February 1963, with scenography by Agustín Ballester and music by Gustavo Pittaluga. In general, Bergamín has been much more successful as a stageable dramatist outside Spain, especially in Uruguay and France. This does not alter the fact, however, that his dramatic works are essentially texts to be read.

5 *Enemigo* was first published in Madrid (Biblioteca Nueva) in 1927, though the texts it contains date from 1925 and 1926. *Los filólogos* was first published in Madrid (Ediciones Turner) in 1978.

6 All quotations from *Tres escenas en ángulo recto* and *Enemigo que huye* are taken from the reprint of 1973 (Madrid, Nostromo) which includes them both under the new title *La risa en los huesos*. Page numbers to references will be given in brackets.

7 The letter is dated 7 March 1928 and is as yet unpublished. I quote from it with the kind permission of Sr Bergamín.

8 *La Gaceta Literaria* 31 (1 April 1928). This number is a special issue devoted to the topic 'Catolicismo y literatura.' The declarations Bergamín made here help

to explain why, for a while in the thirties, he was wrongly associated by certain critics with the ideologues of Spanish fascism and their theories on the Catholic imperialism of Spain. See chapter 6.

9 Bergamín, 'Musarañas del teatro ... in *El Pasajero. Peregrino español en América* 3 (Otoño 1943) (Mexico: Ed. Séneca 1944), 9–27. Page numbers of references to this essay will be indicated in parentheses.

10 The name appears, for example, in a sonnet by Baudelaire and in a short story by Unamuno. Bergamín is likely to have been familiar with both.

11 I take the phrase from the title of the chapter devoted to Bergamín's theatre in the as yet unpublished – and unfinished – doctoral thesis of Florence Delay on Bergamín's work.

12 *La muerte burlada*, for example, is based on certain letters from the correspondence of Saint Catherine Benincasa, letters that Bergamín himself had translated into Spanish and published in the third number of *Cruz y Raya* (June 1933). *La hija de Dios* takes as its point of departure the Spanish translation – entitled *Hécuba triste* – by Fernán Pérez de Oliva of Euripides' *Hecuba*. *Medea la encantadora* has its precedents in the versions by both Euripides and Seneca of the Medea story, while *Los tejados de Madrid* is modelled on Lope's *La gatomaquia*.

13 Florence Delay begins her discussion of *Tres escenas en ángulo recto* with the following remark: 'Le premier personnage auquel nous avons affaire et que nous retrouverons souvent sous la plume de l'auteur, c'est son compatriote Arlequin, originaire comme lui de Bergame.' She goes on to quote this revealing comment by Bergamín himself: 'Je me souviens toujours de l'Arlequin bergamasque qui est un Arlequin noir et sans couleur, un Arlequin squeletique où le masque, j'oserais dire, reste nu, et qui ressemble alors à un squelette. Ce masque bergamasque ... ne vient pas du poème de Verlaine. Verlaine parle d'un paysage de l'âme qui est un paysage choisi et qui engendre masques et bergamasques. C'est une sorte de musique qui convient très bien à la signification arlequinesque du bergamasque. Mais moi, je m'attache à la signification originaire de Bergame de l'arlequin squeletique.'

14 Goethe, *Faust. Part One* (Harmondsworth 1978), 68

15 *La cabeza a pájaros*, 96. The title of the aphorism is in fact taken from the opening line of a sonnet by Lupercio Leonardo de Argensola entitled 'El sueño': 'Imagen espantosa de la muerte, / sueño cruel, no turbes más mi pecho ... '

16 This title even appeared in publicity announcements. For example, in the section entitled 'De la tertulia' of the literary supplement of *La Verdad*, a note was published concerning 'libros buenos próximos a aparecer,' mentioning '*Víspera del gozo* por Pedro Salinas, *Los putrefactos* por Federico García Lorca y Salvador Dalí, *El clave mal temperado* por José Bergamín' (53 [6 June 1926]: 3).

17 Recounted by Bergamín to Florence Delay and reported by her in her thesis.

18 It may be significant that *Mangas y capirotes* is dedicated to Falla.

19 I did in fact use a musical analogy (that of a Bach fugue) to explain the form of Bergamín's prose in my '"Dueño en su laberinto." El ensayista José Bergamín (de la Irreal Anti-Academia).'

20 See, for example, Bergamín's 'Acotaciones a *Medea*': 'Al publicar mis primeros ensayos *teatrales* (para la lectura): *Tres escenas en ángulo recto, Enemigo que huye* ... , acompañados de cuatro o cinco más, que, gracias a Dios, se perdieron durante la guerra en España ... ,' *Primer Acto* 44 (1963): 35–6, at 36.

21 I myself have been on the receiving end of taunts like these from time to time.

22 I had the good fortune to discover the manuscript myself, thanks mainly to the generosity of Rodríguez-Moñino's widow, Doña María Brey. Full details are given in my 'José Bergamín, dramaturgo. (Apuntes sobre la anti-filología),' *Cuadernos Hispanoamericanos*, no. 409 (July 1984): 111–17.

23 Bergamín, in his introduction to *Caballito del diablo*, 11

24 Page numbers to quotations from the text will be given in brackets. It is interesting that by mentioning Aristophanes, Bergamín gives a hint of the literary forebears of *Los filólogos*.

25 Bergamín's condemnation appeared in the first number of his journal *Cruz y Raya* (April 1933). See chapter 6.

CHAPTER 6

1 Quoted by Francisco Javier Díez de Revenga, *Revistas murcianas relacionadas con la generación del 27*, 2nd ed. (Murcia 1979), 36

2 Full details of Altolaguirre's publishing activites are given in Juan Manuel Rozas's excellent introduction to the facsimile reprint of *Poesía* (Vaduz/Liechtenstein 1979).

3 For all relevant information on the journals named, see N. Dennis and L. Albert, 'Literary and Cultural Periodicals in Spain: 1920–1936. A Bibliography,' *Ottawa Hispánica* 4 (1982): 127–70.

4 In a letter to Unamuno of 1 February 1923, Bergamín wrote: 'Me ayudan ya: Ors, Moreno Villa, Abril, Miró, Espina, Marichalar, Ramón Gómez de la Serna ... y espero la colaboración de Ayala, los Machado ... etc.'

5 *El Sol*, 15 January 1933, 2

6 In an interview with César Alonso de los Ríos, 'José Bergamín y su *Cruz y Raya*,' *Triunfo* (Madrid) 615 (13 July 1974): 34–7, at 35.

7 Bergamín, 'Signo y diseño de *Cruz y Raya*,' his prologue to the facsimile reprint of *El aviso de escarmentados del año que acaba y escarmiento de avisados para el que empieza* (Nendeln/Liechtenstein 1974), vii–xv, at viii

8 Bergamín gives details of these consultations in 'Signo y diseño ... ' VIII–IX.

9 It is worthwhile clearing up here the confusion surrounding the date on which this lecture was given. In the most authoritative study of Palencia's work – José Corredor Matheos, *Vida y obra de Benjamín Palencia* (Madrid 1979) – the date is wrongly given (on p. 240) as 1928. The writer confuses the contributions that Bergamín made to the two exhibitions that Palencia had in Madrid in 1928 and 1932. On the occasion of the first, Bergamín gave an untitled '*lectura,*' the invitation to which – dated 30 October 1928 – Corredor Matheos duly reproduces on page 51 of his book. It turns out, however, that this '*lectura*' was not of any text devoted to Palencia, or in fact to painting at all, but was of his own treatise on bullfighting *El arte de birlibirloque*, eventually published in book form in 1930. This is made clear in a brief note (unsigned) entitled 'Palencia, Alberti, Bergamín' that appeared in *La Gaceta Literaria* on 1 November 1928, 8. Concluding a series of references to Palencia's exhibition, and to a '*lectura*' (of poems) by Alberti, the writer comments: 'También José Bergamín dio una finísima disertación al clausurar la Exposición. Se tituló "El arte de birlibirloque," que fue muy gustada y aplaudida.' It was, then, at the conclusion of Palencia's exhibition of 1932 that Bergamín gave a lecture specifically about painting. Extracts from it were immediately published in *El Sol* (14 May 1932, 2) under the title 'Cruz y raya de la pintura.'

10 *Disparadero español* II (Madrid 1936), 225–66

11 On the front cover of *Disparadero español* II, the title 'Un lenguaje de fuego de la pintura' appears in brackets after 'El pensamiento hermético de las artes,' as if Bergamín considered it to be a kind of continuation or appendix to the ideas expressed in the lecture of 1927. It is significant, too, that this volume of the *Disparadero* itself was subtitled *Presencia de espíritu.*

12 Bergamín offers his own version of the different interpretations to which the idiom lent itself in 'Signo y diseño ... ,' VII.

13 It seems reasonable to suppose that *Cruz y Raya*, like the *Revista de Occidente*, had a readership approaching two thousand.

14 The text is unsigned and its authorship has only been clarified in recent years. In 'Signo y diseño ... ' Bergamín explains: '[Falla] empezó por redactar conmigo el texto de la presentación de la revista que encabezaba el primer número, revisándolo y corrigiéndolo minuciosamente con la misma escrupulosidad que lo hacía con su música. Aparte de esa colaboración, que él quería siempre secreta, me dio sus páginas mejores de crítica musical,' IX.

15 Bergamín may well have had in mind the example of *La Gaceta Literaria*, which by 1931 had effectively lost its appeal and prestige because of Giménez Caballero's preoccupation with particular ideological trends and the narrow interpretations of literature and culture that they inevitably imposed.

16 Bergamín had occasionally used the title 'Criba' as a general heading for his contributions to *España* and *La Verdad* (see bibliography), but had not developed the idea systematically. The heading 'Cristal del Tiempo' was taken from Calderón: 'En la forma de las horas / que son cristales del tiempo.' Bergamín regarded this image as something he had practically patented himself and was furious at the way it was appropriated by others after 1936. See his indignant commentary on this point in *Detrás de la cruz. Terrorismo* y *persecución religiosa en España* (Mexico 1941), 161–2.

17 Quoted by Luis Campodónico in 'Manuel de Falla y Bergamín. El contexto de una correspondencia,' *Mundo Nuevo* (Paris) 25 (1968): 15–24, at 21.

18 'Debates,' *El Sol*, 26 April 1933, 2

19 According to Javier Tussell, the concerns voiced by Bergamín and *Cruz y Raya* – particularly their opposition to 'la utilización de la religión por la cultura' – were shared by Catalán Christian Democrats like Cardó and Basque National-ists like Engracio de Arantzadi. Bergamín's journal was apparently given a warm welcome in the Basque press when it appeared. See Tussell's *Historia de la democracia cristiana en España*, 2 vols (Madrid 1974), I, 95.

20 *Hoja Literaria*, June 1933, 10

21 See Bergamín's text on Jiménez entitled 'Sucesión. Discontinuidad,' in *Cruz y Raya* 1 (April 1933): 153–4, and his untitled attack on the Misiones Pedagó-gicas, ibid., 154.

22 Jiménez, 'Prosa inédita,' *El Sol*, 30 April 1933, 2

23 José Herradón, '*Cruz y Raya*, el tentáculo más fino del pulpo monopolista,' *Nueva Cultura* (Valencia) 6 (August–September 1935), quoted by José Carlos Mainer in *La edad de plata (1902–1939)* (Madrid 1981), 318–19

24 In the interview with César Alonso de los Ríos (see note 6), p. 37. J.R. Jiménez also accused Bergamín of having been in league with the Jesuits in *Cruz y Raya*. See his 'Historias de España y México. Carta obligada a mí mismo,' *Letras de México* 4, 20 (1 August 1944): 7, and Bergamín's spirited dismissal of these charges in 'El ensimismado enfurecido. Los puntos sobre las jotas,' *Letras de México* 4, 21 (1 September 1944): 6.

25 There are few documented details concerning the financial administration of *Cruz y Raya*, though Bergamín recalls that the journal had eaten into about one-quarter of its budget by the summer of 1936. The journal's publishing offshoot, the Ediciones del Arbol, seems, in contrast, to have been economically viable. There is evidence that the authors of essays published in the opening section of the journal were paid one thousand pesetas, a generous sum for the time.

26 Marcel Brion, 'L'actualité littéraire à l'étranger,' *Les Nouvelles Littéraires*, 3 March 1934, 8. This same basic distinction is repeated by Rafael Benítez Claros who describes Ortega's journal as 'la ventana cosmopolita por donde desfilan

las más altas figuras de la intelectualidad extranjera' and *Cruz y Raya*'s aim as being 'oponer una zona de independencia frente a esta cultura de importación.' See the introduction to the annotated index '*Cruz y Raya*' (*Madrid, 1933-1936*) (Madrid 1947), x.

27 'De la España peregrina a un peregrino en su patria,' *La Vanguardia*, 17 September 1972. Pérez Minik seems to have reacted in much the same way to Bergamín's own work. Referring to the publication of the latter's essay 'Calderón y cierra España' in *El Sol* in April 1936, he writes: 'Lo que sacaba a uno de sus casillas, nos enfadaba, nos incordiaba, con su mezcla osadísima del más desaforado lirismo, una irracional actitud y su metodología antidialéctica.'

28 See the following in *Cruz y Raya*: P. Claudel, 'Sobre la presencia de Dios,' 11 (February 1934); J. Maritain, '¿Quién pone puertas al canto?' 25 (April 1935); M. Jacob, 'El verdadero sentido de la religión católica,' 13 (April 1934) and 'Las plagas de Egipto y el dolor,' 18 (September 1934); T.S. Eliot, 'Lancelot Andrews,' 12 (March 1934); M. Heidegger, '¿Qué es metafísica?' 6 (September 1933); P.L. Landsberg, 'La libertad y la gracia en San Agustín,' 14 (May 1934), 'Experiencia de la muerte,' 26 (May 1935), and 'Reflexiones sobre Unamuno,' 31 (October 1935); L. Sturzo, 'Fascio lictorio y cruz gammada,' 10 (January 1934) and 'El estado totalitario,' 28 (July 1935).

29 The letter is dated 13 October 1933 and is among the Trend papers kept in the University Library, Cambridge.

30 Trend never did contribute to the journal, nor did Bergamín ever make it to Cambridge to lecture on Bécquer. This does not alter, however, the spirit of the *approchement* between the two. An anthology of texts by Blake did eventually appear in *Cruz y Raya*, translated by Neruda and accompanied by illustrations, in no. 20 (November 1934). It may be of some historical interest to point out that the substitute for Bergamín that Trend found to speak on Bécquer in Cambridge was Altolaguirre.

31 There was one notable deviation from this norm, the supplement to no. 21 (December 1934) being Miguel Artigas's edition of a text entitled *Reflexiones sobre el uso de las palabras nuevas en la lengua castellana* by José Reynoso. The particular interest of this text was that it had been preserved in the Biblioteca Menéndez Pelayo and had not been previously published.

32 Altolaguirre handled, for example, the printing of the two volumes of Bergamín's *Disparadero español*, Pedro Salinas's *Razón de amor*, and the three *fábulas* published in the special collection 'La Rosa Blanca.'

33 This accounts for the physical differences between the books in question, the extremes being represented by the very large format of Lorca's *Llanto por Ignacio Sánchez Mejías* and the diminutive size of Bergamín's *La cabeza a pájaros*.

34 Anon., 'Con Bergamín en *Cruz y Raya*,' *El Sol*, 12 July 1936

35 Bergamín, 'La callada de Dios,' *Cruz y Raya* 29 (August 1935)
36 *Cruz y Raya* 25 (April 1935)
37 *Cruz y Raya* 12 (March 1934)
38 Ibid.
39 'Sí o no, como Cristo nos enseña,' *Cruz y Raya* 14 (May 1934)
40 Ibid.
41 Bécarud, in similar vein, describes *Cruz y Raya's* procedure as 'mimético,' *'Cruz y Raya' (1933–1936)* (Madrid 1969), 56.
42 Bergamín, 'Signo y diseño ... ,' ix–x
43 Idem, 'Un gran vuelo de cuervos mancha el azul celeste,' *Cruz y Raya* 12 (March 1934)
44 Idem, 'Dar que decir al demonio' *Cruz y Raya* 25 (April 1935)
45 Two of *Cruz y Raya's* founding editors were correspondents in Spain for *Esprit*: José María Semprún y Gurrea and Alfredo Mendizábal. *Esprit*, it should be remembered, also devoted space regularly to events taking place in Spain, though Spanish affairs would only really become engrossing during the Civil War itself. On this point see R.W. Ranch, *Politics and Contemporary Belief in Contemporary France: Emmanuel Mounier and Christian Democracy, 1932–1950* (The Hague 1952) and Pierre de Senarclens, *Le Mouvement 'Esprit,' 1932–1941* (Lausanne 1974). *Cruz y Raya's* interest was not limited to *Esprit* and Mounier's circle, as can be seen in this comment by José Antonio Maravall in an essay entitled 'La revolución para el hombre' (no. 15, June 1934): 'Interesa recoger lo que hoy pueda estar aconteciendo con los miembros del *Ordre Nouveau* no por un simple gusto literario hacia el *vient de paraître*, sí por algo mucho más hondo. Por esto: porque estos hombres nos plantean vivamente sobre la misma carne de su pensamiento una serie numerosa de temas del presente. Y a nosotros nos ha de servir mucho poder escuchar bajo el oído de nuestra atención intelectual, aplicado al cuerpo de las cuestiones actuales, la sangre acompasada de otros europeos contemporáneos.'
46 This is the opening sentence of *Pour le bien commun*, quoted by Bergamín in 'Sí o no, como Cristo nos enseña,' *Cruz y Raya* 14 (May 1934)
47 Ibid.
48 Bergamín, in the prologue to his *'Cruz y Raya.' Antología* (Madrid 1974), 9. He makes the same point in the interview with César Alonso de los Ríos, 37.
49 Bécarud, *'Cruz y Raya'* ... , 31
50 Bergamín, prologue to *'Cruz y Raya.' Antología*, 9
51 Quoted by Luis Campodónico, 'Manuel de Falla y Bergamín,' 21
52 Symptomatic of this tendency is the polemical article of 1933 by C.M. Arconada in which Bergamín is grouped together with Giménez Caballero and other figures of the right: 'Las generaciones nuevas de escritores están acentuando

su posición de día en día. Por ejemplo, la contrarrevolución, la reacción, el fascismo o el "catolicismo de la cultura" tiene defensores y adeptos en Montes, Bergamín, Ledesma Ramos, Giménez Caballero, Sánchez Mazas,' in 'Quince años de literatura española,' originally published in *Octubre* (June–July 1933) and reproduced in C.H. Cobb, *La cultura y el pueblo. España, 1930–1939* (Barcelona 1981), 178–88, at 187.

53 See especially page 49 of Bécarud's book, '*Cruz y Raya.*'
54 Oral communication of 9 October 1979 to Ian Gibson, quoted in Gibson's *En busca de José Antonio* (Barcelona 1980), 61–2
55 See the entry of 3 December 1938 in Gide's *Journal (1889–1939)* (Paris 1948), 1327.
56 Bergamín, 'Signo y diseño ... ,' VIII
57 Idem, prologue to '*Cruz y Raya.*' *Antología*, 10
58 *Cruz y Raya* 4 (July 1933)
59 *Cruz y Raya* 19 (October 1934)
60 *Cruz y Raya* 20 (November 1934)
61 Quoted by Bergamín in his 'El estado fantasma y ¿en qué país vivimos?' *Cruz y Raya* 20 (November 1934)
62 The polemic between Bergamín and Serrano Plaja is alluded to, for example, by Marta Bizcarrondo in *Araquistáin y la crisis socialista en la II República. 'Leviatán' (1934–1936)* (Madrid 1975), 316, and by Jean Bécarud and E. López Campillo in *Los intelectuales españoles durante la II República* (Madrid 1978), 111. The fullest account of the exchange is given in Francisco Caudet's introduction to the facsimile reprint of Gide's *Defensa de la cultura* (Madrid 1981), 7–39. Gide's book originally appeared in Madrid in 1936 and contained the text of Gide's speech of 1935, Bergamín's commentary on it, and the letters that passed between him and Serrano Plaja. The book was published at Bergamín's suggestion with the proceeds going to the victims of the repression in Asturias. The texts of the letters themselves had already been published twice in Madrid: in *Leviatán* (September–November 1935) and in *Cruz y Raya* (November 1935).
63 All quotations are taken from Caudet's edition mentioned in note 62. For convenience, page numbers to references are given in parentheses.
64 Bergamín's commentary first appeared in *Cruz y Raya* 28 (July 1935). Quotations from it and from both his letter and Serrano Plaja's are also taken from Caudet's edition.
65 This introductory note does not appear in Caudet's edition. I quote from the text reproduced in Bécarud and López Campillo, *Los intelectuales españoles*, 171. Bergamín also says in the opening paragraph of his reply to Serrano Plaja: 'Lo que yo ... siento más en su carta es esa profunda y veraz, secreta ansia

humana de comunión y comunicación que la impulsa y la anima', Caudet, Gide's *Defensa*, 73–4.
66 Bergamín, 'Signo y diseño ... ,' VIII
67 Tussell, *Historia de la democracia cristiana* ... , I, 207
68 Bergamín, 'Dos amigos del alma,' *El Nacional* (Caracas), 28 February 1953
69 It would be misleading not to point out that there was also a more prosaic reason for the proposed change. Bergamín admitted to me privately that it was becoming an increasing strain in 1936 maintaining the intellectual standards and variety of *Cruz y Raya* on a monthly basis. Had the envisaged change taken place and the journal become tri-lingual, it would have been a quarterly rather than a monthly publication. This would naturally have eased much of the pressure under which Bergamín as director was forced to work, particularly in 1935 and 1936.
70 Anon., 'Una nueva carta de José Bergamín. La calificación reaccionario le resulta injuriosa,' *El Socialista*, 13 July 1936, 4

CHAPTER 7

1 See Bergamín, 'Signo y diseño de *Cruz y Raya*,' prologue to *El aviso de escarmentados del año que acaba y escarmiento de avisados para el que empieza* (Nendeln/Liechtenstein 1974), IX.
2 Bergamín, prologue to *'Cruz y Raya'. Antología* (Madrid 1974), 10
3 See also in this connection the possessive tone of his references to *Cruz y Raya* in *Detrás de la cruz. Terrorismo y persecución religiosa en España* (Mexico 1941), especially p. 161.
4 *El Pasajero. Peregrino español en América* was one of Bergamín's most curious and original undertakings. It was conceived as a journal, to be published on a quarterly basis, but had only one contributor – himself. The issues that appeared had all the variety of *Cruz y Raya*, containing essays, aphorisms, poetry, letters, and general commentaries. While the initiative bears witness to Bergamín's tireless inventiveness, it also suggests the kind of isolation in which he came to languish in Mexico. A total of only three numbers were published, presumably because of financial difficulties that affected his publishing company, the Editorial Séneca. They corresponded to *primavera, verano,* and *otoño* of 1943. The first two appeared in 1943 and the third at the beginning of 1944.
5 Tussell, *Historia de la democracia cristiana en España*, 2 vols (Madrid 1974), I, 251
6 Full details of the differences that emerged between Falla and Bergamín over the running of *Cruz y Raya* are given by Luis Campodónico in 'Manuel de Falla y Bergamín. El contexto de una correspondencia,' *Mundo Nuevo* (Paris) 25

(1968): 15–24. What happened essentially was that Falla, already in 1933, and for a variety of reasons that are not always clear, asked Bergamín to remove his name from the list 'LA EDITAN,' which the journal carried in its early issues. This list became in 1934 'LA FUNDARON' and in the following year disappeared altogether, showing – at least symbolically – how the responsibility for *Cruz y Raya* became concentrated in Bergamín's hands.

7 Quoted by Tussell, *Historia de la democracia* ... , I, 248
8 In a letter to Falla, Bergamín, referring to *El aviso*, put great emphasis on 'el esfuerzo enorme de atención, selección y cuidado que durante un mes me vino costando,' quoted by Campodónico, 'Manuel de Falla y Bergamín,' 21.
9 Bergamín, prologue to *'Cruz y Raya.' Antología*, 9
10 Idem, 'Signo y diseño ... ,' XI
11 Quoted by Campodónico, 'Manuel de Falla y Bergamín,' 21. Notice Bergamín's possessive attitude towards *El aviso* in this passage.
12 G. de Torre, '*El aviso* o un almanaque de caprichos,' *Diario de Madrid*, 6 March 1935. In a letter to Campodónico, Bergamín admitted that he indulged certain personal whims when compiling the material for the almanac. See Campodónico, 'Manuel de Falla y Bergamín,' 19.
13 Falla to Bergamín, quoted by Campodónico, 'Manuel de Falla y Bergamín,' 19
14 Bergamín to Falla, ibid., 22
15 Ibid., 21–2
16 Ibid., 22
17 Bergamín, *La cabeza a pájaros* (Madrid 1934), 109
18 Oscar Wilde, quoted by W.H. Auden and L. Kronenberger in their edition of *The Faber Book of Aphorisms* (London 1962),5.
19 See Bergamín's 'Acotaciones a *Medea*,' *Primer Acto* 44 (1963): 35–6
20 Luis Felipe Vivanco, 'El aforismo y la creación poético-intelectual de José Bergamín,' in G. Díaz-Plaja, ed., *Historia general de las literaturas hispánicas*, 6 vols (Barcelona 1949–68), VI, 599–609, at 600

Bibliography

For convenience and clarity, this bibliography is divided into different sections. Although the heading of each section or subsection is self-explanatory, a few preliminary remarks indicating the problems posed by the presentation of the material, as well as other information, have been added.

A. BERGAMÍN'S WORK (1920–1936)

Some of the notes in this book have already drawn attention to the alarming disorder of Bergamín's published work. A number of his books, for example, have been republished under different titles, with their contents occasionally modified. Certain texts – like *Caracteres* and *La importancia del demonio* – have been reprinted with inexplicable frequency in the last ten years or so, while others have been entirely neglected. The number of articles that have never been collected in book form is truly remarkable. There has been only one attempt at providing a critical edition of a couple of major works – the 1981 edition of *El cohete y la estrella* and *La cabeza a pájaros* – and this left much to be desired. The title and contents of certain individual works can be mystifying: for example, *Poesías casi completas* of 1980 does not contain poetry exclusively, nor is it a collection of Bergamín's poetry up to that date.

These facts stress what will already be obvious to anyone who has tried to follow up even a passing interest in Bergamín's writing: that there is an urgent need to establish some order from this chaos. Ideally, this should be done in two complementary ways. First, an exhaustive bibliography of his writings from the beginning to the present day should be compiled, charting systematically, for example, the movements of particular central texts through the different editions in which they have appeared. To track down all the uncollected material is a daunting but not impossible task; in many ways it should be viewed as a prerequisite for any further research of any substance. The results of this bibliographical work would be voluminous but ultimately invaluable. Second, some initiative should be taken to produce an orderly edition of Bergamín's work as a whole. This could be done either chronologically or by genre, and with a critical apparatus that would correspond to the needs of the texts themselves. Such an edition could include previously uncollected material alongside texts already known, so that a clearer idea of the range and variety of Bergamín's work in particular areas could be presented.

Given the complexity of these problems and the extensive work they require in order to be solved satisfactorily, to say nothing of the embryonic state of Bergamín studies, I have decided to limit the scope of the bibliographical information concerning the writer to be appended here. Essentially, it is limited to the period covered in this book, that is, up to July 1936. The opening section lists (1) eight books published up to that date, with details restricted exclusively to first editions and to whatever subsequent editions referred to in this study; (2) all ninety-seven articles that appeared in separate publications, periodical or otherwise, before 31 July 1936. This list can be regarded as practically complete, though it is still possible that the Madrid press of the period will yield further, though minor finds. I have not encumbered this list with detailed indications of which articles eventually found their way into book form, though this kind of guidance would certainly be useful at some future stage; (3) all texts by Bergamín that were published in *Cruz y Raya*. Given Bergamín's special association with this journal and the attention I have devoted to it in this book, it seems legitimate to list these twenty-six separately.

1 *Books by Bergamín (1923–1936)*

Readers interested in Bergamín's work after 1936 should consult any of the following three bibliographies: (a) that compiled by Florence Delay and published as an appendix to Bergamín's *La claridad desierta* (Málaga 1973), 58–61; (b) that compiled by Gonzalo Penalva, in the appendix to Bergamín's *Por debajo del sueño. Antología poética* (Málaga 1979), n.p.; or (c) that compiled by Carlos Gurméndez and published in *El Libro Español* (Madrid), no. 304 (October 1983): 52–4. All three, however, should be handled with care; although they contain the basic data concerning Bergamín's work published in *book* form, they are in several other respects incomplete and misleading.

El cohete y la estrella. Madrid: Biblioteca de Indice 1923. Second edition in *Caballito del diablo* (Buenos Aires: Ed. Losada 1942), 17–62. Third edition (with *La cabeza a pájaros*), edited by José Esteban (Madrid: Ediciones Cátedra 1981), 51–84

Tres escenas en ángulo recto. Madrid 1925. No details of publisher given. Second edition in *La risa en los huesos* (Madrid: Ed. Nostromo 1974), 9–36
Caracteres. Málaga: Suplementos de Litoral 1927
Enemigo que huye. Madrid: Biblioteca Nueva 1927. Second edition in *La risa en los huesos*, 37–159
El arte de birlibirloque. Madrid: Ed. Plutarco 1930
Mangas y capirotes. Madrid: Ed. Plutarco 1933. Third edition, under same title (Madrid: Ediciones del Centro 1974)
La cabeza a pájaros. Madrid: Ediciones del Arbol 1934. Second edition in *Caballito del diablo*, 89–161. Third edition in the José Esteban edition (with *El cohete y la estrella*), 85–136
Disparadero español. Vol. I, *La más leve idea de Lope.* Madrid: Ediciones del Arbol 1936. Vol. II, *Presencia de espíritu.* Madrid: Ediciones del Arbol 1936.

2 *Articles by Bergamín (1921–July 1936)*

Given the sheer number of periodical publications to which Bergamín contributed during this period and the marginal nature of many of them, I have decided against using abbreviations of any kind to indicate a source.

'Santoral para escépticos.' *Indice* (Madrid) 1, no. 2 (July 1921): 28–30
'Márgenes.' *Indice* 1, no. 3 (1921, no month given): 53–6
'Mirar y pasar.' *Indice* 2, no. 4 (1922, no month given): 9–11
'Los mimos. Clotilde y Alexandre Sakharoff.' *Los Lunes del Imparcial* (Madrid), 21 January 1923, n.p.
'Consideración del comediante. Zacconi, intérprete de Shakespeare.' *Los Lunes del Imparcial*, 4 February 1923, n.p.
'Consideración de la comedia. (Trayectoria estética de la farsa). El teatro como voluntad y como representación.' *Revista de Casa América-Galicia* (La Coruña), no. 29 (May 1923): 2–3
Untitled (included in the series 'Cinco minutos de silencio en honor de Mallarmé'). *Revista de Occidente* (Madrid) 2, no. 5 (November 1923): 254–5
'El cohete y la estrella.' *España* (Madrid), no. 394 (3 November 1923): 6–7
'Márgenes.' *España*, no. 396 (17 November 1923): 7–8
'El mal ejemplo de Azorín. Carta abierta.' *España*, no. 398 (1 December 1923): 5
'Márgenes.' *España*, no. 399 (8 December 1923): 6–7
'Criba.' *España*, no. 400 (15 December 1923): 10–11
'El cohete y la estrella.' *La Verdad* (Murcia), suplemento literario no. 1 (6 January 1924)
'En respuesta a dos cartas' (letter from Bergamín to Juan Guerrero Ruiz). *La Verdad*, suplemento literario no. 1 (6 January 1924)

'Criba.' *España*, no. 403 (12 January 1924): 8–9

'Criba. Literatura y periodismo. Veinte años después.' *La Verdad*, suplemento literario no. 7 (24 February 1924)

'Márgenes y figuraciones.' *España*, no. 412 (8 March 1924): 11–12

'Alusiones aforísticas.' *La Verdad*, suplemento literario no. 11 (23 March 1924)

'Aforística inactual.' *Alfar* (La Coruña), no. 40 (May 1924): 2–3

'La supervivencia de Paul Valéry.' *La Verdad*, suplemento literario no. 22 (8 June 1924)

'Criba. Academus, o ¿cuál de los tres?' *La Verdad*, suplemento literario no. 24 (29 June 1924)

'D. Juan Valera y su prosa.' *La Verdad*, suplemento literario no. 47 (11 January 1925)

'Aforística persistente.' *Alfar*, no. 47 (February 1925): 2–3

'Nominalismo supra-realista.' *Alfar*, no. 50 (May 1925): 2–3

'"Ahijada de la divina ... " (Paisaje madrileño).' *Residencia* (Madrid), no. 1 (January-April 1926): 30

'Caracteres.' *La Verdad*, suplemento literario no. 52 (23 May 1926)

'Arte dramático. El caso de Pirandello.' *La Verdad*, suplemento literario no. 54 (20 June 1926)

'Reconnaissance à Rilke. Hommage.' *Les Cahiers du Mois* (Paris), nos 23–24 (May–June 1926): 85

'Transparencia y reflejo. (El arte poético cristiano de Max Jacob).' *Mediodía* (Seville), no. 5 (October 1926): 1–3

'Hija de la espuma.' *Litoral* (Málaga), no. 1 (November 1926): 6–7

'Miró.' *El Heraldo de Madrid*, 18 January 1927

'Molino de razón.' *Verso y Prosa* (Murcia), no. 1 (January 1927)

'La literatura difunta.' *La Gaceta Literaria* (Madrid), no. 3 (1 February 1927)

'Tres espectáculos distintos y una sola respresentación.' *La Gaceta Literaria*, no. 4 (15 February 1927)

'Veleta de locura.' *Verso y Prosa*, no. 2 (February 1927)

'Márgenes. Figura de cera: el arte romántico de Antonio Espina. La caja de música: el arte romántico de Jean Cassou.' *Verso y Prosa*, no. 3 (March 1927)

'Tres composiciones viendo el lugar.' *Litoral*, no. 3 (March 1927): 9–12

'Epistolario.' *Verso y Prosa*, no. 4 (April 1927)

'Orfeo sin infierno: Jean Cocteau ilusionista (en el escenario).' *Verso y Prosa*, no. 5 (May 1927)

'El idealismo andaluz.' *La Gaceta Literaria*, no. 11 (1 June 1927)

'Patos del aguachirle castellana.' *Verso y Prosa*, no. 6 (June 1927)

'Notas para unos prolegómenos a toda poética del porvenir que se presente como arte.' *Verso y Prosa*, no. 8 (August 1927)

'Martirio de San Sebastián.' *Verso y Prosa*, no. 9 (September 1927)

Untitled *décima. Litoral*, nos 5–7 (October 1927): 19

'Aforústica y epigromética.' *Ley* (Madrid), no. 1 (1927, no month given): 6–8

'Carmen: enigma y soledad.' *Carmen* (Gijon/Santander), no. 2 (January 1928), n.p.

'Hermes, encadenado.' *Mediodía*, no. 9 (January 1928): 4–6

'El grito en el cielo.' *Gallo* (Granada), no. 1 (February 1928): 7–8

'Por debajo de la música.' *Mediodía*, no. 11 (March 1928): 5–7, and continued in no. 13 (October 1928): 9–10

'Un centenario. La influencia de Ibsen en el teatro contemporáneo.' *ABC*, 15 March 1928

'La fe del carbonero o pasarse de listo.' *La Gaceta Literaria*, no. 31 (1 April 1928)

'Ni arte ni parte.' *La Gaceta Literaria*, no. 31 (1 April 1928)

'Contestaciones a la encuesta sobre la nueva arquitectura.' *La Gaceta Literaria*, no. 32 (15 April 1928)

'Solo de Ramón. Trompeta con sordina.' *Papel de Aleluyas* (Huelva), no. 6 (April 1928), n.p.

'Rusia, capital.' *La Gaceta Literaria*, no. 46 (15 November 1928)

'La poética de Jorge Guillén,' *La Gaceta Literaria*, no. 49 (1 January 1929). Also in *La Nación* (Buenos Aires), 21 April 1929

'La importancia artística del cinematógrafo.' *ABC* 16 January 1929

'Literatura y brújula.' *La Gaceta Literaria*, no. 51 (1 February 1929)

'El canto y la cal en la poesía de Rafael Alberti.' *La Gaceta Literaria*, no. 54 (15 March 1929)

'El arte dramático católico de Gil Vicente.' *Criterio* (Buenos Aires), no. 60 (April 1929): 531–3

'El alma en un hilo.' *Litoral*, no. 8 (May 1929): 26–8

'Los tiempos que corren en el teatro. I Genio y figura de Don Juan.' *ABC*, 21 November 1929, and 'Los Tiempos que corren en el teatro. II Génesis dramática del burlador.' *ABC*, 28 November 1929

'De veras y de burlas,' *La Gaceta Literaria*, no. 71 (1 December 1929)

'Ramón y el eco.' *La Gaceta Literaria*, no. 72 (15 December 1929)

'Dios, patria y ley.' *La Gaceta Literaria*, no. 78 (15 March 1930)

'Opiniones de los que fueron a Barcelona.' *La Gaceta Literaria*, no. 80 (15 April 1930)

'Contestaciones a la encuesta ¿Qué es la vanguardia?' *La Gaceta Literaria*, no. 83 (1 June 1930)

'Vallejo y su libro *Trilce*.' *Bolívar* (Madrid), no. 1 (November 1930): 5. Also published as the prologue to Vallejo's *Trilce* (Madrid 1930), 9–17

'Las raíces poéticas del "Teatro independiente revolucionario del XVII."' *Boletín de la Biblioteca Menéndez Pelayo* (Santander), no. 13 (1931): 223–60

'Jesuitismo y masonería. ¡Cuidado con los fantasmas!' *El Sol*, 5 February 1931

'Cruz y raya de la pintura.' *El Sol*, 14 May 1932
'Galdós redimuerto.' *Heraldo de Madrid*, 5 January 1933
'¿Adónde va Vicente?' *Los Cuatro Vientos* (Madrid), no. 1 (February 1933): 58–62
'El arte poético de bailar: La Argentinita.' *Heraldo de Madrid*, 20 April 1933
'Quien más ve, más oye, menos dura.' *Los Cuatro Vientos*, no. 3 (June 1933): 22–31
'Ni más ni menos que pintura.' *Arte* (Madrid), no. 2 (June 1933)
'¡Hay que alambicar!' *Luz* (Madrid), 22 June 1933
'La libertad del miedo.' *Luz*, 3 August 1933
'Dictaduras a la vista.' *Luz*, 19 August 1933
'¡Adelante con los faroles! o los aficionados al fascismo.' *Luz*, 31 October 1933
'Los enemigos de la República y ¡otro gallo nos cantará!' *Luz*, 25 November 1933
'En torno a Juan Ruiz de Alarcón: I. Ruiz de Alarcón en el laberinto de España.' *El Libro y El Pueblo* (Mexico) 11, no. 11 (November 1933): 395–9
'Poesía de verdad.' *Luz*, 30 January 1934
'Este amor que inventamos. Verdad de poesía.' *Luz*, 6 February 1934
'La República traicionada o El Escorial, los gusanos, y el real pudridero de España.' *Luz*, 17 April 1934
'El laburismo español y nueva paradoja del comediante.' *Diablo Mundo* (Madrid), no. 1 (28 April 1934): 3
'Aforística de ideas liebres.' In G. de Torre, E. Salazar y Chapela, and M. Pérez Ferrero, eds, *Almanaque literario*, 162–3. Madrid 1935
'Valle-Inclán.' *El Sol*, 7 January 1936
'Calderón y cierra España. (Contra aventura, ventura).' *El Sol*, 12, 19, and 26 April 1936
'Victor Hugo. La gran campanada romántica.' *Problemas de la Nueva Cultura* (Valencia), no. 1 (April 1936): 41–2
'Homenaje a Lope de Vega.' *El Sol*, 10 May 1936
'Reflexiones sobre la independencia de la tortuga.' *El Sol*, 14 June 1936
'El disparate en la literatura española. El disparate considerado como una forma poética del pensamiento.' *La Nación* (Buenos Aires), 28 June 1936
'El mundo por montera. Cúchares, la vida y la verdad.' *El Sol*, 5 July 1936
'Una nueva carta de José Bergamín. La calificación de reaccionario le resulta injuriosa.' *El Socialista* (Madrid), 13 July 1936
'El disparate en la literatura española. El disparate en Cervantes, Santa Teresa y Lope.' *La Nación*, 19 July 1936
Untitled prologue to Etienne Gilson, *Por un orden católico*. Madrid 1936, vii–xi

3 *Articles by Bergamín in* Cruz y Raya

There does exist a complete and annotated index to *Cruz y Raya*, though it has been out of print for many years: Rafael Benítez Claros, *'Cruz y Raya.' (Madrid, 1933–1936)* (Madrid, 1947).

a) Essays:
'El pensamiento hermético de las artes,' no. 1 (April 1933): 41–66
'La decadencia del analfabetismo,' no. 3 (June 1933): 61–94
'La importancia del demonio,' no. 5 (August 1933): 7–51
'Lope, siguiendo el dictamen del aire que lo dibuja,' nos 23–24 (February–March 1935): 7–52
'Laberinto de la novela y monstruo de la novelería,' part i, no. 33 (December 1935): 7–42; part ii, no. 34 (January 1936): 7–61

b) Anthologies:
'Santa Catalina de Siena,' no. 3 (June 1933): 95–114
'El purgatorio de Santa Catalina,' no. 27 (June 1934): 105–42

c) Critical commentaries (in the 'Cristal del Tiempo' section):
'Las manos vacías,' no. 4 (July 1933): 103–7
'Llamémosle hache. La revolución en entredicho y la contra-revolución en entreacto,' no. 8 (November 1933): 141–5
'Un gran vuelo de cuervos mancha el azul celeste,' no. 12 (March 1934): 144–7
'Sí o no, como Cristo nos enseña,' no. 14 (May 1934): 93–101
'El "tris" de todo y ¿qué es España?' no. 19 (October 1934): 109–19
'El estado fantasma y ¿en qué país vivimos?' no. 20 (November 1934): 127–33
'Dar que decir al demonio,' no. 25 (April 1935): 125–32
'Hablar en cristiano,' no. 28 (July 1935): 73–83
'La callada de Dios,' no. 29 (August 1935): 77–84
'El rescoldo. (Manuel Bartolomé Cossío),' no. 30 (September 1935): 89–92
'Paz con paz, guerra con guerra,' no. 33 (December 1935): 105–12
'Cuatro paredes chamuscadas,' no. 39 (June 1936): 95–9

d) Critical commentaries (in the 'Criba' section):
'Sucesión. Discontinuidad,' no. 1 (April 1933): 153–4
'La letra y la sangre,' no. 1 (April 1933): 154
'No mixtificar y no seréis mixtificados,' no. 3 (June 1933): 165–6
'Por ejemplo,' no. 4 (July 1933): 149–50
'Unas palabras al oído,' no. 6 (September 1933): 155–7

e) Special supplements:
Inventivas: 'La estatua de Don Tancredo,' no. 14 (May 1934): 47 pp.

Incidencias: 'El clavo ardiendo (dos cartas), por Arturo Serrano Plaja y José Bergamín,' no. 32 (November 1935): 33 pp.

B. ABOUT BERGAMÍN AND *CRUZ Y RAYA*

The details given here are limited to those critical texts which (1) refer directly to Bergamín's work prior to 1936, or which (2) were consulted during the writing of this study. Unsurprisingly, no systematic work has yet been done on the critical writings devoted to Bergamín after 1936. In my *'El aposento en el aire': introducción a la poesía de José Bergamín* (Valencia 1983), I have listed the main critical articles that examine different aspects of Bergamín's poetry (pp. 117–18).

1 *About Bergamín*

Alfaro, José María. 'Alrededor de cuatro lecciones sobre teatro español.' *El Sol*, 12 December 1931
– 'España en su laberinto.' *El Sol*, 28 July 1933
Alonso, Cecilio. 'José Bergamín: utopía y popularismo.' *Camp de l'Arpa* (Barcelona), no. 13 (October 1974): 10–16
Anon. 'Palencia, Alberti, Bergamín.' *La Gaceta Literaria*, 1 November 1928
– 'Conferencias. Don José Bergamín en la Residencia de Señoritas.' *El Sol*, 6 May 1932
– 'Una conferencia de José Bergamín en las reuniones de interayuda universitaria.' *Heraldo de Madrid*, 12 April 1934
– 'José Pegamín se define.' *Gracia y Justicia* (Madrid), no. 122 (21 April 1934): 14
– 'José Bergamín habla de "Don Tancredo" en la Residencia de Señoritas.' *Heraldo de Madrid*, 10 May 1934
Arroyo-Stephens, Manuel. 'El Cervantes como premio a la conducta.' *Diario 16* (Madrid), 2 November 1982
Aveline, Claude. 'Présentation de José Bergamín,' Introduction to Bergamín's *Aphorismes* (Avignon 1959)
Azorín. 'España. José Bergamín.' *ABC*, 31 January 1930
Cammarano, Leonardo. 'José Bergamín o l'arte che interpreta se stessa.' *Tempo Presente* (Rome) 7 (July 1963): 65–8
Cañizal de la Fuente, Luis. Untitled review of *Beltenebros y otros ensayos sobre literatura española*. *Insula* (Madrid), no. 329 (April 1974): 4
Carrasco, Bel. 'Presentación de *Al fin y al cabo* y *Poesías casi completas* de José Bergamín.' *El País* (Madrid), 22 February 1981
Cassou, Jean. Untitled review of *El cohete y la estrella*. *Mercure de France* (Paris) 170 (15 February–15 March 1924): 827

- Untitled review of *Tres escenas en ángulo recto*. *Mercure de France* 183 (1 October–1 November 1925): 267
- Untitled review of *Enemigo que huye*. *Mercure de France* 204 (15 May–15 June 1928): 490–1
Delay, Florence. 'Portrait de Bergamín.' *La Quinzaine Littéraire* (Paris), 16–30 April 1970, 10
- 'La crítica citacional de José Bergamín.' *Camp de l'Arpa*, nos 67–68 (September –October 1979): 15–20
Dennis, Nigel. 'José Bergamín y la exaltación del disparate.' *Cuadernos Hispanoamericanos*, no. 288 (June 1974): 539–56
- 'José Bergamín y su conciencia escamoteada.' *Primer Acto* (Madrid), nos 170–171 (July–August 1974): 10–12
- '"Dueño en su laberinto." El ensayista José Bergamín (de la Irreal Anti-Academia).' *Camp de l'Arpa*, nos 23–24 (August–September 1975): 13–19
- '*Popularismo* and *Barroquismo* in the Work of José Bergamín.' Unpublished PH D dissertation, University of Cambridge 1976
- 'José Bergamín: ilustración y defensa de la frivolidad.' *Cuadernos Hispanoamericanos*, no. 342 (December 1978): 603–13
- 'Caracterología bergaminiana. (Verso y prosa en la joven literatura).' *Nueva Estafeta* (Madrid), no. 3 (February 1979): 75–7
- 'Rafael Alberti, José Bergamín y la Eva Gundersen de *Sobre los ángeles*.' *Nueva Estafeta*, no. 15 (February 1980): 60–70
- 'José Bergamín and the Aesthetics of the Generation of 1927.' *Bulletin of Hispanic Studies* (Liverpool) 58 (1981): 313–28
- 'El neo-barroquismo en la prosa española de pre-guerra: el caso de José Bergamín.' *Revista de Occidente*, fourth series, no. 14 (June–July 1982): 85–96
Espina, Antonio. Untitled review of *El cohete y la estrella*. *Revista de Occidente*, first series, 3, no. 7 (January 1924): 125–7
Fernández Almagro, M. 'Nómina incompleta de la joven literatura.' *Verso y Prosa*, no. 1 (January 1927): n.p.
- 'José Bergamín: los juegos de la inteligencia.' *La Gaceta Literaria*, 1 May 1930
Gaya, Ramón. 'Epílogo para un libro de José Bergamín.' In Bergamín's *La claridad desierta* (Málaga 1973), 209–14
Giménez Caballero, E. 'La literatura en la política. José Bergamín, Director de Acción Social Agraria e Inspector General de Seguros y Ahorros.' *La Gaceta Literaria*, no. 112 (15 August 1931)
Gurméndez, Carlos. 'La amistad de Bergamín con Unamuno y Ortega.' *El País*, 10 October 1979, 28
- 'La irreductible personalidad de José Bergamín.' *El País*, supplement of 14 November 1982, 12–14
Jarnés, B. Untitled review of *Enemigo que huye*. *La Gaceta Literaria*, no. 35 (1 June 1928)

Jiménez, Juan Ramón. 'Historias de España y México. Carta obligada a mí mismo.' *Letras de México* 4, no. 20 (1 August 1944): 7

Jiménez Losantos, F. 'El insólito peregrinaje de los libros de Bergamín.' *El País*, 6 September 1978, 20

Maravall, José Antonio. 'Pasión y vida de José Bergamín.' *Literatura* (Madrid), no. 4 (July–August 1934): 127–8

Marfil, Jorge. 'José Bergamín, una inteligencia inclasificable.' *El Viejo Topo*, March 1978, 23–7

Pérez Ferrero, M. 'Ensayo y periodismo de dos nombres de nuestro tiempo.' *Heraldo de Madrid*, 13 July 1933, 13

– Untitled review of *La cabeza a pájaros. Heraldo de Madrid*, 14 June 1934, 6

Pérez Minik, D. 'De la España peregrina a un peregrino en su patria.' *La Vanguardia*, 17 September 1972

Porcel, B. 'José Bergamín, fantasmagórico.' *Destino* (Barcelona), 3 January 1970

Porlan y Merlo, R. Untitled review of *Enemigo que huye. Mediodía*, no 14 (February 1929): 15–16

Romero y Murube, J. Untitled review of *Caracteres. Mediodía*, no. 7 (January 1927): 19

Salas Viu, V. 'Bergamín y su *Disparadero español.' El Sol*, 11 July 1936, 2

Salazar Chapela, E. Untitled review of *Enemigo que huye. El Sol*, 12 April 1928, 2

– Untitled review of *El arte de birlibirloque. El Sol*, 6 August 1930, 2

Salinas, P. 'España en su laberinto.' *Indice Literario* (Madrid) 2, no. 6 (June 1933): 145–50

– 'Los aforismos de José Bergamín.' *Indice Literario* 3, no. 5 (May 1934): 93–8

Santonja, Gonzalo. 'Aproximación a José Bergamín.' *Punto y Hora* (San Sebastián), no. 281 (10–17 October 1982): 12

Sijé, Ramón. 'Péndulo y carbonería.' *El Gallo Crisis* (Orihuela), no. 1 (Corpus 1934): 31–2

Suarès, Guy. 'Un entretien avec José Bergamín. Espoirs et désillusion d'un intellectuel espagnol.' *Le Monde*, 30 November 1963

Torre, G. de. 'Del aforismo al ensayo.' *Luz*, 6 July 1934, 8

Unamuno, M. de. Untitled review of *El cohete y la estrella. Nuevo Mundo* (Madrid), 7 March 1924

Usigli, Rodolfo. 'Un escritor en manos de sus palabras.' *El Libro y el Pueblo* 11, no. 11 (November 1933): 400– 3

Vivanco, Luis Felipe. 'El aforismo y la creación poético-intelectual de José Bergamín.' In G. Díaz-Plaja, ed., *Historia general de las literaturas hispánicas*, VI, 599–609. 6 vols. Barcelona 1949–68

Zambrano, María. 'El escritor José Bergamín.' *El Nacional* (Caracas), 9 May 1961

2 *About* Cruz y Raya

Also included here are details of articles on the two *Cruz y Raya* almanacs of 1934 and 1935.

Alonso de los Ríos, César. 'José Bergamín y su *Cruz y Raya*.' *Triunfo* (Madrid), no. 615 (13 July 1974): 34–7
Anon. 'Debates.' *El Sol*, 26 April 1933, 2
– 'Los escritores españoles contra la tiranía de Dollfus. Comentario y adhesión de *Cruz y Raya* al documento del grupo francés de *Esprit*.' *Heraldo de Madrid*, 19 April 1934, 7
– Untitled review of *El aviso de escarmentados*. *El Sol*, 26 February 1935, 2
– 'Con Bergamín en *Cruz y Raya*.' *El Sol*, 12 July 1936, 2
Bécarud, Jean. *'Cruz y Raya' (1933–1936)*. Madrid 1969
– 'Carta a José Bergamín.' *Triunfo*, 21 August 1974
Benítez Claros, Rafael. *'Cruz y Raya.' (Madrid, 1933– 1936)*. Madrid 1947
Brion, Marcel. 'L'actualité littéraire à l'étranger.' *Les Nouvelles Littéraires* (Paris), 3 March 1934, 8
Campodónico, Luis. 'Manuel de Falla y Bergamín. El contexto de una correspondencia.' *Mundo Nuevo* (Paris), no. 25 (1968): 15–24
Dennis, Nigel. 'Posdata sobre José Bergamín. *Cruz y Raya*: una revista que habla por sí misma.' *Cuadernos Hispanoamericanos*, no. 301 (July 1975): 143–59
– '*El aviso de escarmentados* de 1935 y el futuro de *Cruz y Raya*.' *Insula*, nos 368–369 (July-August 1977): 23 and 26
Mourlane Michelena, Pedro. 'Parabién al grupo que escribe *Cruz y Raya*,' *El Sol*, 11 February 1934
Paniagua, D. 'El más y el menos.' *La Hora* (Madrid), no. 95 (September 1958): 22
– 'Paréntesis sobre la revolución.' *La Hora*, no. 97 (November 1958): 30
Pérez Ferrero, M. 'Actualidad literaria. *El Acabóse* (almanaque).' *Heraldo de Madrid*, 11 January 1934, 6
Torre, Guillermo de. 'El aviso o un almanaque de caprichos.' *Diario de Madrid*, 6 March 1935

C. BOOKS AND ARTICLES

Included in this section are all the texts directly referred to in the notes of the main body of this study, as well as the principal books and articles that I consulted while writing it and which directly or indirectly helped to shape my view of the period and the main issues it raises.

Books

Alberti, R. *Prosas encontradas. 1924–1942*. Edited by R. Marrast. Madrid 1970

– *La arboleda perdida*. Barcelona 1975

Albornoz, A. de, ed. *Juan Ramón Jiménez*. Madrid 1980

Alonso, D. *Poetas españoles contemporáneos*. Madrid 1952

– *Cuatro poetas españoles*. Madrid 1962

Altolaguirre, M. *Las islas invitadas*. Edited by M. Smerdou Altolaguirre. Madrid 1972

Amorós, A. *Introducción a la literatura*. Madrid 1979

Aub, Max. *El teatro español sacado a la luz de las tinieblas de nuestro tiempo*. Madrid 1956

– *Manual de historia de la literatura española*. Madrid 1974

Aubrun, C., and M. Baquero Goyanes et al. *Homenaje a Gracián*. Zaragoza 1958

Auden, W.H., and L. Kronenberger, eds. *The Faber Book of Aphorisms*. London 1962

Ayala, F. *Histrionismo y representación*. Buenos Aires 1944

Aznar Soler, M. (see also Schneider, L.M.). *II Congreso Internacional de Escritores Antifascistas (1937). Pensamiento literario y compromiso antifascista de la inteligencia española republicana*. Barcelona 1978

Bassolas, Carmen. *La ideología de los escritores. Literatura y política en 'La Gaceta Literaria' (1927–1932)*. Barcelona 1975

Bécarud, J., and E. López Campillo. *Los intelectuales españoles durante la II República*. Madrid 1978

Bizcarrondo, Marta. *Araquistáin y la crisis socialista en la II República. 'Leviatán' (1934–1936)*. Madrid 1975

Blanch, A. *La poesía pura española. Conexiones con la cultura francesa*. Madrid 1976

Blanco Aguinaga, C. *Emilio Prados. Vida y obra*. New York 1960

Blanco Aguinaga, C., J. Rodríguez Puértolas, and Iris M. Zavala. *Historia social de la literatura española (en lengua castellana)*. 3 vols. Madrid 1978–9

Bockus Aponte, B. *Alfonso Reyes and Spain*. Austin and London 1972

Bodini, V. *Los poetas surrealistas españoles*. Barcelona 1971

Bonet, J.M., et al. *Juan Guerrero Ruiz y sus amigos*. Madrid 1982

Brihuega, J. *Manifiestos, proclamas, panfletos y textos doctrinales. Las vanguardias artísticas en España, 1910–1931*. Madrid 1979

– *La vanguardia y la República*. Madrid 1982

Brihuega, J., et al. *Orígenes de la vanguardia española: 1920–1936*. Madrid 1974

Buckley, R., and J. Crispin, eds. *Los vanguardistas españoles. (1925–1935)*. Madrid 1973

Cano, J.L. *La poesía de la generación del 27*. Madrid 1970

Cano Ballesta, J. *La poesía española entre pureza y revolución (1930–1936)*. Madrid 1972

– *Literatura y tecnología. Las letras españolas ante la revolución industrial (1900–1933)*. Madrid 1981

237 Bibliography

Capote Benot, J.M. *El período sevillano de Luis Cernuda*. Madrid 1971
Caudet, F. *'Romance' (1940–41): una revista del exilio*. Madrid 1975
Cernuda, L. *Estudios sobre poesía española contemporánea*. Madrid 1957
– *Crítica, ensayos y evocaciones*. Barcelona 1970
– *Perfil del aire*. Edited by D. Harris. London 1971
Chabás, J. *Literatura española contemporánea (1898–1950)*. Havana 1952
Cobb, C.H. *La cultura y el pueblo. España, 1930–1939*. Barcelona 1981
Collard, A. *Nueva poesía. Conceptismo, culteranismo en la crítica española*. Madrid 1967
Connell, G.W., ed. *Spanish Poetry of the 'Grupo poético de 1927.'* Oxford 1977
Correas, G. *Vocabulario de refranes y frases proverbiales*. Edited by L. Combert. Bordeaux 1967
Corredor Matheos, J. *Vida y obra de Benjamín Palencia*. Madrid 1979
Costa, R. de, ed. *Vicente Huidobro y el creacionismo*. Madrid 1975
Dehennin, E. *La Résurgence de Góngora et la Génération Poétique de 1927*. Paris 1962
Del Río, A. *Historia de la literatura española*. 2 vols. New York 1963
Deschner, K. *Med Gud og Fascisterna*. Oslo 1971
Díaz, E. *Pensamiento español 1939–1973*. Madrid 1974
Díaz-Plaja, G. *El espíritu del barroco*. Barcelona 1940
– *El poema en prosa en España. Estudio crítico y antología*. Barcelona 1956
– *El barroco literario*. Buenos Aires 1970
– *Vanguardismo y protesta*. Barcelona 1975
– *Estructura y sentido del novecentismo español*. Madrid 1975
– *Memoria de una generación destruída (1920–1936)*. Barcelona 1976
Diego, G. *Primera antología de sus versos*. Buenos Aires 1941
– ed. *Antología poética en honor de Góngora*. Madrid 1927
– ed. *Poesía española. Antología 1915–1931*. Madrid 1932
– ed. *Poesía española. Antología (contemporáneos)*. Madrid 1934
Díez de Revenga, F.J. *Revistas murcianas relacionadas con la generación del 27*. 2nd ed. Murcia 1979
Espina, A. *El alma garibay*. Santiago de Chile and Madrid 1964
– *El genio cómico y otros ensayos*. Santiago de Chile and Madrid 1965
Esteban, J., and G. Santonja. *Los novelistas sociales españoles (1928–1936)*. Madrid 1977
Fagen, P.W. *Exiles and Citizens. Spanish Republicans in Mexico*. Austin 1973
Fernández Cifuentes, L. *Teoría y mercado de la novela en España del 98 a la República*. Madrid 1982
Fuentes, Víctor. *La marcha al pueblo en las letras españolas 1917–1936*. Madrid 1980
Gallego Morell, A. *Vida y poesía de Gerardo Diego*. Barcelona 1956
García Lorca, F. *Obras completas*. 2 vols. 18th ed. Madrid 1974

Geist, A.L. *La poética de la generación del 27 y las revistas literarias: de la vanguardia al compromiso (1918– 1936)*. Barcelona 1980
Gibson, I. *En busca de José Antonio*. Barcelona 1980
Gide, André. *Journal (1889–1939)*. Paris 1948
– *Defensa de la cultura*. Edited by F. Caudet. Madrid 1981
Gil-Albert, J. *Memorabilia*. Barcelona 1975
Giménez Caballero, E. *Julepe de menta*. Madrid 1927
– *Junto a la tumba de Larra*. Madrid 1971
– *Genio de España*. 7th ed. Madrid 1971
Goethe, J.W. von. *Faust. Part One*. Harmondsworth 1978
Gómez de la Serna, G. *Ramón. Vida y obra*. Madrid 1963
Gracián, B. *Oráculo manual y arte de prudencia*. Edited by M. Romero-Navarro. Madrid 1954
– *Agudeza y arte de ingenio*. Edited by E. Correa Calderón. 2 vols. Madrid 1969
– *El criticón*. Edited by E. Correa Calderón. 3 vols. Madrid 1971
Guerrero Ruiz, J. *Juan Ramón de viva voz*. Madrid 1961
Hernando, M.A. *'La Gaceta Literaria' (1927–1932). Biografía y valoración*. Valladolid 1974
– *Prosa vanguardista en la generación del 27. (Gécé y 'La Gaceta Literaria')*. Madrid 1975
Hollingwood, R.J., ed. *A Nietzsche Reader*. Harmondsworth 1977
Ilie, P., ed. *Documents of the Spanish Vanguard*. Chapel Hill 1969
Jarnés, B. *Ejercicios*. Madrid 1927
Jiménez, J.R. *Españoles de tres mundos*. Edited by R. Gullón. Madrid 1969
– *Libros de prosa: I*. Madrid 1969
– *Selección de cartas (1899–1958)*. Edited by F. Garfias. Barcelona 1973
Jiménez Fajardo, S., and John C. Wilcox, eds. *At Home and Beyond: New Essays on Spanish Poets of the Twenties*. Lincoln, NE 1983
Jiménez Fraud, A. *La Residencia de Estudiantes. Visita a Maquiavelo*. Madrid 1972
Lechner, J. *El compromiso en la poesía española del siglo XX.* 2 vols. Leiden 1968
López Campillo, E. *La 'Revista de Occidente' y la formación de minorías, 1923–1936*. Madrid 1972
Mainer, J.C. *Literatura y pequeña burguesía en España, 1890–1950*. Madrid 1972
– *La edad de plata (1902–1931); ensayo de interpretación de un proceso cultural*. Barcelona 1975. Second edition, revised to cover the period 1902–1939: Madrid 1981
– *Falange y literatura (antología)*. Barcelona 1971
Maravall, J.A. *La cultura del barroco*. Barcelona 1975
Marichal, J. *La voluntad del estilo; teoría e historia del ensayismo hispánico*. Madrid 1971
Moreno Villa, J. *Vida en claro. Autobiografía*. Mexico 1944

Morla Lynch, C. *En España con Federico García Lorca. (Páginas de un diario íntimo, 1928–1936).* Madrid 1958
Morris, C.B. *A Generation of Spanish Poets. 1920– 1936.* Cambridge 1969
– *Surrealism and Spain. 1920–936.* Cambridge 1972
– *This Loving Darkness. The Cinema and Spanish Writers 1920–1936.* Oxford 1981
– *El manifesto surrealista escrito en Tenerife.* Tenerife 1983
Mounier, E. *Révolution Personnaliste et Communautaire.* Paris 1935
Mourgues, O. de. *Metaphysical, Baroque and Précieux Poetry.* Oxford 1963
Mousacchio, D. *La revista 'Mediodía' de Sevilla.* Seville 1980
Neira, J. *'Litoral,' la revista de una generación.* Santander 1978
Orozco Díaz, E. *Temas del barroco.* Granada 1947
– *Lección permanente del barroco.* Madrid 1952
Ortega Y Gasset, J. *Obras completas.* 6 vols. 4th ed. Madrid 1957–8
Ossorio, A. *La guerra de España y los católicos.* Buenos Aires 1942
Palau de Nemes, G. *Vida y obra de Juan Ramón Jiménez* (Madrid, 1957)
Pascal, B. *Pensées.* Paris 1964
Pastor, M. *Los orígenes del fascismo en España.* Madrid 1975
Pérez Ferrero. *Tertulias y grupos literarios.* Madrid 1975
Pérez Ferrero, M., G. de Torre, and E. Salazar Chapela, eds. *Almanaque literario.* Madrid 1935
Pérez Merinero, C. and D. *En pos del cinema.* Barcelona 1974
– *Del cinema como arma de clase. Antología de 'Nuestro Cinema,' 1932–1935.* Valencia 1975
Pérez Minik, D. *Facción española surrealista en Tenerife.* Barcelona 1975
Rama, C. *La crisis española del siglo xx.* Mexico 1960
Ramos, V. *Vida y teatro de Carlos Arniches.* Madrid 1966
Ranch, R.W. *Politics and Belief in Contemporary France: Emmanuel Mounier and Christian Democracy, 1932–1950.* The Hague 1952
Redondo, G. *Las empresas políticas de José Ortega y Gasset.* 2 vols. Madrid 1970
Ridruejo, D. *Casi unas memorias.* Barcelona 1976
Rodrigo, A. *García Lorca en Cataluña.* Barcelona 1975
Rougemont. D. de. *Politique de la personne.* Paris 1934
Rozas, J.M. *La generación del 27 desde dentro.* Madrid 1974
– *El 27 como generación.* Santander 1978
Ruiz Ramón, F. *Historia del teatro español. Siglo xx.* Madrid 1975
Ruiz Salvador, A. *Ateneo, Dictadura y República.* Valencia 1977
Ruthven, K.K. *The Conceit.* London 1969
Santos Torroella, R. *Catálogo de revistas. Medio siglo de publicaciones de poesía en España.* Segovia 1952
Sbarbi, J.M. *El refranero general español.* 10 vols. Madrid 1874–8

- *Monografía sobre los refranes, adagios y proverbios castellanos.* Madrid 1891
- *Diccionario de refranes, adagios, proverbios, modismos, locuciones y frases proverbiales de la lengua española.* 2 vols. Madrid 1922
Schneider, L.M. *II Congreso Internacional de Escritores Antifascistas (1937). Inteligencia y guerra civil española.* Barcelona 1978
Schneider, L.M., and M. Aznar Soler, ed. *II Congreso Internacional de Escritores Antifascistas (1937). Ponencias, documentos y testimonios.* Barcelona 1979
Semprún y Gurrea, J.M. *República, libertad y estatismo.* Madrid 1931
Senarclens, P. de. *Le Mouvement 'Esprit,' 1932–1941.* Lausanne 1974
Siebenmann, G. *Los estilos poéticos en España desde 1900.* Madrid 1973
Sobejano, G. *Nietzsche en España.* Madrid 1967
Symons, J. *The Thirties.* 2nd ed. London 1975
Tandy, L., and M. Sferrazza. *Giménez Caballero y 'La Gaceta Literaria' (o la Generación del 27).* Madrid 1977
Torre, G. de. *Literaturas europeas de vanguardia.* Madrid 1925
- *La aventura estética de nuestro tiempo.* Barcelona 1962
Torrente Ballester, G. *Panorama de la literatura española contemporánea.* Madrid 1956
- *Literatura española contemporánea.* Madrid 1964
Tuñón de Lara, M. *Medio siglo de cultura española (1885–1936).* 3rd ed. Madrid 1973
- *La España del siglo XX.* Paris 1973
- ed. *Sociedad, política y cultura en la España de los siglos XIX y XX.* Madrid 1973
- ed. *Movimiento obrero, política y literatura en la España contemporánea.* Madrid 1974
Tussell, J. *Historia de la democracia cristiana en España.* 2 vols. Madrid 1974
Valbuena Prat, A. *La poesía española contemporánea.* Madrid 1930
- *Historia de la literatura española.* 3 vols. 6th ed. Barcelona 1960–2
Valencia Jaén, J. *Indice bibliográfico de la revista 'Mediodía.'* Seville 1961
Vallejo, C. *Espistolario general.* Edited by J.M. Castañón. Valencia 1982
Vela, F. *El arte al cubo y otros ensayos.* Madrid 1927
Videla, G. *El ultraísmo.* Madrid 1971
Weinstein, L. *The Metamorphoses of Don Juan.* Palo Alto 1959
Wilde, Oscar. *Plays, Prose Writings and Poems.* Edited by I. Murray. London 1975
Zulueta, E. de. *Historia de la crítica española contemporánea.* Madrid 1966

Articles

Abril, M. 'Itinerario del nuevo arte plástico.' *Revista de Occidente*, first series, 14 (1926): 343–67

Aleixandre, V. 'Mundo poético.' *Verso y Prosa*, no. 12 (October 1928)

Alonso, D. 'Claridad y belleza de las *Soledades*.' In L. de Góngora, *Soledades*, 7–36. Madrid 1927

Anon. 'De la tertulia.' *La Verdad*, no. 53 (6 June 1926): 3

– 'Los intelectuales y la represión de las huelgas de Asturias.' Special issue of *Boletín Informativo del Centro de Documentación y Estudios* (Paris), no. 19 (November 1963)

Aranguren, J.L. 'Evolución espiritual de los intelectuales españoles en la emigración.' *Cuadernos Hispanoamericanos*, no. 38 (1953): 123–37

– 'Antonio Marichalar y la generación de 1927.' *Informaciones* (Madrid), 28 November 1974

Ayala, F. 'Apuntes para una visión de la joven literatura.' *Síntesis* (Buenos Aires), no. 13 (July 1928): 8–15

Azocoaga, E. 'Sentido antisocial del poeta. Fragmentos.' *Hoja Literaria* (Madrid), no. 2 (April 1933): 4–5

Behar, H. 'L'Espagne au coeur. (Le deuxième congrès international des écrivains).' *Europe* (Paris), no. 637 (May 1982): 179–200

Buckley, R. 'Francisco Ayala y el arte de vanguardia. (Hacia una nueva valoración de la generación de 1927).' *Insula*, no. 278 (January 1970): 1 and 10

Cano, J.L. 'La generación poética de 1925. Noticia histórica.' *Revista Nacional de Cultura* (Caracas) 12 (1954): 75–80

– 'Cernuda y la publicación de *Perfil del aire*.' *Nueva Estafeta*, no. 2 (1978): 54–60

Cano Ballesta, J. 'Poesía y revolución: Emilio Prados (1930–1936).' In *Homenaje universitario a Dámaso Alonso*, 231–48. Madrid 1970

Cavallo, S. 'Un antecedente del 27: Gómez de la Serna y la greguería.' *Insula*, no. 368–69 (July–August 1977): 26

Chabás, J. 'Elegía a las revistas.' *El Sol*, 15 January 1933, 2

Corbalan, P. 'Los escritores y el cine (1925–1933).' *Informaciones* 12 September 1974

Cossío, J.M. 'Recuerdos de una generación poética.' In *Homenaje universitario a Dámaso Alonso*, 189–202

Costa, L.F. 'La deshumanización del arte y la generación de 1927.' *Los Ensayistas* 4, VI–VII (1979): 39–49

Croll, M.W. 'The Baroque style in prose.' In *Studies in English Philology. A Miscellany in Honour of F. Klaeber*, 427–56. Minneapolis 1929

Dennis, Nigel. 'Los intelectuales y la República. El semanario *Diablo Mundo* (1934).' *Ottawa Hispánica*, no. 3 (1981): 1–42

Dennis, Nigel, and Lorraine Albert. 'Literary and Cultural Periodicals in Spain: 1920–1936. A Bibliography.' *Ottawa Hispánica*, no. 4 (1982): 127–70

Díaz Fernández, J. '1930. La nueva generación.' *El Sol*, 16 July 1930, 2

Diego, G. 'La vuelta a la estrofa.' *Carmen*, no. 1 (December 1927): n.p.

- 'Crónica del centenario gongorino.' *Lola*, nos 1 and 2 (December 1927 and January 1928): n.p.
- 'Mínimas estéticas.' *Meseta* (Valladolid), no. 1 (January 1928): 5
- 'Defensa de la poesía.' *Carmen*, no. 5 (April 1928): n.p.
- 'La nueva arte poética española.' *Síntesis*, no. 20 (January 1929): 183–99
Domenchina, Juan José. 'Poetas españoles del 13 al 31.' *El Sol*, 12 March 1933, 2 and 19 March 1933, 2
- 'Soliloquio en retazos alrededor de la poesía.' *El Sol*, 2 April 1933, 2
- 'Poesía y crítica.' *El Sol*, 21 May 1933, 2
- 'Poesía o yugo.' *El Sol*, 11 June 1933, 2
Espina, A. '¿Incompatible? La cultura y el espíritu proletario.' *El Sol*, 18 July 1930, 1
Fuentes, V. 'La novela social española (1931–1936): temas y significación ideológica.' *Insula*, no. 288 (November 1970): 1 and 4
- 'Los libros y los lectores durante la II República.' *Arbor* (Madrid) CIX, nos 426–427 (June–July 1981): 85–94
García de la Concha, V. '*Alfar*: historia de dos revistas literarias (1920–1927).' *Cuadernos Hispanoamericanos*, no. 255 (March 1971): 500–34
Garfias, F. 'Las revistas juanramonianas.' *Poesía Española* (Madrid), second series, nos 140–141 (August–September 1964): 9–10
Gili Gaya, S. 'Agudeza, modismos y lugares comunes.' In *Homenaje a Gracián*, 89–97. Zaragoza 1958
Giménez Caballero, E. 'Bellas letras.' *Poesía* (Madrid), no. 3 (November–December 1978): 72–80
Grady, H.H. 'Rhetoric, Wit and Art in Gracián's *Agudeza*.' *Modern Language Quarterly* (Seattle) 41, I (March 1980): 21–37
Guillén, J. 'Carta a Fernando Vela.' *Verso y Prosa*, no. 2 (February 1927): n.p.
Gullón, R. 'Ambiente espiritual de la generación española de 1925.' *Revista Nacional de Cultura* XXI, no. 136 (September–October 1959); 28–49
- 'Los prosistas de la generación de 1925.' *Insula*, no. 126 (May 1957): 1 and 8
Hatzfeld, H. 'A Clarification of the Baroque Problem in the Romance Literatures.' *Comparative Literature* 1, 2 (Spring 1949): 113–39
- 'The Barroquism of Gracián's *El oráculo manual*.' In *Homenaje a Gracián*, 103–18
Jiménez, J.R. 'Prosa inédita.' *El Sol*, 30 April 1933, 2
Jowers, R. 'Las revistas literarias.' *Revista de Occidente*, fourth series, nos 7–8 (November 1981): 133– 54
Laporta, F.J. 'Los intelectuales y la República.' *Historia 16* (Madrid) 6, 60 (April 1981): 86–93
Larrea, J. 'Epílogo' to the facsimile reprint of *España Peregrina*. Mexico 1977. Appended to no. 10 (1941), 75–86
López Campillo, E. 'Apuntes sobre la evolución en la temática del ensayo

español (1895–1930).' *Cuadernos Hispanoamericanos*, no. 255 (March 1971): 445–60
– 'Esquema de los criterios intelectuales bajo Primo de Rivera.' *Cuadernos Hispanoamericanos*, no. 291 (1974): 690–7
– 'El antimilitarismo de los intelectuales en la revista *España*.' *Revista de la Universidad Complutense* (Madrid) 26, no. 108 (1977): 157–79
Machado, A. '¿Cómo veo la nueva juventud española?' In *Los complementarios*, 152–6. Buenos Aires 1957
Mark, J. 'The Uses of the Term "Baroque."' *Modern Language Review* 33 (1938): 547–63
May, T.E. 'An Interpretation of Gracián's *Agudeza y arte de ingenio*.' *Hispanic Review* 16 (October 1948): 275–300
Montseny, F. 'Los intelectuales y la revolución.' *Estafeta Literaria*, no. 350 (13 August 1966): 40
Osuna, R. 'Las revistas españolas durante la República (1931–1936).' *Ideologies and Literatures* 2, no. 8 (1978): 47–54
Pérez Ferrero, M. 'Dos poetas españoles en América y uno americano en España.' *Tierra Firme* (Madrid) 2, 1 (1936): 23–45
Rodriguez Padrón, J. 'Juan Ramón Jiménez-Luis Cernuda: un diálogo crítico.' *Cuadernos Hispanoamericanos*, nos 376–378 (October–December 1981): 886–910
Rozlapa, A. 'El arte deshumanizado 1925–1975.' *American Hispanist* 2, no. 10 (1976): 13–16
Salazar, A. 'Bocetos: Jeroglífico y arabesco.' *Indice*, no. 3 (1921): xi–xii
Salazar y Chapela, E. 'A buena política, mejor literatura.' *El Sol*, 26 April 1931, 2
Sampelayo. 'Los pombianos del exilio.' *Tiempo de Historia* (Madrid) 7, no. 85 (December 1981): 102–15
Silver, P. 'La estética de Ortega y la generación de 1927.' *Nueva Revista de Filología Hispánica* 20, no. 2 (1971): 361–80
Torre, G. de. 'Las ideas estéticas de Ortega.' *Sur* (Buenos Aires), no. 241 (July–August 1956): 79–89
Tuñón de Lara, M. 'Los intelectuales, de 1926 a 1936.' In *Estudios de historia contemporánea*, 177–204. Barcelona 1977
Varela, L. 'Defensa de la cultura. La voz de España.' *El Sol*, 22 July 1936, 2
Villar, Arturo del. 'A los veinte años de su muerte. Un enfado y dos textos olvidados de Juan Ramón Jiménez.' *Estafeta Literaria*, no. 236 (15 May 1978): 4–7
Vivanco, L.F. 'Prólogo' to the facismile reprint of *Los Cuatro Vientos*, 7–18. Glashütten im Taunus 1976
Wellek, R. 'The Concept of Baroque in Literary Scholarship.' *Journal of Aesthetics and Art Criticism* 5, no. 2 (December 1946): 77–109
Yndurain, F. 'Gracián, un estilo.' In *Homenaje a Gracián*, 163–88
Zulueta, Luis de. 'La generación de la dictadura.' *El Sol*, 20 January 1931, 1

Index

UNIVERSITY OF TORONTO ROMANCE SERIES